Angels and Absences

ANGELS AND ABSENCES

Child Deaths in the Nineteenth Century

LAURENCE LERNER

VANDERBILT UNIVERSITY PRESS • *Nashville & London*

This publication is made from recycled paper and meets the minimum requirements of American National Standard for Information Sciences—Permanence of Paper for Printed Library Materials. ∞

Library of Congress Cataloging-in-Publication Data

Lerner, Laurence.
   Angels and absences : child deaths in the nineteenth century /
Laurence Lerner. -- 1st ed.
      p. cm.
   Includes bibliographical references and index.
   ISBN 0-8265-1287-9 (alk. paper)
   1. English literature--19th century--History and criticism.
   2. Death in literature. 3. Children--Great Britain--Mortality-
   -History--19th century. 4. American literature--19th century-
   -History and criticism. 5. Dickens, Charles, 1812-1870--Characters-
   -Children. 6. Children--Death--Psychological aspects.
   7. Sentimentalism in literature. 8. Children in literature.
   I. Title.
   PR468.D42L47 1997
   820.9'3548'09034--dc21   97-4572
                                   CIP

Manufactured in the United States of America

to Wayne Booth

CONTENTS

LIST OF ILLUSTRATIONS

(following page 113)

1. "The Child," by Otto Runge

2. "Rachel Weeping," by Charles Wilson Peale

3. "An Anxious Hour," by Alexander Farmer

4. "The Doctor," by Luke Fildes

5. "Angel faces smile," by Elizabeth Hawkins

6. "The Empty Cradle," by W. Archer

7. "Little Nell," by George Cattermole,
for first edition of *The Old Curiosity Shop*

8. "Little Nell," another version by George Cattermole

9. "Kit's First Writing Lesson," by Robert Martineau

10. "Felix Grundy Eakin," by John Wood Dodge

11. "Paul and Mrs. Pipchin," by Hablot Browne,
from the first edition of *Dombey and Son*

12. "What Are the Wild Waves Saying,"
tinted lithograph by C. W. Nicholls

PREFACE

Life has two gates: to stand before either is to stand on a threshold. The newborn child and the dying old man or woman mark the point at which awareness has just begun or is about to cease. How are these two points related? If we see life as a linear movement, then the point of beginning is the farthest from the point of ending, and the two are opposites. But if we see life as a space, demarcated by the fact that it abuts, at either end, on silence and unawareness, then the two extreme points are identical. In the first case, childhood is a beginning: the child has left nothingness behind and with every moment will become more alive; it embodies energy and vitality, and nothing is more remote from the idea of childhood than death. But in the second case, where the child exists on the margin, it embodies frailty and is always liable to be snatched back into the darkness from which it has barely emerged.

If then the child dies, we can react either with deep shock (this one least of all should be touched by mortality) or with sad understanding (not yet fully emerged into life, it was always in danger of slipping back into nonexistence). This ambivalence has always been with us, prior to and independent of the facts about child death. But nothing is quite free of history; in studying the death of children in the nineteenth century, this book will necessarily glance before and after, to ask how far even what seem unchanging qualities of childhood may change. It is an attempt to describe the deaths of actual children, to understand some of the issues that such deaths raised then and raise now, and to study the way in which they were represented in writing.

Easily the fullest and most complex representation of experience is found in literature, and most of the book deals with poetry and fiction; but the study of literature is enriched by an awareness of historical context, and the first chapter therefore relates some actual deaths that are well documented and can teach us something about how nineteenth century society coped with premature death. History is not fiction, but writing fiction and writing of what actually happened have a great deal in common, and this material therefore confronts us with important questions about the way grief is represented in words: what is the difference between public and private feeling, and how far can we deduce past feelings from the words that have been left us? Beginning with actual deaths should prepare us for asking what is fictitious about fiction.

The second chapter looks at poems about the death of children, studying them primarily as strategies of consolation, and discusses the theology and psychology of dealing with grief. At the same time it relates the poems, where this is known, to the poets' own experience of bereavement and so is enabled to ask whether the truest poetry is the most feigning. A concluding discussion of Wordsworth's lines "There was a Boy" suggests that an interest in poetry as poetry, though it draws on such context, also moves away from it.

Chapter 3, on Dickens, tells the stories of Little Nell and Paul Dombey, adds some account of the many other child deaths in Dickens, and attempts to use this as a point of entry to understanding Dickens's literary art. Is it an accident that the great humorist was also a great sentimentalist? Why was Dickens so fascinated by girls on the threshold between childhood and womanhood?

Chapter 4 looks at other novelists, studies the variations that can be played on the theme of child death, and asks why it is so prominent in nineteenth century fiction, when it was so rare earlier. One answer looks at what is happening in terms of actual child mortality and draws on what is known about the demographic history. It is easy to make bold claims about this, and after making one I conclude the discussion rather skeptically. A quite different kind of explanation would be in terms of the steady expansion of the subject matter of fiction. The chapter concludes with an account of child death in twentieth century fiction and of the very different way it is represented.

Finally, I look at the reception history of Nell, Paul, and all those other children in nineteenth century novels whose life was in more danger, according to Fitzjames Stephen, than the troops who stormed the Redan. The contempt with which twentieth century criticism has dismissed them as sentimentalized contrasts vividly with the enthusiasm and tears of contemporaries. What does this tell us? Is it simply the verdict of one age upon another, to be replaced in its turn by the verdict of a future age on our own (arguably this has already begun), and to be explained in terms of the needs and values of the age that responds? Or is some kind of objective criterion possible in such judgments? I have come across no topic that raises this issue so acutely as child deaths, because it is the topic on which the difference between contemporary and modern judgments is most extreme: the once great popularity of *The Fairchild Family* and the overwhelming impact of the deaths of Nell, Paul, and Eva now leave us puzzled, indifferent, even vaguely resentful. The question of value judgments and the permanence of the canon, once so central and so unquestioned in literary criticism, now so profoundly interrogated and explained as the rationalization of power, takes us to the heart of literary controversy today. So whereas in the first four chapters I have tried to write directly about the original material, allowing these often moving stories and wonderful novels to affect the reader directly, mentioning modern scholars and critics only when they impinge directly on the discussion, and then only briefly, in the last chapter I confront recent critics explicitly and use the matter of child death to enter into current controversies. For some readers this may seem the most important chapter, for others it may the one to skip.

No one writes a book like this all by himself; and I am more than usually conscious of how much I owe to others. Impersonal thanks are due to those whose published work has helped me to cope with my ignorance, especially to the historians who have gathered together some of the material I have used. Although I have tried to go to the original sources where feasible, I owe much to the editorial and scholarly work of Robert Cecil, Philip Collins, Leonore Davidoff and Catherine Hall, David Grylls and Linda Pollock. Peter Wright and Warren Lenney did their best to correct my medical ignorance, and the late David Eversley my ignorance of demography; they must of course not be held responsible if it still shows. The deepest and most important thanks are due to those who read my first draft and offered much good advice: John Burrow, Philip Collins, Tony Thorlby, and above all Wayne Booth, who is as conscious of how much of his good advice I did not take as I am of how much I did.

1

Real Deaths

Princess Charlotte

ON THURSDAY 6 November 1817 Princess Charlotte, only child of the Prince Regent, died a few hours after giving birth to a still-born son; and all England was plunged into grief (that is how, for the moment, we will put it). For several days the newspapers were filled with details of her illness and death, the sorrow of her husband and father, the arrangements for the funeral, and accounts from all over Britain of the widespread mourning. "We never recollect," wrote the *Times*, "so strong and general an expression and indication of sorrow";[1] and a correspondent from Brighton wrote that "chilling regrets and unavailing laments seem the mournful inmates of every mansion house and cottage" (*Times*, 17 Nov.). The funeral took place on the 19th, the newspapers printing a very detailed account of the procession, the coffin and the order of service; and funeral services were held all over the country, in churches often draped in black, and in front of large congregations. National grief does not necessarily produce national harmony: in St. Paul's cathedral there was very nearly a riot, and the newspapers were full of complaints—about the bad Latin of the inscription on the coffin ("in the fifty-eight words of which the inscription is composed there are forty-four genitive cases"), about the rapacity of the officers at the Royal Chapel, who made people pay for their seats "as at a Theatre," and, most important, about the medical attention received by the Princess.

The bulletins issued during her labor were short and resolutely optimistic, announcing first that labor was "going on very slowly but, we trust, favorably," then that she had been delivered of a still-born male child, followed by the sentence, "Her Royal Highness is doing extremely well." Four hours later she was dead. The only cause given by the newspapers for the death was exhaustion. Jesse Foot, a well-known surgeon, wrote a letter to the *Sun*, which he later published as a pamphlet, proposing a public inquiry and probing the details of the bulletins to ascertain whether Sir Richard Croft, the obstetrician, was present all the time (*Sun*, 12 Nov.). Foot's letter was careful not to make any direct accusations, and even suggested that the medical men themselves should be in favor of such an inquiry; but it is clear that public sentiment was convinced that Croft had been negligent. The *Morning Chronicle* tells us that this question was the topic of every assembly; and a year later Croft shot himself.

Such a national calamity naturally gave rise to discussions of Providence. "How dark and mysterious are the ways of Providence," wrote a correspondent from Exeter. "Who can tell why virtue in the bloom of spring is so often suddenly snatched away?" (*Times*, 13 Nov.). A number of other correspondents were quite confident that they knew why. "Civis" wrote to the *Times* on 11 November asserting "the certainty of retributive justice in one form or another upon national guilt," and describing the forms of guilt that, in his opinion, had led to this particular retribution: "the state of the parks at night— . . . an evil which can only here be adverted to," causing the metropolis of the British Empire "to bear too near a resemblance to the profligate and polluted capitals of Italy and France." To this he added profanation of the Sabbath, the licensing of public houses that were applied to purposes which cannot be named, and the lottery: the death of the unfortunate Princess being a "fearful admonition" from God about these national vices. A similar but more generalized indignation appears in a paragraph in the *London Chronicle*:

> Arrogant and self-conceited criticism delights to assign imaginary causes for these unexpected and extraordinary events; but it usually overlooks the great cause of all, the Will of the ALMIGHTY. (*London Chronicle*, 19 Nov.)

The logic of attributing a death to the anger of God is obviously tricky, as we see if we ask whether the Will of the Almighty is equally the cause of all deaths or whether poor Charlotte was singled out from others dying "in the bloom of spring" for special admonition. the *Times* was more cautious in its wording: "That she died by natural causes is true; but that she died for some moral purpose or end, is no less so" (19 Nov.). More cautious, but no more logical: yet this is an area in which rigorous logic could too easily be seen as dangerous. The *Times* editorial insists that there is no half-way house between "full and complete Christianity" and "absolute Atheism," and that unless one grants that there is a moral purpose in such a death one will be reduced to a complete denial of God and Providence. This is an issue that untimely deaths continued to raise throughout the century.

Most of what we have so far looked at could be described as the Establishment response to the death of the Princess. The *London Chronicle*, an extremely conservative paper, in the course of its contemptuous dismissal of the criticisms of Sir Richard Crofts and his colleagues, criticisms "which sink to nothing before the high medical reputation of the Gentlemen who attended her Royal Highness," attacked the "reptiles" who break in upon the occasion of national sorrow to preach sedition, blasphemy, obscenity, "and whatever else shocks decency and outrages public morals" (17 Nov.). Many of these reptiles now make livelier and more intelligent reading than the orthodox. Leigh Hunt's paper, the *Examiner*, provides a mild example: much of what it says about the event is conventional enough, and its insistence that we should feel infinitely more for Leopold as a man than as a prince is, after all, the same point that the *Times* and the *Morning Chronicle* make, though the rhetorical emphasis has shifted when the *Examiner* exclaims, "What are kings and dynasties to us, especially in an age like the present . . . compared with this abrupt reminding us of the naked humanity of us all?" (9 Nov.). Reminders of our common humanity have always been common to both conservative and radical rhetoric, the difference being that in the one case they are intended as a distraction from politics, in the other as having political consequences. And we have moved from rhetoric to explicit politics when the *Examiner* launches its complaint against "the indecent advantage taken of the Princess's death by the Ministerial Papers to keep a comparative silence, day after day, on all other subjects." What aroused particular indignation in the *Examiner* was the proposal that people should conduct themselves "*as if* some dear relative were lying dead—as if people had not hundreds of causes of grief *besides* this!" (16 Nov.). That fiery radical Thomas Wooler in *The Black Dwarf* went further: not only did he refuse to mourn "merely for a Princess" while being very ready to regret "the helpless fate of the wife and mother," he also took issue with those editors who demanded the cessation of public business as a sign of mourning. Most newspapers reported that shopkeepers had spontaneously closed their shops, and many expressed indignation at those who had not. The *Times* rebuked the citizens of Norwich for their feverish commercial activity to meet the demand for bombazines, a favorite material for mourning, insisting that "it is not in common nature to have the heart and mind so absorbed by the love of gain" (13 Nov.); *The Black Dwarf* observed caustically that this writer "forgets himself to drop his avocations, and exhibit the extent of his affliction by dropping his pen, and closing the office of his publication" (19 Nov.).

The most scathing contempt came from William Cobbett, then in America, but continuing his choleric attacks on the political establishment. An innkeeper at Esher called Carpenter, who had been largely supported by her patronage "was so affected when he heard of the demise of the Princess, that he nearly fainted. He was seized with indisposition, and talked of nothing but the death of the Princess. On the next day he expired!" (*Observer*, 28 Nov.). One can hear Cobbett snorting as he read this story:

> Coupling this fact with the sight of the news-papers lined all round with black, I really began to fear that a considerable portion of the nation were actually dead, or in a dying state. (*Cobbett's Political Register*, 25 April 1818)

On the day Princess Charlotte died, three working class leaders of the ineffectual Pentridge Rising were executed at Derby. The coincidence provides obvious material for radical comment on the national calamity, and it was well exploited in the *Examiner*; it also provides the main argument of Shelley's *Address to the People on the Death of the Princess Charlotte*, which he wrote on 11–12 November but never published. The conventional view distinguished clearly between the compassion for personal loss aroused by the death of the Princess and the political judgment that would condemn the Pentridge insurrectionists for threatening the basis of society. But Shelley, with some ingenuity, subverts this contrast, first by political comment on Charlotte:

> She was born a Princess, and those who are destined to rule mankind are dispensed with acquiring that wisdom and that experience which is necessary even to rule themselves. . . . She had accomplished nothing, and aspired to

nothing, and could understand nothing respecting those great political questions which involve the happiness of those over whom she was destined to rule.

Then comes the comment on the executions, which claims that they are quite as infused with private grief as the Princess's death:

> They had sons, and brothers, and sisters, and fathers, who loved them, it should seem, more than the Princess Charlotte could be loved by those whom the regulations of her rank had held in perpetual estrangement from her.[2]

Princess Charlotte was the only legitimate grandchild of George III, and therefore virtually certain to succeed to the throne: the son she bore, if he had lived, would one day have been king of England. The newspapers now indulged their passion for research by printing lists of the heirs to the throne of England, right down, in the *Times*, to no 123: after the sons and daughters of George III (all of them over forty) none of the names are English. It looked as if England would once again have to import its king from Germany. The matter was, of course, resolved by the Duke of Kent dismissing his mistress and taking a wife who gave birth to Victoria two years later, so that the ascent of a pious and respectable young woman to the throne (also with a foreign husband) simply took place in 1837 instead of 1830; but at the time it looked as if the political consequences of the double death would be enormous. All the newspapers were careful to distinguish between the personal and the political aspects of the calamity, and all of them observed the proprieties by insisting respectfully that the personal came first—all, that is, except the rumbustious Cobbett:

> The *political consequences* of the death of the Princess is all that we, any of us, can have anything to do with. We cannot have any *personal* feeling upon the occasion. It is a young wife dead in child-birth; and this happens, in many parts of every great country, every twenty-four hours. It is nonsense, and, indeed, worse: it is vile hypocrisy to talk about *personal sorrow*, or personal feeling of any sort. (*Cobbett's Political Register*, 25 April 1818)

It was obvious to contemporaries that the event posed the question of how to distinguish between the public and the private, and it is to this that I now turn; but it will not be possible to be as clear cut as either the conventional papers, on the one hand, or Cobbett, on the other. The distinction

is one that constantly needs to be deconstructed and reasserted: its bound-
aries are established even as they are transgressed. There is, first of all, the
very conception of public grief. What does it mean to speak of a "universal
burst of sympathetic grief," as the *Scotsman* did? What persuaded the
Brighton correspondent of the *Times* that "chilling regrets and unavailing
laments seem the mournful inmates of every mansion, house and cottage"
(17 Nov.)? And how can we judge if such claims are true? Several papers
drew an interesting distinction but put it to questionable use:

> To assert that we, or that the whole British nation, is at this moment dissolved
> in tears . . . would be absurd, though many a tear will be shed for her fate by
> those who have never seen her; but if we say that deep regret, that calm sorrow,
> produced by pity for her sufferings, and a rational calculation of the loss we
> have sustained in her death, are universally prevalent, we say no more than
> every tongue confirms.(*Times*, 7 Nov.)

This seems a commonsense observation, but in one respect it is the opposite of the truth: for it is perfectly possible to say whether people are in
tears, but whether they are feeling deep regret or pity or are calculating
rationally can only be a deduction. We can always ask of references to
national grief or public mourning whether they refer to emotions or to
behaviour, to the internal experience that others must deduce or to external signs that can be observed; but once we draw this distinction, it is striking how much of the relevant vocabulary is ambiguous. The clearest example is the term "mourning" itself. The claim that the expression of public
sympathy is genuine, unlike the usual mourning for princes, clearly refers
to the sentiment, but when we are told that in Carlisle "mourning has
become general," the word refers to clothing and means that most people
are wearing black. The claim that in Plymouth "every thought of amuse-
ment ceases" possesses the same ambiguity: it can mean that very few
amusements are going on or that no one wants any. To speak of "most
solemn and devout observance" can refer either to feelings of devotion or
to the ringing of bells and the saying of prayers. When we speak of the feelings of a group or a community, something in language itself discourages us
from being too confident about the distinction between emotion and
behaviour.

The public/private dialectic concerns not only the relating of national
grief to individual emotions, but also the relation between the individual
sorrow of those personally involved and the process of its becoming a spec-

tacle to the world: that is, it involves both the internalizing of national grief and the publication of individual grief. So I turn now to the Princess's family. The two people most concerned were her husband and her father, and the press not only reported their actions but speculated about their feelings. Running through all the comments there is, not surprisingly, an element of doubt about what is proper to say—whether personal grief should be published at all. When the Prince Regent left Claremont to visit his mother and sisters at Windsor, he "went alone, and travelled with the blinds of his carriage down" (*Times*, 10 Nov.). That glimpse could be seen as one version of the right relationship with the public: his need for privacy and the impropriety—even the impossibility—of finding out what he felt.

The newspapers certainly toyed with this opinion. Both the *Times* and the *Observer*, stating that they had not heard the particulars of the interview between Leopold and the Prince Regent, added, "nor are we curious to intrude upon the overwhelming grief of a father and a husband" (12 Nov.). But to expect such lack of curiosity to govern everything in a newspaper is virtually to ask journalism to self-destruct; and for the next few days the private feelings of Prince Leopold, at least, led a very public existence. Here, for instance, is the account in the *Times* of his behaviour at the funeral:

> Prince Leopold followed the coffin as chief mourner; his appearance created the deepest interest; his countenance was dejected; his manner was full of despondency; and though he made evident efforts to preserve calmness and fortitude, yet he every now and then burst into a flood of tears. He walked along with unsteady steps, and took the seat provided for him at the head of the coffin. . . . During the whole time of the funeral service he preserved one fixed but downcast look towards the coffin of his beloved wife: he never once raised his eyes to the congregation: he was totally absorbed in his grief. The Royal Dukes who sat or stood beside him, watched him with much solicitude, as if they were afraid he would sink under his affliction. His distress, however, was tolerably subdued till the moment when the coffin was gradually lowered into the grave; at this awful crisis, when his deeply regretted consort was to be separated from him for ever, he was alarmingly moved, but by a strong effort he seemed also to conquer this emotion.(*Times*, 19 Nov.)

There are two struggles taking place here: Leopold's struggle to control his emotion and the observers' struggle to interpret his appearance. In the former, the subject is aware of his feelings and struggling for an outward comportment that will not betray them; in the latter, the Dukes are aware of the comportment and have deduced the feelings from it. This puts them in a position similar to that of the writer, who knows what Leopold's behaviour was and concludes that it partly hid, partly revealed his inner turmoil. Here we encounter a question that will constantly recur in this book: what can we know about the feelings of real people by observing—or reading about—their behaviour? To study past deaths and how they were responded to is to explore the relation between the texts we have and the experience of past generations to which they provide the only access. Like the Dukes, we are eager to know what Leopold felt; but whereas their concern was practical and immediate (would he fall down?), we have the leisure to reflect on our own acts of interpretation, to pause and ask how one can know such things and whether such knowledge can be reliable.

Shortly after Charlotte's death, Leopold had sent a message to his friend the Earl of Lauderdale, who arrived at Claremont the day after the funeral. The following account of this meeting follows shortly after the description of his behaviour at the funeral:

> It is said that on his entering the room, his Serene Highness rushed into his Lordship's arms with the violence of a heart-broken man, and remained in that situation for a full half-hour, during which time his grief found vent only in sobs and moans. Lord Lauderdale at last gently tore himself away, and endeavoured to lead the Prince's mind to the consideration of minor objects. "How delightful it is," said his Lordship, "to breathe the sweet odour of these flowers, so diversified, so rich. An eternal spring seems to embellish these domains; it is a terrestrial paradise." It is added that these observations aroused Prince Leopold, and, for the first time, he found himself momentarily relieved. "I will," exclaimed he, "live and die at Claremont. I will devote every moment of my future life to carry into effect all the ideas of that blessed angel whom I have lost for ever!" Here he burst into a flood of tears. (*Times*, 19 Nov.)

Here the situation is different. Whereas the writer may well have been present at the funeral, we are now, as the passage goes out of its way to make plain, dealing with hearsay. The exclamatory sentences of Lauderdale, flowery in more than one sense, and the polished parallels of Leopold, show that the dialogue is not meant to be literally accurate (especially since it immediately precedes a flood of tears!). The conventionalized style, though it deprives us of authenticity, could be thought of as a way of making the intrusion less impertinent, as if we are seeing a Leopold who already conforms to a stereotype and so to a more public role. His true grief is, then, left private.

And are we being told the truth? The question thrusts itself upon us when we compare the accounts of Leopold with those of his father-in-law. The assurances about the Prince Regent's emotions are almost as emphatic as those about Leopold's. When he saw the body of his daughter, we are told, he had a stroke of apoplexy; and the *Gentleman's Magazine* went so far as to write,

> If there be one trait which is more marked than another in the character of the Prince Regent, it is his affection for all the members of his family; and if there was one individual in whom that affection was more intensely centred than another, it was his beloved and only Daughter. (*Gentleman's Magazine*, Nov. 1817)

This is (not to put too fine a point on it) a pack of lies. The Prince's treatment of some of his family had been notoriously callous, and, having taken little notice of Charlotte for much of her life, he had quarreled with her for her refusal to accept the arranged match with the Prince of Orange. So what are we to think of his apoplexy? It is hard to believe that it was a burst of true fatherly feeling and unkind to assume that it was calculated hypocrisy. Should we see it as the expression of a histrionic and shallow character, or an example of the inherent difficulty of relating behaviour to emotion?

If we cannot believe the newspapers about the Prince Regent, why, it seems natural to ask, should we believe them about Leopold? The cynical answer is that we know less about Leopold and therefore have less reason to question them; but there are other reasons: that the motive to cover up is much less powerful in his case, since he was not the sovereign (as the Prince was in fact and would soon be in name); that the much fuller descriptions of his behaviour have not the blandness of the lies about the Prince Regent; and also that since he was a foreigner the press might feel less need to conform him to a stereotype, might even feel some satisfaction in reporting his slightly un-English feelings.

The two important members of Charlotte's family are her husband and her father, but there are three others who form a shadowy presence in the reports. One is King George III, now almost eighty years old and hopelessly insane. Two papers (the *Observer* and the *Examiner*) inserted a paragraph about the illustrious and venerable personage "who is not dead, and yet who partakes not of the joys or the afflictions of his kindred or his people." The author of this paragraph, which attempts to probe the consciousness of the mad king, did not know what he was talking about and realized that he did not know: "It is said—but who can tell whether truly or not, for nothing concerning his mysterious insulation can be affirmed except the meagre fact of his perpetuated existence in a general state of forlorn tranquillity and occasional perturbation . . . " (after that parenthesis, it does not seem to matter what "is said"). This ignorance enables him to end on a pious note, claiming that the king is not forsaken "by Him whose loving kindness is better than life" but also, and more interestingly, lends the paragraph a certain power, deriving from the correspondence between the writer's inability to make contact with the king's consciousness and the king's inability to make contact with the external world.(*Observer*, 16 Nov.)

The second shadow in the story is Caroline, the estranged wife of the Prince Regent. She was kept out of the picture for political reasons, and it is therefore the radical "reptiles" who bring her in. She may have been almost as much to blame as her husband for the collapse of the marriage, but this did not prevent her from being seen as a victim when the Prince's unpopularity was being emphasized. So when the inhabitants of Reading met in the town hall to send an address of condolence to the Prince Regent, an attempt was made to propose sending a similar condolence to Caroline, "the unfortunate and highly to be pitied mother." It was voted down, because it "would much diminish the compliment to be paid to the Prince Regent" (*Examiner*, 30 Nov.). Since there is not even mention of a condolence for Leopold, I take it the motivation of the whole event was clearly political (and conservative). In New York, I am glad to report, where the royal influence was naturally weaker, a gathering of loyal merchants condoled with the Prince, and the English reformers, to Cobbett's delight, responded by sending a similar address "to the royal mother instead of the father" (*Cobbett's Political Register*, 25 April 1818).

Finally, the most shadowy figure of all: the dead child, who provides the link between this episode and the rest of this book. He was not even given a name, and does not figure in the royal genealogies; yet politically, his loss was in the long run the most important. The hopes placed on him can perhaps be seen from this somewhat bizarre detail: the bulletins declared him to be "perfect, and one of the finest infants ever brought into this world" (*Times*, 7 Nov.)—as if a dead Prince is finer than a living commoner! If there is any one point on which it would be revealing to penetrate the inaccessibility of the private feelings of the dead, it would be to find out if there was any grief for this infant. Leopold cared only for his wife: when the news of the child's death was brought him, he exclaimed, "Thank God, thank God, the Princess is safe!" (*Times*, 7 Nov.). Charlotte received the news of the child being born dead "with much resignation." In the light of what this book will go on to explore, it is extraordinary that this baby died so unmourned.

We even have a comparison to hand; four years later, another infant heir to the throne died. William, Duke of Clarence, the third son of George III, who later became king when George IV died, married in 1818, at the age of 53, as did his younger brother, the Duke of Kent, because the need to produce an English-born heir was now considered urgent. Adelaide, Duchess of Clarence, gave birth to a daughter in 1820, but though she lived long enough to be given a name, the young Elizabeth died on 4 March 1821. Nothing remotely like national grief took place, and if we ask why, there seem several possible answers. First, the mother was still alive. As we shall go on to see, the death of a child alone could be a cause of intense grief, but not—are we to conclude?—of public grief. Second, William and Adelaide were by no means such popular figures as Charlotte: they were not young and serious, and they did not contrast with a dissolute and unpopular father. And third, William was not the immediate heir to the throne (Frederick, Duke of York, the second son, lived until 1827), though there is no doubt that the daughter, Elizabeth, had she lived, would have succeeded in 1837. As far as I have been able to trace, no poems on the occasion were published in the national press, whereas the death of Princess Charlotte produced dozens, including one by Thomas Campbell, one by the ever-popular Felicia Hemans, and an adaptation of Milton's "Lines on a Fair Infant" to make it fit the occasion. In the *Times* on 12 March 1821 we read that Elizabeth was buried without fuss at Windsor, the coffin being put into a coach belonging to the king, "in which were two gentlemen of the Duke's household. Only one mourning coach and six followed."

* * *

This book is about the death of individuals and the grief of parents: unless we have individual records, we can only study child deaths statistically, not as a matter for grief. But to place the study in context, I will for a moment follow the lead of Shelley, Cobbett, and Wooler, and point out that around the Princess the poor were dying every day in their thousands, unchronicled and (except by their unchronicled families) unremembered.

> Sir, it is not possible for any man, whatever be his station, if he have but a heart within his bosom, to read the details of this awful document without a combined feeling of shame, terror, and indignation.

The awful document is the report of the Commission on the Employment of Children in Mines and Factories of 1842, perhaps the most horrifying of the great series of government reports on the Condition of England that appeared in the 1840s; and the remark was made by Lord Shaftesbury, speaking in Parliament, and quoting descriptions of the conditions, almost unimaginable to us today, in which women and children worked in the mines.

> They carry coal on their backs on unrailed roads, with burdens varying from 3/4 cwt to 3 cwt,—a cruel slaving, revolting to humanity. I found a little girl, only six years old, carrying 1/2 a cwt, and making regularly fourteen long journeys a day. With a burden varying from 1 cwt to 1 1/2 cwt, the height ascended and the distance along the roads, added together, exceeded in each journey, the height of St Paul's Cathedral. . . . And it not unfrequently happens that the tugs break, and the load falls upon those females who are following, who are struck off the ladders into the depths below.[3]

The denunciation of the conditions of labor by the conservative evangelical Shaftesbury had much in common with that of the radical and atheist Friedrich Engels. In *The Condition of the Working-Class in England in 1844* he describes suffering and death through an accumulation of factual detail: the final chapter, on the workings of the New Poor Law of 1834, describes the death of a man dismissed from the workhouse, of a patient "tied fast with cords passed over the covering and under the bedstead, to save the nurses the trouble of sitting up at night," and concludes:

> As in life, so in death. The poor are dumped into the earth like infected cattle. . . . The paupers are thrown into a ditch fourteen feet deep; a curate rattles through the Litany at the top of his speed; the ditch is loosely covered in, to be re-opened the next Wednesday, and filled with corpses as long as one more can be forced in.[4]

The Reverend John Skinner, writing in the first third of the nineteenth century, did not share the distress of Shaftesbury or the indignation of Engels:

> But happy is it that people in the lower ranks of life are not possesed of the same sensibility as their superiors. . . . If enjoyment be less, privation is in proportion.[5]

Since this book does not deal with the very poor, I must insert a sharp dismissal of this complacency. Skinner applies to class the same comfortable point that Lawrence Stone makes about chronology. In his influential *Family, Sex and Marriage in England 1500–1800*, Stone claims that strong, affective family bonds date only from the eighteenth century; before that, he believes, most people found it very difficult to establish close emotional ties to any other person.

The necessary reply to both Skinner and Stone is that "the grief which does not speak Whispers the o'erfraught heart, and bids it break." We do not possess, from the poor in the nineteenth century, or from almost anyone in earlier times, much in the way of detailed accounts of intimate affection or of grief, the sort of account that moves us so profoundly and tells us how deeply Catherine Tait and Josephine Butler loved and mourned their children, but this does not entitle us to deny the feelings. The girls who fell off the ladder into the depths below were falling into oblivion as well as to their death; the poor who were dumped into the earth like infected cattle left no memorial and no name behind them (even Engels is only able to put a name to one of his examples). We can pay them the passing tribute of a sigh, and offer them the respect of believing that their grief was as great as that of the articulate whose records we possess; but we cannot explore what we have no evidence of.

If the contrast between rich and poor is no longer so extreme in our society, it is still with us on a world scale. The typical child death in our time is the photograph of the victim of famine in Africa—emaciated, disturbing and anonymous. Such children are thrust in front of us, on television and in newspapers, because it is believed we can do something to help. But the impact of the image is not merely practical; it also serves to arouse our unease and even our guilt—what have we done to deserve our freedom from such distress? In 1839 Thomas Carlyle made his famous plea for politicians to attend to the Condition-of-England question: "the condition of the great body of people in a country is the condition of the country itself."[6] Today it is the people in other and poorer countries of whose condition we need to be reminded. In both cases, the dying child who is thrust into our attention is not an individual. Such children are important because there are so many of them, "dying thus around us every day," wrote Dickens. In both cases the child is voiceless—more so in the case of today's third world child, for if she, or her parents, could speak to us, we would not understand. And in both cases the call on us to act may succeed in doing good but may also produce a kind of hopelessness: the comfortable reader, trying to see the starving child as one of her own, may be confronted with a gap that the imagination cannot cross.

The Tait Children

In 1856 Archibald Campbell Tait, who later rose to be Archbishop of Canterbury, was Dean of Carlisle; he and his wife had five daughters and one son, ranging in age from ten downwards, and a sixth daughter was born in February, just before the terrible events now to be narrated. On Monday 3 March the third daughter Charlotte (Chatty) fell ill with what turned out to be scarlet fever, and three days later she was dead. Then, one by one, the remaining girls fell ill and died: Susan (aged one and a half) on March 11, Frances (nearly four) on March 20, Catharine (Catty), the oldest, on Easter Tuesday, and May (nearly 8) two weeks later. The only survivors were the one boy, Craufurd, and the new baby, Lucy.

Mrs. Tait wrote a narrative of these events, which was printed in the memoir of her and her son by William Benham (1879). It is the longest and most detailed account of child deaths in the nineteenth century that I have come across, filled with warm family affection and grief, and with an insistent religious faith that appears to be shared by the children. Chatty's illness began by her declaring that she was tired, then vomiting, then sleeping most of the night, but restlessly at times. After she had said her prayer, and "in a voice of exceeding clearness said the poem she been learning the day before," Mrs. Tait began to feel alarmed; and when the doctor announced that it was scarlet fever, the other children were isolated (but too late). Chatty's descent was rapid: she had a "spasm," and "looking at me in a strange wild manner, began to open her mouth in a fearful way"; when this was over, she looked at her parents and said "I must go away." "Yes darling," the narrative adds, "away from your happy home on earth to that much brighter home above."[7]

Mrs. Tait appears to have had a premonition of the next death. When the children were reading to her out of the Bible, "just then there rushed to my heart a feeling of separation from them which I could not bear, and an intense faintness." Both she and her husband attributed this to her own illness, accentuated by weakness from the recent childbirth, but when she was told that Susan was ill she immediately felt well again, "and this came like light to my mind, 'We are in God's hands.'"

As death moves inexorably through the children, the narrative grows more and more painful to read. "It seemed, now," she writes at one point, "as if every look of health was of untold value to us." To the modern reader, the distress is increased by the obvious helplessness of medical science. Attempts to prevent the disease spreading by removing each child from the others as she falls sick are quite ineffective; there are no drugs that will help, and all that the doctor can prescribe is something to "strengthen" the patient (usually port wine); when more distinguished doctors are brought in to consult, there is obviously no further expertise that they can bring. As each child fell ill, her hair was cut off, which may have increased her comfort, and certainly saddened the mother, but can have done little else. The ineffectualness of the palliatives makes distressing reading:

> He then desired us to give her a vapour-bath by bottles filled with hot water, and wrapped in damp flannel put all about her; but alas! no relief to the fever; no moisture on the skin.

Mrs. Tait's religious faith was intense:

> Craufurd said even little children were martyrs. I, putting my arms round Chatty, said, "Yes, even such little ones as Chatty died gladly, that they might go to be with Jesus." She looked up with a look I never shall forget, it was so sweet. Yes, my little lamb was ready for her Saviour's call! Before the week was half over, she was with him.

This moment takes place before any of the children fall ill, though it was of course written afterwards. By inserting it at the beginning of her account, Mrs. Tait (with perhaps half-conscious artistry) is providing a framework for our acceptance of the ensuing tragedy.

She cannot think about death except as a reuniting, and she speaks of it in that way to the children: when the dying May asks, "Where is Catty?"

> I said, "May dear, the Good Shepherd has come and taken your dear Catty." She said with a voice of astonishment, "What!" I said, "The Lord Jesus Christ has taken your dear Catty to heaven. He has taken her to Chatty and Frances and Susan; shall you like to go to her?" She became very silent, and did not answer me, but her mind seemed satisfied.

Though her role as a clergyman's wife may have laid on her an especial duty of faith, and of being seen to have faith, there is no reason to doubt the genuineness of these assertions. Such language, which seems clearly to spring from her own beliefs, and not to be there merely to comfort the children, recurs constantly in Victorian accounts of child death. Later we shall be confronted with attempts to resist it.

One glimpse of Mrs. Tait's theology is interesting, more interesting perhaps than she would have been comfortable with. It occurs half way through the series of deaths:

> Earnestly we prayed that God would now stay His hand and spare to us the rest. . . . No doubt he heard that prayer, though he could not grant us what we so earnestly asked for.

The revealing words here are "could not." The dilemma of postulating a God who is both all-powerful and all loving is as old as Christian theodicy; and in her need to cling to her God as all-loving she seems to glide, probably without noticing, into a belief that he is not omnipotent.

How much can we know about Catherine Tait's suffering? How much, indeed, can we know about the suffering of any of the mothers in this book? There are some strong and heart-rending expressions of grief, often accompanied by equally firm statements of religious faith. Elizabeth Prentiss, wife of the Reverend George Prentiss, who published a posthumous memoir of her in 1883, lost two children in 1852, her young son Eddy, and, five months later, her baby daughter Elizabeth. Her journal alternates outbursts of grief with assertions that "it would be most unchristian and ungrateful in us to even wonder at that Divine will which has bereaved us of our only boy—the light and sunshine of our household." The most painful outburst of grief comes after the second death:

> Here I sit with empty hands. I have had the little coffin in my arms, but my baby's face could not be seen, so rudely had death marred it. Empty hands,

empty hands, a worn-out exhausted body, and unutterable longings to flee from
a world that has had for me so many sharp experiences. God help me, my baby,
my baby! God help me, my little lost Eddy![8]

There are two kinds of comment possible about such writing. The first is
immediate and untheoretical, to record how moving it is: for some purposes
this is all we want to say, and it may, given the original document, not be
necessary to say anything. But for other purposes we might want to make a
theoretical point: that as readers we are confronted only with words, from
which we derive the visceral experience of a mother's grief, and can be
moved to a similar, if less intense, visceral experience of our own.

Fact and Fiction

When Elizabeth Prentiss writes "God has been most merciful to us in
this affliction, and, if a bereaved, we are still a *happy* household and full of
thanksgiving," this claim will sound, to many a modern reader, like the rote
repetition of a formula. Are we entitled to demand something more than
rote formulae before we can be convinced of the reality of grief? That is
clearly a literary question, and in later chapters it will be thrust on us. We
know that such faith was expected (especially from clergymen's wives), and
therefore we can say that, however despairing the women felt, they would
still feel obliged to affirm the strength of their faith. The fact that we are
reading a private diary does not affect this, not only because the possibility
of publication might well have been present to her mind (justifiably, in this
case) but also because conforming to expectations is best done if consis-
tent. These women inhabited their public belief system even when alone.

The Tait and Prentiss children really lived and really died, and there is
no hint of fiction in the accounts; I shall now, for comparison, turn to a narrative which hovers between fact and fiction.

William Canton had two daughters, and lost them both. In 1874, at the
age of twenty-nine, he married Emma Moore; their small daughter Violet
died in 1877, and his wife died in 1880. Two years later he married again,
and his wife Annie bore two children, a daughter, Winifred Vida (known
usually as W.V.) in 1890, and a son, Guy, in 1896. W.V. died in 1901, just
before her eleventh birthday.

The sketches, stories, and poems that Canton wrote about her are now
more or less forgotten but were very popular at the time. Many of these

pieces found their way into *Everyman's Library*, including *The Invisible Play-mate* and *W.V. Her Book*, written during her lifetime, and *In Memory of W.V.* in 1901.[9] It is not easy to classify them as memoirs or fiction: both father and daughter made up stories for each other, and sometimes these are printed as they stand; sometimes the book is about the making up of stories. The truth-status of a story concerns W.V. herself at one point, in terms appropriate to a young child:

> How amazingly W.V. has grown in a twelvemonth! Even to her the Forest is no longer quite the same vague enchanted region it used to be. . . . I notice a growing impatience at "sham stories," and a preference for what has really happened—"something about the Romans, or the Danes, or Saxons, or Jesus." When I begin some wonderful saga, she looks up alertly, "True?"—then settles down to her enjoyment.

One of the stories the father tells is of a father and daughter who were separated in the forest,

> and the forest grew older and older and older; and the great trees decayed and fell down with age . . . and at last the country became the Fenland, and the Romans, when they conquered Britain, made a roadway across it with trunks of trees and a bed of gravel, and that was fifteen hundred years ago.
> "True?"
> Why, yes.
> How did I know?

With impeccable positivism he gives an archeologist's answer to this, then reverts to the little girl, who

> wandered on and on till she came to an old quarry, and there she lit a fire, and when she had done she turned round, and there was her father sitting beside it.
> W.V. laughed incredulously: "Father, you said it was true!"

If we look at the texture of the writing, we can easily date this, with its mixture of whimsy and domestic affection, of historical feeling and fin-de-siècle charm, that links it to William Morris and Kipling and Andrew Lang; but on the one point of truth-status it can be seen as a curious anticipation of something much more modern. The narrative glides from the true to the fictitious in a way that subverts the distinction between them, while using W.V. to reassert it. Yet what she asserts is the validity of the distinction rather than its importance: she needs to know if the narratives are true, but her enjoyment does not altogether depend on that.

Along with the gliding between truth and fiction there is a gliding between the living and the dead. The title story begins with a familiar device, the assertion that what follows is taken from "a series of letters which I received a year or two ago." The writer of the letters (like the writer of the book) "was twice married, and . . . just before the death of his first wife their only child, a girl, died at the age of six weeks." In his idolatry of her, he declares, he "clean forgot the savage irony of existence" (Christian belief seems here to be a fiction tenable only during happiness). He has therefore "petrified [him]self against disaster" by deciding that he will never again be taken unawares:

> Sometimes even when I am putting the latch-key into the lock, I stop and hear an inward voice whispering "Baby is dead," and I reply, "Then she is dead." The rest I suppress, ignore, refuse to feel or think. It is not pleasant schooling; but I think it is wise.

But as the anecdotes of the new daughter unfold, it becomes clear that it is not by suppressing feeling that he has "petrified" himself: he is "growing imbecile under the influence of the Pinaforifera." He reports that the girl has got a new plaything, "an invisible 'iccle gaal' (little girl) whom she wheels about in her toy perambulator, puts carefully to bed, and generally makes much of," and whom she treats with intense literalism: "She won't sit on my right knee at all until I have pretended to transfer the playmate to the other."

W.V. falls ill and dies, and the last "letter" describes his final conversation with her:

> Can you believe this? *I* cannot; and yet I saw it. A little while before she died I heard her speaking in an almost inaudible whisper. I knelt down and leaned over her. She looked curiously at me, and said faintly: "Pappa, I not let her fall." "Who, dearie?" "Yourn iccle baby. I gotten her in here." She moved her wasted little hand as if to lift a fold in the bedclothes. . . . Close beside her lay that other little one, with its white worn face and its poor arms crossed in that old-womanish fashion in front of her. Its large suffering eyes looked for a

moment into mine, and then my head seemed filled with mist and my ears buzzed.

I saw that. It was not hallucination. It was *there*.

Just think what it means, if that actually happened. Think what must have been going on in the past, *and I never knew*. I remember, now, she never called it "mamma's baby"; it was always "yourn." Think of the future now that they are both—what? Gone?

The mingling of truth and fiction in this narrative is far more complex than the sentimental charm of the writing would suggest. There is, first, the old device of attributing the story to "a friend," whose situation turns out to be exactly that of the author. Then there is the identity and truth-status of that unseen playmate: is this a ghost story, in which the spirit of the dead child appears first to the living half-sister and then, finally, once, to the father? or did the young daughter make it up and then talk her father into a hallucination at the end? or did she invent a being who then turns out to be real? Or did the father make it all up—in self-deception, or deliberately, as fiction?

And there is another complication. *The Invisible Playmate* was published in 1894; W.V. died in 1901. When the story was written she was still alive, and the death in which it culminates is an anticipation of later fact. The writer's claim that he has "petrified himself against disaster" is wildly and ironically untrue: he has imagined a disaster that had not yet occurred but later did. In thought, at least, he killed his second daughter.

Next to this winsome narrative, I now place a sophisticated piece of theory. Paul Ricoeur's distinction between the semiotic and the semantic is useful here. When a text is analyzed as a self-contained unit, as it is by structuralism, its elements are understood only in relation to one another, that is, as "a system of signs defined by their differences alone": this is the semiotic. Semantic analysis regards the text not as closed in on itself, but as "opening out onto other things," and semantic understanding is "to understand oneself in front of the text." Though Ricoeur respects semiotic analysis as a way of moving us from surface semantics to depth semantics, he does not believe that texts are self-contained, for that would be to reduce analysis to a "sterile game." The world we inhabit, for Ricoeur, is not locked up in a prison house of language.[10]

In the texts of Catherine Tait and Elizabeth Prentiss, we find two emotions, faith and grief. Now what will the response be of the skeptical reader who cannot use Christian faith to "understand himself in front of the text"? To such a reader the faith may seem like a statement of what one was expected to say, whereas the grief can leave us convinced of its genuineness and immediacy. This does not mean that the statements of faith were hypocritical: it means that if we view them from the outside, we shall see them as a semiotic system, governing systematically the way experience is talked about, but pouring no meaning into our world. Even the modern Christian, if he is of a sophisticated, demythologizing turn of thought, might say this. But to say the same of grief would open us to the charge of reading as desiccated, inhuman computers: a computer can analyze with ever-increasing competence, but does not inhabit a semantic world. Computers do not grieve.

But this distinction can in its turn be challenged—and in two ways. In the first place, there is the reader for whom religious experience is as real as any other experience, who will refuse to reduce the statements of faith to the purely semiotic. And second, there is the reader who will be prepared to treat grief as I have proposed treating faith and who can cite, as support for his position, the case of fiction.

For it is easy enough to imagine that the text of these journals came from a novel, and in Canton's narrative we see this transition taking place; in later chapters we shall come across abundant examples. If the accounts were fiction, we would subject them to a kind of examination that when applied to actual bereaved mothers seems impertinent. We would ask if they were mere repetitions of the clichés of grieving or if they showed any verbal distinction, were linguistically inventive and the result of literary talent. We might even make this point by asking if they sounded like real grief, but if we did we would need reminding that actual grieving does not require any literary talent.

That truth and fiction have much in common has been one of the insights of recent literary theory; but it is necessary to remember that they are not identical. This is true not only in the obvious sense that we sometimes want, like W.V., to know whether events actually took place; it is also true when we are considering the relation between texts and the emotion they arouse. We need to say that a text can move us in two ways. The first is by its semiotic properties: it may command our response because it is powerfully written. The second is by our knowledge that it has a real referent, that Catherine Tait and Elizabeth Prentiss really did lose their children. We can, that is, be moved because we are sensitive to literature, or because we respect real suffering. This difference is important and necessary, but it is not watertight. Literature that impresses us because we enjoy the verbal skill operates on the semiotic level only; literature that speaks to our condition moves us by requiring us, in Ricoeur's formulation, to understand ourselves in front of the text. Analysis of technique, whether in terms of traditional literary devices or in those of structuralism, deals with the former; much of this book is an attempt to deal with the latter too.

The Sudden Cry, and Then the Silence

The death of little Eva Butler came not from illness but from an accident—an accident so painful that it is frightening to think about it. George and Josephine Butler returned home from a dinner party one evening in 1864, and Eva leapt out of bed to greet them. The banisters gave way, and she fell onto the tiled floor. She died after convulsions a few hours later, never regaining consciousness. She was five years old.

> It was difficult to endure at first the shock of the suddenness of that agonising death. Little gentle spirit! the softest death for her would have seemed sad enough. Never can I lose that memory—the fall, the sudden cry, and then the silence. It was pitiful to see her, helpless in her father's arms, her little drooping head resting on his shoulder, and her beautiful golden hair, all stained with blood, falling over his arm. Would to God that I had died that death for her!

George Butler was a clergyman, and Josephine was deeply religious, so it was inevitable that they should feel led to question their God and speculate about his providence:

> It was a wonderful repose for me, a good gift of God, when troubled by the evils in the world or my own thoughts, to turn to the perfect innocence and purity of that little maiden. But that joy is now gone for us. I am troubled for my husband. His grief is so deep and silent; but he is very very patient. He loves children and all young creatures, and his love for her was wonderful.[11]

F. D. Maurice's letter of condolence is interesting both for itself and for its glimpse of the parents' response:

> I am not surprised that you cannot acquiesce in the notion of your own growth in goodness being the reward of separation from the child who was so dear to

you. As far as my experience goes, we want to be united to each other more, to love each other better and better. . . . You cannot think that your child is really severed from you. The yearning you feel is the pledge and assurance that it is not so.[12]

Maurice was a Broad Church clergyman, responsive to the skeptical and secularizing currents of his time, and this reference to reunion with the child is so hesitant that it seems to suggest a corresponding hesitation about the belief. Yet even the Broad Church Christian of 1864 probably still believed in an afterlife: the hesitation points to a greater undermining of faith than has yet taken place. It contrasts vividly with the detailed scenarios of reunion in heaven that we shall notice in the next chapter.

The Butlers found it very difficult to accept Eva's death. In her old age, Josephine wrote to her son Stanley that Eva's death "had a horrible sting in it. She was 5 1/2, never had a day's illness—healthy, strong, beautiful, our only daughter—father and I just adored her, and in a moment she fell, *smashed*, her head broken, and after hours of awful convulsions she died."[13] For the next twenty-five years she had never woken from sleep, she said, without a vision of Eva's falling figure and without the sound of her head hitting the ground ringing sickeningly in her ears. She dreamed constantly of Eva; and she worried about her silent, brooding husband. When a "ray of light" appeared—presumably a feeling that his grief was growing less intense—she gave the credit to God with a passion that shows how desperate she must have been.

Josephine claimed that this event was what turned her to the social work for which she is now so famous, her campaign against the Contagious Diseases Acts and her work on behalf of prostitutes and against licensed prostitution. Despite what she had said to Maurice, then, she did come to believe that her own growth in goodness was the reward of her loss, and when she claimed that she could not acquiesce in this, she was clearly fighting against herself. There is obviously no way of testing the truth of that belief, and if we say that she needed to believe it in order to be able to accept the death (even though she also, at first, needed not to believe it), that does not diminish its emotional importance for her. To the modern reader, this death may be the most painful of all those recorded in this chapter, because it cannot be locked up in its century: death in childbirth and child death from illness are so much less likely today, but accidents will be with us as long as there are children, and no modern parent can fail to hear the sound of that head hitting the ground ringing sickeningly in the ear.

"I cannot write"

Margaret Oliphant bore six children and outlived them all. Three died in infancy; the eldest, Maggie, died in 1864, aged ten; her two sons died in their thirties, when she was over sixty, leaving her desolate: "all gone, all gone, and no light to come to this sorrow any more." Shortly after Maggie's death, she wrote an account of her feelings; and in the last ten years of her life she incorporated this into an autobiographical sketch, much of which dealt with her children's deaths, and her reaction to them. The pages about Maggie's death are a cry of pain. Her husband had died in 1859, after only seven years of married life, and just before the birth of the last child; the further blow of losing her "one woman-child" seemed at times unbearable:

> The hardest moment in my present sad life is the morning, when I must wake up and begin the dreary world again. I can sleep during the night, and I sleep as long as I can; but when it is no longer possible, when the light can no longer be gainsaid, and life is going on everywhere, then I, too, rise up to bear my burden. How different it used to be! When I was a girl I remember the feeling I had when the fresh morning light came round. Whatever grief there had been the night before, the new day triumphed over it. Things must be better than one thought, must be well, in a world which woke up to that new light, to the sweet dews and sweet air which renewed one's soul. Now I am thankful for the night and the darkness, and shudder to see the light and the day returning.[14]

Sometimes her sorrow breaks into exclamations ("Help me, Oh help me Lord"), sometimes into despairing questions ("Where are you, oh my child, my child"), sometimes into puzzlement over the after-life: "She is with God, she is in his hands. I know nothing, cannot even imagine anything. Can I trust her with Him? Can I trust Him that He has done what was best for her?"

Some of the funeral notices on Princess Charlotte had tried to suggest that a death such as hers might be a blessing: "If she has been suddenly taken," wrote the *Sun*, "by the awful visitation of God, from all the pleasures and high distinctions of this transitory life, she is, mercifully, spared from its future trials, cares and sorrows." This is a rather half-hearted version of what some stern preachers stated much more aggressively, that since the world is a vale of sinfulness, we should give thanks for an early death because it enables the young person to avoid temptation (though the theology of this assertion is, as we shall see, tricky.) And in the pages of Catherine Tait and Elizabeth Prentiss we have met, without the specious argument that it was for the best, the effort to accept the death without repining, to believe that it would be "unchristian and ungrateful" to feel anything like discontent.

As we read Margaret Oliphant's autobiography, these pious assurances crumple before our eyes. Preachers can urge resignation, because God decreed the death: she writes, "I have not been resigned, I cannot feel resigned, my heart is sore as if it was an injury." Preachers can know it is all for the best, because God means everything for the best, and if we cannot see the blessing that is because our mortal sight is limited: she writes, "I keep on always upbraiding and reproaching God. I can't help thinking of the question somebody once asked a grieving woman, Have you not yet forgiven God? I feel like that myself." In the end, she does not trust God: "I come round again to the one misused unfailing answer—God must ever have a reason."

Thirty years later, facing the loss first of one son then of the other, she was still thinking of Maggie's death and of the two children who died in infancy. Of her "dear little Marjorie," who died at eight months, she writes, "I have never forgot the look with which that baby died." Her elder son Cecil had been a disappointment, the younger had had bad health, but it was the sheer fact of losing them that overwhelmed all previous disappointments and worries, and led to a recurrence of the despair she had felt after Maggie's death. She is clear-sighted enough to see how helpful people are trying to be, but she knows it is useless: "Everybody is very kind of course—people are always kind and I am like Job, such a monument of endless sorrow, always beginning and beginning once again." Reading Scott's account of his wife's death in his journal she is deeply impressed, but she adds: "No child died before him. It occurs to me that anything in the world could be lightly borne with that exception."

Margaret Oliphant wrote nearly a hundred novels, and though none has quite become a classic they deserve their modest place in literary history as well as the mild revival they have recently had. They are carefully plotted with a good deal of melodrama, some sharp social observation, and some effective comedy. But you will search in vain in the pages of *Miss Marjoriebanks* and *Hester*, probably her two best, for anything like the raw power of this autobiographical sketch. The meticulous plots of the novels are of course totally absent from the disjointed fragments of autobiography, which she never published or even arranged into a coherent whole; but the contrast shows us what perhaps we have always known—that plot is after all a kind of substitute for death, a way of producing in fiction the emotional intensity that is thrust into our lives by the death of those we love.

This reading of the *Autobiography*, I must now pause to observe, is directly at odds with that of its most recent editor, Elisabeth Jay. In her Introduction, she insists that it is a literary artifact and that the self it offers to us is a deliberate creation:

> It is important to make this point about the literariness of the *Autobiography* if only to dispel the long-held notion that this fragmented self-disclosure is merely a naive compilation of diary, chronicle and anecdote, eliciting compassion for a series of personal tragedies. . . . The self that Oliphant presents in the *Autobiography* is a deliberate creation.

Jay even sees the work as an anticipation of modernism, suggesting that this accounts for Virginia Woolf's praise of it, because it approached the condition to which she believed fiction should aspire, with "no plot, no comedy, no tragedy, no love interest or catastrophe in the accepted style."

Jay's reading of the *Autobiography* is so consonant with current critical theory, and so much at odds with mine, that it seems necessary to offer a short discussion of it, and a defense of what may be seen as a naive reading. The theoretical question at issue concerns the determinants of any piece of writing: how far it is the result of preceding, often nonverbal experience that was there before the act of writing began, and how far it is the result of the strategies of the act of writing itself—in other words, how far our world is shaped by the language we use to articulate it.[15] Once we grant that any act of writing has a double input, from experience and from the strategies of writing, we can then observe that the respective share of each can vary from one writing act to another. I claim that the *Autobiography* derives far more from experience than the novels do and that it *does* "elicit compassion for a series of personal tragedies." To deny this is (I return to Ricoeur's terminology) to confine ourselves to the semiotic—and, in a case like this, would be deeply insulting to Oliphant's grief. To assert it is not to refuse interest in writing strategies but to see them as a way of exploring the interface between text and experience.

This enables me to claim what Jay's position would have difficulty in claiming (even had she wished to, which it appears she does not), that the

Autobiography is the most powerful of Oliphant's writings because it is the least literary, the closest to experience, refusing the stereotypes she employed so competently in her novels. I do not want to make this claim in its extreme, anti-literary form, to assert that the language of even the greatest poet "must often, in liveliness and truth, fall short of that which is uttered by men in real life, under the actual pressure of those passions": in this notorious passage, Wordsworth is indeed being naive, overlooking the likelihood that the immediacy of real language will fall into cliché.

Trying, then, to step briefly outside the hermeneutic circle, I propose that there are moments in the *Autobiography* when the power of the writing comes from sheer immediacy. Such a moment occurs in the last two sentences. A long paragraph rehearses her son's faults, his virtues, their intimacy, and the progress of his illness, and ends, "but all through he was getting weaker; and I knew it, and tried not to know." After all this come two brief one-sentence paragraphs:

> And now here I am all alone.
> I cannot write any more.

The isolation of those two blunt statements into separate paragraphs is a stroke of genius. I have no proof, but I feel sure it was not pondered, it resulted from the author forgetting her craftsmanship and her principles of construction and letting her grief speak. It is misleading, therefore, to call it a strategy of writing (though it is one). For the reader, that touch of genius in the writing creates the emotion; for the writer, it was the emotion that shaped the writing. For both, the total experience is semantic, not just semiotic.

I will add a word on Jay's parallel with modernism. Modernist narrative strategies, as is well known, disperse and disintegrate the unitary characters of traditional realist fiction. We can explain this either by saying that modernism was a revolution in sensibility, in our awareness of ourselves, and that human beings today are less certain of a coherent identity than were their great-grandparents; or by saying that experience has always been more fragmentary than the conventions of narrative have found convenient, so that modernism is actually more realistic than realism. Has human nature changed, or has its representation?

It would be an oversimplification to choose one of these views and reject the other, but the shift of emphasis is important. On the one hand,

Jay clearly leans towards the first view, that the modern self has disinte-
grated and that a fragmentary narrative is therefore a sign of proto-mod-
ernism. I, on the other hand, regard literary revolutions as less fundamen-
tal than that. There has always been a fragmentary quality to experience,
and random jottings have always been a natural way of recording experience. I see no reason to believe that if Oliphant had published her *Autobiography* she would have left her jottings unarranged. I do not see her as
anticipating modernism; I see her as making random jottings and not
arranging them, in a way that modernism has subsequently legitimated.

Josephine & Noel

Josephine Kipling, eldest child of Rudyard and his wife Caroline, died
in New York on Sunday 6 March 1899, at the age of six. The death came
just as her father was recovering from an attack of pneumonia that had
almost killed him, and as a result it achieved world-wide publicity. Kipling
was perhaps the most popular living writer, and when it was known that he
was dangerously ill in a New York hotel, letters and telegrams of concern
poured in from all over the English-speaking world. The unfortunate doctors and the even more unfortunate wife, as if fending off the reporters
were not difficult enough, were bombarded with exhortations to put raw
onion poultice on his chest and the bottom of his feet, to "use oxygen by
the bowel" and to inject 1 per cent common salt solution "and save husband's life." The news that he was recovering was accompanied by the
news that his daughter had died (this was known to the world before it was
told to Kipling himself); consequently, the flood of letters grew even
greater, congratulations on recovery followed by sympathy at the loss. The
masters and boys of St. Edmund's School, Canterbury, begged respectfully
"to be allowed to express to Mr. Rudyard Kipling our thankful pleasure at
his recovery from recent severe illness, and our hope that he may be spared
to write many more books which may be, like those of the past, the delight
of boys both of larger and smaller growth. At the same time, we write to
offer our deep sympathy to Mr. and Mrs. Rudyard Kipling in the great loss
which has come upon them. . . ." The military attaché at the British
Embassy in Washington sent "a soldier's heartfelt congratulations on your
stubborn gallant fight, and on your truly British victory—the most popular,
I believe, since Waterloo." Henry James wrote two emotional, very Jame-
sian and illegible letters, one congratulating the "dear demonic indestruc-

tible youth" on the fact that he had "visited the mountains of the moon and come back on a taut wire, in the cold light of that satellite and with every opera-glass on earth fixed on you—with no balancing pole but your inimitable genius," followed next day, when he heard about Josephine, by a rueful letter to Caroline wishing that he could recall the first:

> Please believe in the abounding sympathy with which I think of you. Dear little vanished delightful Josephine and dear little surrendered sacrificed soul! Forgive this incoherent expression—I am only thinking of her being worsted in the battle, and of the so happy form in which I saw her last winter at Rottingdean. But how can I even seem to allude to what you feel? . . . Magnificent have you both been and still more will have to be now. But I believe in you up to the hilt. The best and kindest day to my sense will be when you are at peace together again in this corner of the land. Don't read my other letter—read this. More than ever constantly and tenderly yours, Henry James.

In most of the letters, the balance tilts more to congratulation than to consolation—understandably enough from those who read the father and did not know the daughter. So delight in his recovery tends to be followed by a mere concessive clause, "though the shadow of the dear little lost one is over it." (Josephine is described as "little" in letter after letter, a verbal detail I shall revert to).

Josephine attained her sudden world-wide fame by accident. Her death would not have attracted anywhere near so much attention if it had not been for the coincidence of her father's narrow escape. Yet though this made her, briefly, the most celebrated dead child in the world, the letters that matter are clearly those that would have been written anyway, such as the note from Kipling's neighbor in Rottingdean ("My little Molly and your sweet little maid were such friends and Molly now talks so constantly of her that we cannot but feel very deeply ourselves the loss"), and above all those from Kipling's mother and his aunt Georgiana, wife of Edward Burne-Jones.

Here is Alice Kipling to her sister:

> My darling Georgie,
> Deeper and deeper yet. There has come a telegram from New York— telling us that little Josephine died this morning at 6.20. The apple of her father's eye—the delight of his heart! How will he bear it? and poor Carrie

already worn with sorrow and crushing anxiety. In the letter which I asked Margaret to send on to you—Carrie makes no mention of Josephine being *ill*—except for whooping cough—but from the moment I knew the poor child had pneumonia I have been afraid. The dear-bright-pretty child—six little happy years—and now a memory only!

Georgie wrote an affectionate, emotional letter to Carrie:

There is not a heart untouched with sympathy for you I am sure. Here where she has lived, the news has sent a chill through everyone. Many refused to believe it, and some came almost trembling to ask if it could be true. . . . Oh my poor darlings, this great distance makes it feel as if I was talking to the stars. . . .

What is striking in all this material, especially if we compare it to the Tait or Butler deaths, is the disappearance of God. There is as much tenderness, as much grief and as much need for consolation, but there are no reassurances that she has joined her heavenly Father or that those who mourn for her will later be reunited with her, and there is no hint that she is better dead. There is, to be sure, one letter from a clergyman which refers to "the profound faith of Mr Kipling," but even this is almost withdrawn again: "I know too well the profound faith of Mr Kipling and his unfaltering courage to doubt as to his power to accept this bereavement." If the faith is profound, we might comment, then there is no need for courage. The letter continues: "A new wonder will arise in his soul, and new sweetness and depth in his poetry. He will reveal some new, clear, indubitable vision upon which many mourners for children will look and be comforted." This seems carefully balanced on the edge of making credal statements: "wonder," "sweetness," "depth," "vision" are all terms that could, but need not, imply Christian belief and, perhaps, rather carefully avoid doing so. I know nothing about that clergyman, Charles Orris Day, but without questioning the genuineness of his belief we can see his letter as illustrating the tendency of Christian consolation to become secularized. When he writes, "Alas! that this sweet flower is transplanted; though growing eternally more lovely somewhere, I must believe," we can wonder if there is an element of skepticism in the last three words—which could mean, "As a clergyman I am not allowed to say otherwise."[16]

Almost forty years earlier, T. H. Huxley's eldest son Noel died of scarlet fever, shortly before he turned four. Huxley took consolation for his grief in the memory of the life:

So end many hopes and plans—sadly enough, and yet not altogether bitterly. For as the little fellow was our greatest joy so is the recollection of him an enduring consolation. It is a heavy payment, but I would buy the four years of him again at the same price.

A letter of condolence from Charles Kingsley produced from Huxley what is probably the most interesting and eloquent letter he ever wrote, a passionate defense of his agnosticism (a few years later, he was to coin the term). In contrast to the Kipling consolations, Christian belief is here quite explicitly considered and rejected. The arguments are familiar enough nowadays, and we shall revert to them in the next chapter: that our passionate wish for personal immortality, so far from being an argument in favor of it, is precisely the reason we should be especially skeptical about it; that arguments based on the nature of personality as the surest thing we know and therefore, in some sense, enduring lead to "mere verbal subtleties"; and that the claim that belief in future rewards and punishments is necessary to morality on this earth is a "mischievous lie." This last conviction is directly linked to the child's death:

> As I stood behind the coffin of my little son the other day, with my mind bent on anything but disputation, the officiating minister read, as a part of his duty, the words, "If the dead rise not again, let us eat and drink, for tomorrow we die." I cannot tell you how inexpressibly they shocked me. . . . I could have laughed with scorn. What! because I am face to face with irreparable loss, because I have given back to the source from whence it came, the cause of a great happiness, still retaining through all my life the blessings which have sprung and will spring from that cause, I am to renounce my manhood, and, howling, grovel in bestiality? Why the very apes know better. . . .

There are two ways for God to disappear. As we read the Kipling correspondence, we can observe that God has slipped, silently and unnoticed, out of human consciousness. As we read Huxley's letter, we can see that God has been defiantly expelled. The motive for the latter has often been political: the radical atheism that runs from the French Revolution through Shelley, Richard Carlile, and Huxley's contemporary James Thomson claims that priests have often been the allies of kings in their oppression of humanity. Huxley's irreligion has no such explicit political content (despite his intellectual radicalism, Huxley held fairly conservative political views), but there is no doubt about the defiance: he even strikes a heroic posture that is appropriate to this radical tradition and quotes Luther's famous "Gott helfe mir, Ich kann nichts anders"; and after a half-ironic suggestion that if he had lived a couple of centuries earlier he could have fancied a devil scoffing at him, "asking me what profit it was to have stripped myself of the hopes and consolations of the mass of mankind," he ends the thought very earnestly:

> Oh devil! truth is better than much profit. I have searched over the grounds of my belief, and if wife and child and name and fame were all to be lost to me one after the other as the penalty, still I will not lie.[17]

All trace of irony has now disappeared from this self-dramatizing heroism. How utterly different from Georgie Burne-Jones, responding to Josephine's death: "Mystery it all is—but we are part of it, and no trouble that happens to us is a new one in the world." She does not know whether the mystery is a Christian one: Christian belief has merged into a kind of humanist pantheism ("I wonder . . . whether you felt behind you any breath of the sympathetic support from the great tides of feeling that your trouble has set in motion"). But she would have fed the clergyman's pieties into her grief whether she believed in them or not, not even perhaps knowing if she believed, but accepting the vocabulary as appropriate to the occasion. The smile that lingered on after the Cheshire cat had vanished may have been intended by Lewis Carroll as a joke, to show that everyone in Wonderland is mad, but it can also be seen as a brilliant metaphor for our cultural history: Christian doctrine may fade away, but the sentiment of consolation it had given rise to lingers on.

* * *

> My period of intense religiousness, although not by design, helped me through the first year of Robby's death in a very practical manner. . . . I began to develop a routine, to plan my day around the evening Kaddish service. . . . The advantage of religious belief when a child dies is enormous. It is a source of comfort. . . . If your faith offers no daily religious service, or if you do not choose to partake in one, set aside ten minutes a day, at the same time every day.[18]

Why is it immediately obvious that this comes from the twentieth century? Neither Catherine Tait nor Elizabeth Prentiss, nor any other bereaved parent of a hundred or a hundred and fifty years ago, though they would not actually have disagreed with these statements, could have thought in this way. What is here assumed is that religion is an option among others. In the humane and thoughtful book from which this is taken, *The Bereaved Parent*, written in 1977 by Harriet Sarnoff Schiff, herself a bereaved parent, coping with a child's death is seen as a psychological problem for the survivor, needing treatment like any other problem. The dead child is purely an absence; religion is not a matter of belief but of ritual and psychological function (even the sentence about the advantages of "religious belief" does not really refer to belief but to ritual and institutional practices). It is seen as a method that will work very well for some, not at all for others, and in the secularized, tolerant world of modern America no blame attaches to the choice. Concentrating in this way on the psychological function of religion—calling it "religion," as if the choice between the Christian or Muslim or (as here) the Jewish version was a secondary matter—does not seem to have weakened that function at all. Religious belief has faded like the Cheshire Cat; but religious sentiment, like the smile, continues as strong as ever.

A *Child Speaks*

The great limitation in our study of these children, is, of course, that they do not speak to us directly: we normally hear only what the bystanders say about them. In discussing the difference between one child death and another, we are mainly dealing with differences between the narrators, who are usually the parents. This is most obviously true in the case of infant death, for the human being in the first year of life is literally *in-fans*, unable to speak. But even in the case of the Tait children, we only have access to their consciousness through what Mrs. Tait tells us they said; will there not therefore be a special interest in those records that are left by the child? Of course, there are a host of reasons for treating these with skepticism: the children who write them will not be typical, will not be young, obviously will not be dead, and we must take it on trust that adults have not tampered with the writing.

Emily Shore was certainly an exceptional child. She kept a journal from the age of eleven until she died of consumption in 1839, at the age of nineteen. The extracts published by her sisters in 1891 run to 350 pages, and she had also written romantic novels, histories of Greece and Rome, and a great deal of natural history. The journal is rich in botanizing observations, along with much family detail: her father was a clergyman who had refused a living because of his doubts about the Thirty-nine Articles and who supported himself and his family by taking pupils. The last half-year of her life was spent in Madiera: the reasons she gives are her father's health and the cheapness of living there, but her own health must have been a consideration, perhaps the main one.

There is so much enthusiasm for living, learning, and observing in her journal, and she was so obviously a fluent and relaxed writer, that the occasional gloomy entries come with a real shock. The first of these occurs less than a year before the end:

> Journalizing has lost its interest with me. I am dreary, dispirited, and ill. The only occupation I pursue with any interest is that of increasing my knowledge of chronology. I have in the last few days learned perfectly a hundred dates.

The gloom did not last: on the very next day she is reading Nichol's book on the solar system with obvious interest, and by the following week she records that in reading Nichol, "astonishment, delight, admiration, almost overpowered my imagination and thoughts." On 29 January 1839 she writes:

> While they went to church in the morning, I was as usual left alone, and sank into a long melancholy reverie on subjects which will intrude themselves whenever I am alone. . . . I ought to esteem myself happy; but all the enjoyment of happiness is gone, and cannot return. . . . There is nothing in Madiera which is dear to me; the land, the people, are new and unknown and strange. Nay, it makes no little difference to me that in every room of the house I look round on strange furniture, which belongs to another, instead of our own, which I remember from earliest childhood. . . . Oh there are moments when visions start up before me of sweet well-known spots—woods where the anemone and bluebell grow; streams shaded with ash-trees and hawthorn, where I have wandered alone in early spring mornings, on violets and primroses and grass drenched with dew, myself the happiest of the happy, listening to the songs of the birds, and shaking over me a shower of bright drops, as I gathered the branches of the willow or bullace. . . . Oh, how many happy hours, which seem to me but as yesterday, start up in contrast with the present! . . . I live it all over again, and I cannot avoid weeping. There is no language to describe the sharp pain of past and regretted happiness. I was much happier as a child than I am now, or ever shall be. . . .

That is the most moving passage in her journal, yet perhaps nothing in it has the bleakness of that account of her learning a hundred dates because a purely mechanical, even pointless, task, is all she can bring herself to perform. This passage was written six months before her death on July 7, and though she went on writing until a fortnight before the end, there is nothing as extended or powerful as this. It surely owes much of its impact to the fact that it is less about impending death than about actual illness: future experience can (obviously) never be as real as present experience. At times, indeed, it hardly seems to be about illness but simply about growing up, about the nostalgic vision of lost childhood, the "meadow grove and stream . . . apparelled in celestial light—the glory and the freshness of a dream." We could even claim that Wordsworth's celestial light is less immediate than the shower of bright drops that falls from a very earthly tree on the young Emily.

As befits a clergyman's dutiful daughter, there are elements of piety, but there is very little about a future life. She asks God to be merciful to her a sinner, she praises God for "giving me such excellent parents," but she does not seem to anticipate union with God, and no light is shining on her as she goes. Her final entry, after a few brief, telling details, looks forward not to her own future, but to being remembered:

> I suppose I am beginning to sink; still I can at times take up my pen. I have had my long back hair cut off. Dear Papa wears a chain of it. Mamma will have one too.

In one sense at least, this is the most actual of all the child deaths. Emily was no longer a child, but at nineteen she remembered her childhood with such intensity that we can feel that the Emily who is dying is not the young adult who is writing the journal; that child is present in the dying writer, not through sympathy but in a more literal sense, through memory. This is the nearest thing we have yet had to a child's account of her own death.[19]

A Postscript: Diagnosis and Non-diagnosis

What did these children die of? Almost all of them died of infectious diseases, and we know in statistical terms what these diseases were. Smallpox was the biggest killer until the introduction of vaccination early in the nineteenth century. Even then, smallpox remained the most common cause among poor children until well into the century, because the practice of vaccination only spread slowly down the social scale. After that came pulmonary tuberculosis ("consumption"), which was also endemic. Then came diseases that swept England in epidemics (especially cholera), and those that came in waves of greater and less severity (measles, scarlet fever). Typhus, diphtheria, and whooping cough were also important. Frequency of all these diseases dropped dramatically with improvements in public health after the mid-century: it is of course prevention not cure that has lowered the child death rate so dramatically in our time. Even antibiotics do not cure all of them.

All that is well-known, but what did particular children die of? Often we know, but often we do not. I have looked at some dozens of child deaths in memoirs and letters and am struck by how often we are told that a patient died of "spotted fever of the most malignant character," of "fever and brain disorder," of "inflammation of the bowels," of "convulsions," or simply of a serious illness.[20] It is common practice today, especially in America, when mentioning a death (even in the case of the very old, and certainly in other cases) to state the cause of death; clearly this was not the case in Victorian times.

There are three, perhaps four, reasons for this. The first is medical ignorance: the further back in time we go, the less capable medical science is of classifying and diagnosing—indeed, the more alarming medical science is in every respect! Some of the doctors we meet in the pages of these memoirs do not inspire much confidence: Elizabeth Prentiss told Dr. Watson that she thought her little son had "water on the brain": her description is fairly detailed, and suggests either a brain tumor or tubercular meningitis. To expect the doctor to diagnose this would be asking too much, but it is alarming to read that, even in 1852, "he said it was not so, and ordered nothing but a warm bath"; twelve days later the child was dead. We have already seen how little Sir Richard Croft could do for Princess Charlotte and how dearly he paid for his presumed incompetence. The official bulletin, presumably provided by Croft himself, attributed her death to "exhaustion of vital energy, occasioned by excessive and insupportable pain."[21] This appears to suggest a blockage in the course of delivery, but the fact that the child was born normally and was "one of the finest infants ever brought into this world" makes that very unlikely. The Princess must surely have died of sepsis or a hemorrhage: it looks as if Croft did not realize this—or was he being vague in order to preserve what he saw as the proprieties? Of course, the occasional bland or incompetent physician is not of great historical significance: more interesting is to observe how far medical science itself was or was not able to diagnose.

The second reason for vague and general description could be, simply, the Victorian belief that diagnosis is not important. If death is the release of the soul from the body, if it is to be welcomed as being received into the presence of God, then the body has ceased to matter, and one need waste no attention on what caused it to cease functioning. Here for instance is Mrs. Tait's description of the dead Chatty:

> There she lay in the room in which I had given her birth; but that day I felt indeed the spirit was gone, and the little form before us looked so different now the bright spirit which had breathed through it, and given it such exceeding beauty, had flown to a region far more suited for it than this world of sin and sorrow.

Almost every detail tells us that the body, having released Chatty's spirit, no longer matters. Whatever she had died of, the description would have been much the same: all that needs to be said about the empty shell is that it has lost the bright spirit which breathed through it.

To say that something does not matter can, of course, be a defense mechanism: it might matter very much, and hence be a topic we would rather avoid. The great avoidance in nineteenth century linguistic practice, as everyone knows, was sex. Dismissing sex as a mere animal impulse, not worthy of serious attention and shameful to talk about, must have served several purposes: for instance, allowing men to indulge in it without too much fuss being made, allowing women not to talk about it and so, it is presumably hoped, not to have the discomfort of thinking about it. I do not find it easy to decide whether something similar is true of illness—whether the malfunctioning of the body was regarded as an indelicate topic, and so repressed, enabling us to think of the human being as essentially spiritual.

And then there is a final possibility, the most interesting of all, though the hardest to pin down: a skepticism about diagnosis springing from skepticism about the classification of disease. To explain this, I turn to Florence Nightingale's *Notes on Nursing*, published in 1860.

This admirable book is packed with keen observation and sensible advice, revealing how carefully and sensitively Nightingale had thought about every detail in the sick room. It treats the patient as a frail but responsible person, suggesting, for instance, that his stomach, even if expressed as whims and fancies, may be a more reliable guide to diet than chemistry; and it explores what every aspect of nursing practice must look like to the person for—and to—whom it is done. Most striking, for our purpose, is the emphasis placed on hygiene. The health of a house depends on five essential points: pure air, pure water, effective drainage, cleanliness, and light. This, Nightingale claims, is what every schoolgirl should be taught (rather than "the coxcombries of education" such as the elements of astronomy) and what every nurse should concern herself with. The first rule of nursing is to "keep the air [the patient] breathes as pure as the external air, without chilling him," because foul air is the cause of disease—not contagion but foul air:

> Is it not a fact, that when scarlet fever, measles or smallpox appear among the children, the very first thought is "where" the child can have "caught" the disease. . . . They never think of looking at home for the source of the mischief. If a neighbour's child is seized with smallpox, the first question which occurs is whether it has been vaccinated. No-one would undervalue vaccination; but it becomes of doubtful benefit to society when it leads people to look abroad for the source of evils which exist at home.

Florence Nightingale is here taking sides in an important medical controversy on the cause of disease, that between the believers in miasma and the believers in contagion. Miasma describes the state of the environment in general terms; contagion refers to something specific. The reason Nightingale resisted it so strongly is that it would introduce an element of pure chance into the battle between order and disorder:

> The causes of the enormous child mortality are perfectly well known; they are chiefly want of cleanliness, want of ventilation, want of whitewashing; in one word, defective household hygiene.[22]

These are the words of a moral crusader, and Charles Rosenberg has pointed out how central such moral fervour is to Nightingale's conception of nursing.[23] If we put our lives in order, we shall not catch scarlet fever or measles or smallpox. Looking back more than a century later, we can see that she was both right and wrong. Of course foul air and foul water are the causes of disease, because there are airborne and waterborne infections. It is not foulness as such that we must be protected from, but the microorganisms that carry these diseases. But for her, to maintain that would be to reify disease:

> Is it not living in a continual mistake to look upon diseases, as we do now, as separate entities, which *must* exist, like cats and dogs, instead of looking upon them as conditions, like a dirty and a clean condition, and just as much under our control. . . . I was brought up, both by scientific men and ignorant women, distinctly to believe that smallpox, for instance, was a thing of which there was once a first specimen in the world, which went on propagating itself, in a perpetual chain of descent, just as much as there was a first dog. . . . Since then I have seen with my eyes and smelt with my nose smallpox growing up in first specimens, either in close rooms or in overcrowded wards, where it could not be any possibility have been "caught" but must have begun.[24]

Here we hear the commanding voice of experience, authoritative, impressive, and wrong. For a counterstatement from modern times to set against it, I choose not a medical writer but Susan Sontag's vigorous and personal essay, *Illness as Metaphor.* This stirring defense of scientific medicine attacks multicausal theories of disease, along with theories that diseases are caused by mental states, because they moralize what should be seen as pathology and "make people irrationally fearful of effective measures such as chemotherapy, and foster credence in thoroughly useless remedies such as diets and psychotherapy." All moral or mental explanations, which Sontag sees as examples of metaphor, "are always an index of how much is not understood about the physical terrain of a disease,[25] and she has, as one would expect, no respect for the outmoded "miasma" theories that Nightingale still clung to.

The contrast tells us a great deal. It is the contrast between scientific medicine and public health, two institutions that (fortunately) collaborate in practice but between which, as I have tried to show, a deep gulf of principle can open. Perhaps too it is the contrast between the human being seen holistically and morally (what do diagnostic details matter to the spiritual self?) and the human being anatomized by experimental science. And is it going too far to suggest that it is, in part, the contrast between the nineteenth and the twentieth centuries?

2

Strategies of Consolation: The Dead Child in Poetry

CHILD DEATHS, then, were common enough in the nineteenth century and were brooded on; so it is hardly surprising that they figure so
prominently in nineteenth century literature. (Whether we should
nonetheless be surprised will be discussed in chapter 4.) In this chapter I
shall look at some of the many poems on the subject.

All deaths bring to the survivors a need for consolation, and child deaths
most of all because of the feeling that it is unnatural as well as distressing
for the mother to outlive her child. Consolation is at least the apparent
theme of poems on the subject; so imagine yourself a bereaved mother
reading the following poem by Felicia Hemans:

> No bitter tears for thee be shed,
> Blossom of being! seen and gone!
> With flowers alone we strew thy bed,
>   O blest departed One!
> Whose all of life, a rosy ray,
> Blushed into dawn and passed away.
>
> Yes! thou art fled, ere guilt had power
> To stain the cherub-soul and form,
> Closed is the soft ephemeral flower

That never felt a storm!
The sunbeam's smile, the zephyr's breath,
All that it knew from birth to death.

Thou wert so like a form of light,
That Heaven benignly called thee hence,
Ere yet the world could breathe one blight
          O'er thy sweet innocence:
And thou, that brighter home to bless,
Art passed, with all thy loveliness!

Oh! hadst thou still on earth remained,
Vision of beauty! fair as brief!
How soon thy brightness had been stained
          With passion or with grief!
Now not a sullying breath can rise
To dim thy glory in the skies.

We rear no marble o'er thy tomb;
No sculptured image there shall mourn;
Ah! fitter far the vernal bloom
          Such dwelling to adorn.
Fragrance, and flowers, and dews must be
The only emblems meet for thee.

Thy grave shall be a blessed shrine,
Adorned with Nature's brightest wreath;
Each glowing season shall combine
          Its incense there to breathe;
And oft upon the midnight air,
Shall viewless harps be murmuring there.

And oh! sometimes in visions blest,
Sweet spirit! visit our repose;
And bear, from thine own world of rest,
          Some balm for human woes!
What form more lovely could be given
Than thine to messenger of heaven![1]

Is it not insensitive to insist, with the aid of so many exclamation marks, that the death of a child is not matter for grief but rather of acceptance, even rejoicing? Certainly when Hemans wrote to a bereaved mother in sober prose, she made no mention of rejoicing and gave no hint that the child was better dead:

> I can feel deeply for the sorrow you communicate to me; it is one which Heaven has yet graciously spared me; but the imagination . . . has often brought all the sufferings of that particular bereavement before me, with a vividness from which I have shrunk almost in foreboding terror. And I have too (though not through the breaking of *that* tie) those sick and weary yearnings for the dead, that feverish thirst for the sound of a departed voice or step, in which the heart seems to die away, and literally to become a "fountain of tears."[2]

There is a difference, evidently, between writing about "the child" and a particular child. Rejoicing belongs to the imagined child death, tears are in order for an actual death. The writing of Hemans's poem is not in itself insensitive, but the act of showing it to a mother who had suffered such a loss might be.

There are many such poems. They all urge the parents not to weep because the dead child is now an angel ("and treads the sapphire floors of Paradise"), has left behind a happy memory ("the shrine of pleasing thoughts, soft as the scent of flowers"), and will through its death have a beneficial effect on the survivors ("They that have seen thy look in death / No more may fear to die").[3] The second and third of these consolations are compatible with Christianity, the first is explicitly Christian.

I propose to use these poems to examine the ways in which Christianity performs the function of consolation for the bereaved parent. What enables a poem to perform this function effectively is not its artistic excellence: so the discussion is not offered as literary criticism in the evaluative sense—it is not primarily concerned with distinguishing good poems from bad. The reader who believes that judgment of quality is inescapable, and who therefore finds this omission unpardonable, must be asked to suspend condemnation, since I shall address this point explicitly in the last chapter (and occasionally before). The reader who rejoices in the omission, as freeing us from the ideological bias that disguises itself as aesthetic judgments, is encouraged to rejoice, but may be in for disappointment later.

Furthermore—and this is trickier—the discussion is about the social and emotional function of religion and attempts to set aside the question of truth or falsehood. Whatever functions we attribute to religion can always be seen either as evidence that religion is a human invention or that it is a part of God's plan. And the agnosticism from which I have tried to write is not, in this case, simply a methodological strategy: it is a posture from which I do not intend to emerge. I fear that both Christian and atheist readers may find themselves dissatisfied with this, but there is no compensation that can be offered them except the intrinsic interest of the arguments.

Coleridge and the Dead Infant

"Be rather than be called a child of God"
Death whispered. With assenting nod,
Its head upon its mother's breast,
       The Baby bowed without demur—
Of the kingdom of the Blest
Possessor, not Inheritor[4]

If we read this poem as orthodox Christian, which it clearly is, Death is seen as helpful, listening to the words of the baptism service and offering to go one better, and so doing the infant a good turn. But no such poem can protect itself against the defiantly atheist reader, and if we give it an unchristian reading (if we pretend, say, that it was written by Hardy) then Death becomes not helpful but sardonic, and the poem is a chuckle, saying, "If that's what they think, let's act on it." Reverse the interpretative context, in other words, and we can reverse the poem. Our knowledge that Coleridge (who was orthodox enough by 1799, when these lines were written) did not mean it that way, and would no doubt have been indignant at such a reading, is knowledge extrinsic to the text, telling us not that it will not bear this meaning but that responsible historians would not dream (or would only dream) of propounding it.

That this reversal of meaning, if we insisted on imposing it, would not be mere whim is confirmed by the "Epitaph on an Infant" of 1811 (by which time Coleridge was even more orthodox):

Its balmy lips the infant blest
Relaxing from its Mother's breast,
How sweet it heaves the happy sigh
Of innocent satiety!

> And such my infant's latest sigh!
> Oh tell, rude stone! the passer by
> That here the pretty babe doth lie,
> Death sang to sleep with Lullaby.

Once again, Death is doing the child a good turn, but not, this time, for Christian reasons. There is no Christianity at all in this proto-Freudian poem about the satiety of the child removed from the breast, which Freud would later compare with sexual satiety (and which in its turn has often enough been compared to death). The parallel with the first epitaph consists in the wiliness of Death. The baptismal service and the bliss of being breast-fed both contain a promise of ensuing happiness, that of heaven in the first, of sleep in the second. Death hears the service, sees the infant, and in both cases fulfils the promise in a way we did not expect but cannot logically object to. He has played a benign trick on us—or rather a trick that should be benign to the Christian, and will seem a bad joke to the this-worldly reader.

In neither of these poems is there any statement that living in the world is a danger from which the child has been released, as there is in the earliest of Coleridge's three child epitaphs:

> Ere Sin could blight or Sorrow fade,
> Death came with friendly care:
> The opening Bud to Heaven conveyed
> And bade it blossom *there*.

The promise that Death decides to grant immediately, which was textual in the first poem and physiological in the second, is now presented through the image of plucking (or transplanting) a flower, with, this time, an explicit mention of the dangers of living on. Though these dangers are not mentioned in the other two epitaphs, it would not be misreading to import them: it could even be claimed that they are clearly implied—why else would Death be doing a kindly act? (In the reversal I have proposed, where Death's motive is malevolent, the view of life as a vale of tears and danger is still implied: In that case, Death is not rescuing the infant, but cunningly exploiting the logic of such a view).

What Coleridge merely implies is spelled out at great length by Hemans: her poem is a celebration of Death's benign rescue. It too uses the image of a flower being transplanted, and as in Coleridge's epitaph the flower blooms only in infancy; she then develops the implication that it can go on blooming in Heaven. The image clearly springs from otherworldliness, the conviction that what happens in this world is of only minor or temporary importance; or, more strongly still, that life on earth is a corrupting experience, from which we should be glad to be rescued. If our true fulfillment lies in Heaven, then the sooner we get there the better: suicide needs to be forbidden to Christians because a true Christian ought naturally to desire to die as soon as possible. The child, too young to be tempted by suicide, was lucky to be given immediate access to Heaven, without having to sin in order to get there. And if this world is not merely a delay but actually a danger, then to dwell in it might diminish our chances of reaching Heaven at all. Hemans's poem does not quite say that; but it does say that if the child had lived, then its brightness would have been "stained with passion or with grief":

> Now not a sullying breath can rise,
> To dim thy glory in the skies.

These lines, if scrutinized, seem to say that there are degrees of being saved: that those unfortunate enough to live longer would have their glory "stained"—presumably meaning either that they will be less glorious as angels or (more probably) that our memory of them will include the imperfections of being human as well as the fact that they are now in Heaven. The lines do not quite say that their chances of attaining Heaven will be diminished if they live on—an opinion we shall encounter later.

Before we leave Coleridge, we ought to know that he did actually lose an infant son. So as well as exploring the implications of meaning that his epitaphs offer, we can relate them to the poet himself. Coleridge spent the winter of 1798–1799 in Germany, learning the language and collecting material for one of the many proposed books he never completed, a life of Lessing. He left his wife Sara and their two small sons in Nether Stowey, where their friends the Pooles kept an eye on her. While he was away, his infant son Berkeley was inoculated against smallpox, and the inoculation went wrong; he grew feverish, and the pustules began to appear on the skin by hundreds. Sara was distracted, especially since she herself caught a violent cold ("I was seized with a pain in my eye; it in a few hours became quite closed—my face and neck swollen, my head swimming")[5], as well as finding that the pustules had broken out on her nipples. It looked as if the child would die: he recovered, then a month or so later was seized with a violent suffocation and fever, from which he did not recover, dying in February 1799. During this long trouble, Thomas Poole insisted that Coleridge should not be distracted from his studies. He urged Sara not to tell him of the child's illness (which meant that for a long time she did not write at all), and he himself wrote one deliberately misleading letter, assuring Coleridge that his family were well. Sara was not, however, able to stop herself writing a long truthful account in November, followed by another in December when Berkeley seemed to be recovering, in which she admits that Poole

> *insists* on my not telling you about the child until he is quite well—I am sorry I let my feelings escape me so—Be assured, my dear, that I am as comfortable as my situation (with respect to the child) will admit, and that I am truly glad that you are not here to witness his sufferings, as you could not possibly do more for the boy than has been already done for him.

Coleridge eventually learned the news of Berkeley's death in a letter from Poole, written on March 15.

The contrasts revealed by this three-cornered correspondence are very sharp. Sara's letters are by far the most direct and matter-of-fact: they contain vivid and accurate descriptions of the child's symptoms, along with outpourings of how much she feels the need of her husband's presence during her troubles. These are sometimes very painful to read:

> God almighty bless you my dear Samuel! Pray continue to cherish affection for us; and be assured that tho' I long to see you, I should be much hurt if you were to return before you had attained the end of your going—and I am very proud to hear that you are so forward in the language—and that you are so gay among the Ladies: you may give my respects to them and say that I am not at all jealous, for I *know* my dear Samuel in her affliction will not forget entirely, his most affectionate wife, Sara Coleridge. (Sara to Coleridge, 13 Dec. 1798)

Poole's letter informing Coleridge of Berkeley's death is well-meaning but reveals a very different worldview:

> I have thus, my dear Col., informed you of the whole truth. It was long contrary to my opinion to let you know of the child's death before your arrival in Eng-

land. And I thought, and still think myself justified in that notion, by the OVER-anxiety you expressed in your former letters concerning the children. Doubtless the affection found to exist between parents and *infant* children is a wise law of nature, a mere instinct to preserve Man in his infant state. . . . But the moment you make this affection the creature of reason, you degrade reason. When the infant becomes a reasonable being, then let the affection be a thing of reason, not before. Brutes can only have an instinctive affection. (15 Mar 1799)

What he regards as "mere instinct," the brutish element in human feeling, was for Sara the bond of nature. Poole, it is true, also speaks of "nature," but in his usage the term is merely condescending:

You will feel, and lament, the death of your child, but you will only recollect him a baby of fourteen weeks, but I am his Mother, and have carried him in my arms, and have fed him at my bosom, and have watched over him by day and by night for nine months. . . . (24 Mar 1799)

It may be an accident of orthography, but it seems a significant one, that Sara capitalizes the word "Mother," whereas Poole, capitalizing the generic "Man," writes "parents" with a lower case.

A comparison that seems thrust upon us here is that between a mother's experience of losing an infant and a father's. This could easily turn into an unseemly wrangle ("I suffered more than you"), but in this case, as we shall soon see, it is important to pause and think about the question. There are two reasons for expecting a mother's grief to be the more intense. The biological reason, that giving birth and suckling results in an intense physical bond, will presumably be stronger the younger the infant; the social reason, that the mother will have seen much more of the child, will vary according to circumstances, but the facts of parental contact before (and even through) the twentieth century are almost certain to confirm it, and none more so than the case of Berkeley Coleridge.

Poole no doubt wished to pay a compliment to Sara when he assured Coleridge that she had not given way to grief:

Mrs Coleridge felt as a mother . . . and, in an exemplary manner, did all a mother could do. *But she never forgot herself.* She is now perfectly well, and does not make herself miserable by recalling the engaging, though, remember, mere instinctive attractions of an infant a few months old. Heaven and Earth! I have myself within the last month experienced disappointments more weighty than the death of ten infants.

Feeling as a mother, we observe, is a feeling to be tolerated rather than admired, and perhaps only tolerated if it does not go too far. It is disappointing that Poole does not tell us what his "weighty" disappointments were, so that we could measure them against "mere instinct." He would no doubt have characterized his attitude as Stoical: orthodox Stoicism regards grief as mere irrationality, a philosophy that can never have had many female adherents.

And Coleridge? Absent during the whole episode, pouring out his loneliness and his solicitude in his letters, desperately worried when he does not hear from his wife—yet constantly postponing his return, not only to continue his researches but to go on a walking tour in the Harz mountains. While there, he wrote in the album at Elbingerode some lines of blank verse about how he longed to be back in England:

> Yea, mine eye swam with tears: that all the view
> From sovran Brocken, woods and woody hills,
> Floated away, like a departing dream,
> Feeble and dim! Stranger, these impulses
> Blame thou not lightly.

He does not of course believe that a stranger will "blame" this outpouring of sentimental homesickness: blame attaches to acts, not to feelings, and the act he was avoiding in order to indulge these feelings was that of returning to the native land he so much missed, and where his bereaved wife was waiting. No "stranger" would know about that.

The view that to linger on the expression of sad emotions is culpable because it interferes with doing something positive (the view, crudely, that we ought to pull up our socks and stop whining) is hardly one that any reader of poetry can accept; but if we are looking for a case to which it could with some justice apply, we could hardly do better than this one.

On April 6 Coleridge had received the news of the death, and he wrote to Poole about his reaction:

A mass of Pain was brought suddenly and closely within the sphere of my perception. . . . I read your letter in calmness, and walked out into the open fields,

oppressed, not by my feelings, but by the riddles, which the Thought so easily
proposes, and solves—never! A Parent—in the strict and exclusive sense a *Parent*-! to me it is a *fable* wholly without meaning except in the *moral* which it suggests. . . . [6]

It is not easy to follow this train of thought; the very confusion might
leave us wondering whether he suffered acutely and pushed the suffering
aside in an attempt to philsophize about it, or whether personal grief was
soon, and easily, swallowed up into the contorted reflections on religious
belief and Pascal's rejection of Pyrrhonism and dogmatism into which the
letter then drifts, leading to the observation that "my Baby has not lived in
vain." The reason for that claim is impressive (though hardly Christian): the
belief that however short the life it has an intrinsic value: "this life has been
to him what it is to all of us, education and development." And Coleridge,
we can observe, has had the grace to spell "Parent" with a capital—though
this could easily be undercut by observing how many other nouns the letter capitalizes, and remembering that he was busy learning German.

Does all this change the way we read Coleridge's child epitaphs? To
resituate a poem in the biographical situation from which it has emerged is
always illuminating, but should not lead us to lock it up there, as if it had
never emerged. How we read poems depends not just on the discovering
of evidence, but on our practice as readers, on whether we treat a poem on
the death of an infant as a biographical document or as part of the practice
of consolation in that (or any) social world.

The Future (and the Past) of an Illusion

Christian belief in an afterlife offers heaven as reward for the blest and
hell as punishment for the reprobate. Philippe Ariès claims that in the later
Middle Ages the emphasis fell on Hell and by the nineteenth century had
shifted to Heaven, and, in an argument having some resemblance to
Lawrence Stone's view, he attributes this to the growth of "affectivity," "a
new type of family relationship in which affection outweighed every consideration of self-interest, law or propriety." As a result, a new type of paradise was created, "which is not so much the heavenly home as the earthly
home saved from the menace of time."[7] This is the background to Victorian attitudes to death in general, and child death in particular.

Like any system of rewards and punishments, the Christian afterlife
can be seen as serving a moral and psychological function in this life. Belief

in hell, thundered from a thousand pulpits, has been used to cow not only thieves and whoremongers but also those who question constituted authority; belief in heaven has offered comfort against fear and grief—fear of one's own annihilation, grief for the loss of loved ones. There is of course an asymmetry in the system: the function of hell is moral, whereas that of heaven is consolatory. Because being too confident of one's own salvation is pride, it is mainly for others that we can indulge in confident dreams of heaven: religion as consolation tells us that the lost one is now in a happier state, and this is especially necessary if the lost one is a child. A life lived out to term can be regarded as blessed simply by seeing it as a whole and accepting that the end came when it had to, but a life cut off before it had really begun offers no such possibility of consolation. The only reassurance is that the child is now an angel.

And what would heaven be like? Faith in a future life must naturally lead to speculation on its nature. The Victorians discussed this endlessly, and sometimes with surprising confidence. In a book edited by the Bishop of Ripon in 1866, called *Recognition of Friends in Heaven*, the authors all claim that the experience of heaven will be recognizable to our present selves. Most of the essays begin with a confident declaration of belief in an afterlife. "The instant horror with which the soul recoils from the thought of annihilation, its ardent longing after a perpetuity of existence . . . are so many facts on which to found a very plausible conjecture that the soul of man shall live when the body is no more."[8] They then go on to make equally confident assertions about what the afterlife will be like. "The heart cannot admit for a moment," the Preface asserts, "that we shall never see or know them [our loved ones] again." "Since man is a social being," writes the Rev. Norman Macleod, "so in Heaven there will be society:

> It is unnecessary to prove what is assumed as so evidently true, and which I cannot really understand how anyone should doubt, and that is the recognition of our Christian friends in Heaven. . . . What! shall memory be obliterated, and shall we forget our own past histories? (46)

And if we ask what alleviates the pain that we and our dying friends (including of course our children) experience when bidding farewell, the answer is, "the assurance that we shall very soon follow them, and in a short time shall meet again to part no more for ever."

Two points are particularly striking in these essays. The first is the assurance with which the authors know what the afterlife will be like. It holds no mysteries, and the Rev. W. S. Thomson even knows the reasons why souls in bliss do not wish to rejoin us:

> It is not that they become forgetful of their friends upon the earth—it is not because their affection for them cools or abates,—it is not because they become indifferent as to their happiness or their welfare. No, very far from it; but it is because they can now measure time as they never measured it before, and see it to be a point not worth estimating, . . . it is because, when they leave us, they know we are left in good hands. (58)

To know not only what happens in heaven but also why, to offer statements on the motives of the souls in bliss, removes all element of mystery from the kingdom of God. At times this confident knowledge becomes comic. As we listen to those we meet in heaven, writes the Rev. A. M. Aslane, "we may from their conversation discover who they are, [and] from whence they came into this world"—just as when a British soldier in India, hearing a fellow soldier remark, "That is a Glendore thaw," realized that he was a fellow Scot and even a fellow parishioner. As well as retaining our local dialect, we shall also retain the conventions of making new acquaintances, and embarrassment will be avoided because Jesus Christ will be there to perform the necessary introductions:

> Then can I suppose this friendship renewed too by introductions. Go back to the time when Jesus, with his three disciples, went up into Mount Tabor, where Jesus was transfigured: the disciples did not know Elijah and Moses, for they had never seen them before, and how then did they come to know the two worthies of a bygone age? I suppose the Saviour introduced the disciples to them, and if the Saviour condescended to introduce some of His people to others on Mount Tabor, do you not think that He will condescend on Mount Zion to do the same thing, or employ some of His angels, at least, to do it. (167)

Second is the frankness with which the belief is based on wishful thinking—not only the general belief in immortality but also the details of its nature, including recognition and retaining of identity.

> There is something that instinctively urges us to hope that in heaven we may see and know each other again; and as it cannot but be a source of the highest and most refined gratification for friends on earth to meet as friends in heaven,

I cannot believe that a source of happiness such as this will be denied by God
to his people. (60)

The Bishop of Ripon and his colleagues limited themselves to discussion,
but in America this view of heaven was turned into fiction, most famously
by Elizabeth Stuart Phelps. In her novel *The Gates Ajar*, published in 1868,
a young woman loses the brother to whom she is passionately devoted, and
after enduring "that most exquisite of inquisitions, the condolence system,"[9] she eventually finds real consolation from her young aunt Winifred.
Winifred's success in comforting her is due not only to her sensitive personality but also to her view of heaven: she assures the heroine that "if
there is such a thing as common sense, you will talk with Roy as you talked
with him here,—only not as you talked with him here, because there will
be no trouble nor sins" (51). This is contrasted with the sermon on heaven
by the clergyman Dr. Bland, which declares that "Heaven is an eternal
state" where "we shall study the character of God," assuring his listeners
that he expects "to be so overwhelmed by the glory of the presence of God
that it may be thousands of years before I shall think of my wife"—at which
point, we are told, "poor Mrs Bland looked exceedingly uncomfortable"
(44). The moment seems worthy of Dickens; and Phelps takes her view of
heaven even nearer to the edge of parody when she inserts a conversation
between children, in which Winifred's daughter insists that she is going to
have little pink blocks made out of the sunset clouds when she gets to
heaven: "P'r'aps I'll have some strawberries too, and some ginger-snaps,—
I'm not going to have any old bread and butter up there" (114). Her mother
defends this as the best way of leading children towards a positive view of
religion, and although the book was a best seller it attracted, not surprisingly, some stern clerical disapproval.[10]

    That this cosy view of heaven was widespread in the nineteenth cen-
tury is shown by Colleen MacDannell and Bernhard Lang in *Heaven: a History*, which documents not only the widespread assurances that one will be
able to meet one's friends and relations in a heaven full of nursery treats for
children, military service in India for working men, and a gentlemanly
Christ to perform introductions, but also notes the scorn of some religious
thinkers (and some satirists) for what Mark Twain called "a mean little ten-
cent heaven about the size of Rhode Island."[11] And lest we think it was an
Anglo-Saxon eccentricity, I here quote Aries' observation, based mainly on
French sources, that "in the nineteenth century everyone seemed to

believe in the continuation of the friendships of life after death." He finds examples of pious deaths among young girls and children, along with uplifting family groups gathered round a dying child, represented not only in writing but on Italian tombs.[12]

If we read this material with post-Freudian eyes, we can suggest that the argument these apologists give as the strongest support for their belief can also be seen as its greatest weakness: the fact that it fulfils our deepest wishes.

> The renewal of Christian acquaintance, at the coming of Christ, is a thought which corresponds with the best wishes and emotions of the human heart. . . . And shall this hope . . . prove to be but a delusion? No, this cannot be.[13]

> Religious ideas are illusions, fulfilments of the oldest, strongest and most insistent wishes of mankind. . . . It is characteristic of the illusion that it is derived from men's wishes. . . . It would indeed be very nice if there were a God, who was both creator of the world and a benevolent providence, if there were a moral order and a future life, but at the same time it is very odd that this is all just as we should wish it ourselves.[14]

As so often happens with subversive theories, Freud's attack on religious belief turns out to be virtually a restatement of one of its traditional defenses. The Bishop of Ripon and his collaborators believe in an afterlife for the very reason that Freud uses to undermine their belief—and they say so![15]

And there is another, and some may feel a profounder, reason for rejecting the comfort offered by these assurances that we shall recognize our loved ones in heaven. In the most powerful and disturbing account of grief I have come across, C S Lewis wrote: "Don't come talking to me about the consolations of religion, or I shall suspect that you don't understand." A lifelong bachelor, Lewis had married a woman from a totally different background at the age of fifty-eight, and after four years of intense and (to him) astonishing happiness, she died of cancer: he then wrote, and published anonymously, *A Grief Observed*, in which he dryly dismisses "all that stuff about family reunions 'on the further shore' pictured in earthly terms."[16] The positive side of this is Lewis' conception that communion with God will be unimaginably different from any individual experience we have known. Lewis was not a mystic, but in this claim he has all the mystics on his side.

Mystical writing—the attempt to articulate direct experience of communion with the divine—is faced with the problem that such experience is ineffable, and linguistic strategies are therefore necessary to confront the paradox of expressing it. The two main strategies have been the use of imagery and the negative way. Images—sometimes accompanied by an admission of their inadequacy—attempt to give at least an analogy for the experience. Much the commonest are images of light:

> It is a great thing, an exceeding great thing, in the time of this exile, to be joined to God in the divine light by a mystical and denuded union. This takes place when a pure, humble and resigned soul, burning with ardent charity, is carried above itself by the grace of God, and through the brilliancy of the divine light shining on the mind, it loses all consideration and distinction of things and lays aside all, even the most excellent images; and all liquefied by love, and, as it were, reduced to nothing, it melts away into God. It is then united to God without any medium, and becomes one spirit with Him, and is iron changed into fire, without ceasing to be iron. It becomes one with God, yet not so as to be of the same substance and nature as God. Here the soul reposes, and ceases from its own action; and sweetly experiencing the operation of God, it abounds with ineffable peace and joy.[17]

This is not offered as an actual experience of heaven, for no earthly creature, not even Louis de Blois, has been to heaven and returned to "the time of this exile" to tell of it. It is offered as the experience of prayer, which is the nearest we can come to communion with God. This excerpt from Louis's *Spiritual Mirror* is characteristic mystical writing, using not only the image of light but also that of metal heated in the fire to convey the idea that the soul admitted to divine communion both is and is not identical with the godhead. The idea is conveyed through images, but at the moment of most intense communion the soul "lays aside all, even the most excellent images": here Louis adumbrates the opposite method, the use of negatives, of denials that this unique experience is like anything earthly, which results in a series of paradoxes. Associated especially with St. John of the Cross, this strategy is most familiar to English readers through Eliot's *Four Quartets*:

> In order to possess what you do not possess
>   You must go by the way of dispossession.

In order to arrive at what you are not
> You must go through the way in which you are not.
And what you do not know is the only thing you know
And what you own is what you do not own
And where you are is where you are not.[18]

The two strategies bear a kind of symbiotic relationship to each other, for the images of light are almost always accompanied by an insistence that it is unlike any earthly light: it does not illuminate anything except itself:

> The soul delighteth unspeakably therein, yet it beholdeth naught which can be related by the tongue or imagined in the heart. It seeth nothing, yet seeth all things, because it beholdeth this Good darkly—and the more darkly and secretly the Good is seen, the more certain is it, and excellent above all other things. Wherefore is all other good which can be seen or imagined doubtless less than this, because all the rest is darkness.[19]

The rest is darkness: yet the light itself is a kind of darkness. Because communion with the divine shuts out all earthly interests, even all awareness of anything else, it can be compared with darkness as well as with light. Hence Vaughan's famous lines:

> There is in God (some say)
> A deep but dazzling darkness[20]

—lines aptly chosen by Patrick Grant to provide the title of the anthology of mystical writing from which I have taken these extracts: *A Dazzling Darkness*

Now such communion, though infinitely more precious to the mystic than any human experience, is quite useless as a cure for human ills. Lewis realized this, and said so with characteristic bluntness:

> If a mother is mourning not for what she has lost but for what her dead child has lost, it is a comfort to believe that the child has not lost the end for which it was created. And it is a comfort to believe that she herself, in losing her chief or only natural happiness, has not lost a greater thing, that she may still hope to "glorify God and enjoy him forever." A comfort to the God-aimed, eternal spirit within her. But not to her motherhood. The specifically maternal happiness

must be written off. Never, in any place or time, will she have her son on her knees, or bathe him, or tell him a story, or plan for his future, or see her grand-child.

Lewis's account of grief can stand as an emphatic Christian alternative to, even a contemptuous dismissal of, the recognition of friends in heaven, a standard by which to look at such attempts at comfort, and lay them aside as merely bogus. It is a modern traditionalist's dismissal of Victorian senti-mentality, but it can be matched from the nineteenth century. Elizabeth Fry, grieving for her young daughter Betsy, drew great consolation from her religious faith (and even uses the word "consolation") but she was aware of its limitations:

> Although faith tells us that the spirit is indeed fled from its earthly house, yet the distress felt in parting with the body, I can hardly describe; for the body of little children, their innocent and beautiful faces and forms, we are prone to delight in; and there is a sort of personal attachment towards little children, that partakes of the nature of animal life, which I believe is hardly to be described, but only fully known to parents.[21]

Lewis, whom one would not think of as intuitively aware of women's feel-ings, turns out to be uncannily accurate in his account of a mother's "nat-ural unhappiness" (Fry's "distress felt in parting with the body"). Religious faith may transcend this grief but cannot eliminate it.

Freud, then, and Lewis: unlikely allies. And not really allies, for though they both reject a view of religion as consolation, they do so for opposite reasons: the lower reason and the higher reason? or the honest reason and another form of wish-fulfillment? No scholarly study can settle that for us.

Reversals

In discussing Coleridge's epitaphs I used the term "reversal" to claim that the same poem could, if we shift the way we look at it, turn into some-thing like its opposite. A well-known graphic figure, that of the duck-rab-bit, produces this effect in experiments on perception. A blink or other minor stimulus can cause the long ears to turn into a bill and, thus, the same drawing to turn from one animal into the other. Such a cartoon figure, for use in a joke or a simple experiment, may suggest triviality, but it is so apt that I offer it, quite seriously, as an image for this reversal of meaning. Here, for instance, is a simple example, unfictitious, blunt and moving:

> "I have none but God left now!" said a poor widow, who had been freely pouring out her troubles to an aged friend. . . . By the poor widow's account, she had passed through deep waters of affliction, and endured, as she said, more than her "share of trouble." One of her two children had been drowned, and the other was then in a lunatic asylum. She had lost her brother and sister, and only three weeks before had buried her husband, being left alone, and in poverty. "All the day long," said she, "I am grieving; and when I wake in the morning, my pillow is wet with tears. Everything seems to have melted away, and I have none but God left now."[22]

The author of this improving anecdote in *The Young People's Treasury* of 1896 points out to her (or, more probably, his?) readers that the poor widow could have no greater blessing than the Lord, who is her strength and shield, and urges her:

> Up and be doing, broken hearted pilgrim. Onward and upward, desolate widow. If thou hast God left, then hast thou more need to praise Him on an instrument of ten strings, than to hang thy harp on the willows.

We are listening here to an exhortation that must have been delivered innumerable times in the cottages of the poor by well-meaning Christian comforters. The comforter in this case has seen that the duck of despair can be made a rabbit of consolation, and his hectoring tone is designed to produce this reversal. But the shift can run in either direction; and the old widow's remark, if we hear it as a response to the comforter, turns the rabbit into a duck, pointing out that God is a concept offered to those who have lost everything else.

The old widow spoke with the inadvertent accuracy of despair. There must have been thousands of occasions when her remark would have sounded to the "broken hearted pilgrim" like a palpable hit. Since we have not many records of such actual visits, I will turn to a poem (anonymous, dating from the mid-century) that is clearly intended to serve the same function:

The Gathered Flower

A Gardener day by day had watched with care
A favourite rose, so fragrant and so fair,
That when to full perfection it should come
He thought to send it to his master's home:
It was the rarest flower the tree had borne—
He marked its glaring beauties every morn;
But ah! one day he missed his garden gem;—
A hand unknown had plucked it from the stem.

Some servant stole the rose, the gardener thought,
And he, with angry brow, the culprit sought;
But soon his feelings of displeasure turn'd
To joy and satisfaction when he learn'd
That 'twas his master who had pass'd the bower,
And for its special beauty cull'd the flower:
Now at his mansion, in some gorgeous room,
The gardener's favourite sheds its rich perfume.

Then said his master, "You with gladness spare,
To grace my home, your rose so bright and rare;
And yet, because my hand of late removed
From your home bower one blossom that you loved,
Your heart rebels; you are unreconciled
To God's wise will in reference to your child;
Think rather is it not an honour given
That he should take your flower to bloom in heaven?"

How often parents, like this gardener, find
Rebellious feelings rising in the mind,
When the Almighty's gracious, sovereign hand
Removes a babe from out their household band!
Mourners, 'tis hard to part from those you love,
But this remember—they are best above;
No frost, no blight, no stormy winds are there—
All these on earth your flowers might have to bear.

God takes your babes, and they—oh! think of this—
Are by creation and redemption His;
Christ shed for them His blood—a wondrous price;
His spirit sweetened each for paradise;
There, no destructive canker-worm of sin
Can carry on its deadly work within,
But pure and perfect in the realms on high,
Your flowerets bloom, and they shall never die.[23]

The analogy between earthly and heavenly master is old and familiar: it was a commonplace of medieval and Renaissance ideas of order and degree that God was the ruler of the world, the father was a God to his family, and the monarch was the father of his people: a threefold analogy that could be invoked when speaking of theology, of state, or of domestic politics. This poem, coming at the end of a long tradition, exposes with simplistic clarity the ambivalence of the parallel. It makes a double comparison: first, that a child is like a rose, and because a rose is plucked to serve a higher purpose, shedding its perfume in a gorgeous room, so the child was plucked to adorn God's mansion; and second, that the master who took the rose was behaving like God, whose power is absolute and exercised only for good. Now which element in this analogy explains the other? Do we know about God and therefore use the parallel to understand the human master better, or do we (this is surely the more realistic case) explain our idea of God's authority by invoking the earthly master? But if we do not start by viewing this master as godlike, he might not greatly impress us as a model. Who, after all, owns a garden? In the legal sense, of course, the master does, but there is another sense in which a garden belongs to the person who cultivates it, and a thoughtful owner will remember this and will not (surely) steal up behind his gardener's back to remove the flowers without a word. Either the divine parallel tells us that this master is not high-handed, or the earthly parallel tells us that God is.

Consolation can be direct or indirect: directly, it addresses the grief of the survivor; indirectly, it looks at the departed and claims that all was for the best, even in the case of a child. Heaven was "benign," in Hemans's poem, to call the child hence, "E'er yet the world could breathe one blight / O'er thy sweet innocence." Hemans's abstract nouns "passion" and "grief" and the dead metaphor of "blight" in both Hemans's poem and in

"The Gathered Flower" are poeticisms for sin; the theological point is simply that the less you live in the world, the less you will be tainted. Better dead: the view could be held without belief in an afterlife, in which case it will be deeply pessimistic—like those gloomy assurances by the chorus in Greek tragedies that it is best not to be born, and second best is to die as early as possible.

It is perhaps surprising to find something very close to this in a letter of George Eliot's, written to Cara Bray on the death of her only daughter in 1865:

> I don't know whether you strongly share, as I do, the old belief that made men say the gods loved those who died young. It seems to me truer than ever, now life has become more complex and more difficult problems have to be worked out. Life, though a good to men on the whole, is a doubtful good to many, and to some not a good at all. To my thought, it is a source of constant mental distortion to make the denial of this a part of religion, to go on pretending things are better than they are—like talking of "your Majesty's happy reign" to a successful monarch whose reign has been one of blood and fire to half a population, who happen to be at a distance and out of sight. So to me, early death takes the aspect of salvation—though I feel too that those who live and suffer may sometimes have the greater blessedness of *being* a salvation.[24]

This paragraph is preceded by an explanation that she has let some weeks go by without writing a letter of condolence because "If I could have been with you in bodily presence, I should have sat silent, thinking silence a sign of feeling that speech, trying to be wise, must always spoil"; not writing has therefore been a way of avoiding presumption. "There is no such thing as consolation, when we have made the lot of another our own as you did Nelly's." This is something one could only say to a close and understanding friend, and to such a one it might be the best thing to say. It is then followed by the knotty paragraph quoted above, George Eliot at her most thoughtfully pessimistic and agnostic. She begins with pagan pessimism and then shows her deep emotional attraction to the Christianity she rejected—above all through the play on the meaning of salvation: the first instance meaning, I take it, salvation from the pain of living (Greek tragic pessimism) and the second a kind of imitation of Christ, joining the "choir invisible / Of those immortal dead who live again / In minds made better by their presence." It is almost an impertinence to call this purely humanist point a belief in "salvation"; but it is in its way a strategy of consolation.

The most ingeniously tortured theological consolation I have come across is that of T Binney (of whom I know nothing): "It would be a terrible world, I think, if it was not embellished by little children; *but* it would be a far more terrible one *if little children did not die*!" (his italics). Granting that death is the punishment for sin, he then explains that God looked for ways of making mortality tolerable. The two solutions he came up with were, first, that death happens alike to all, and second that it occurs at all ages. "It is important both for happiness and virtue that no one should know when he is to die"; and "to be thoroughly kind" [*sic*], that law must apply from the very earliest age. It is therefore necessary that some children, along with those of other ages, should die, in order to carry out God's benevolent plan; and to the grieving mother he therefore points out that "all thy life thou hast been reaping advantages that came to thee by the death of the infants of others."[25]

Catherine Tait, after the first of her daughters had died, read to the others a poem by Lydia Sigourney, the "sweet singer of Hartford," which is strikingly similar to "The Gathered Flower":

The Mother's Sacrifice

"What shall I render Thee, Father Supreme,
For thy rich gifts, and this the best of all?"
Said the young mother, as she fondly watched
Her sleeping babe. There was an answering voice
That night in dreams:—
    "Thou hast a tender flower
Upon thy breast—fed with the dews of love:
Send me that flower. Such flowers there are in heaven."
But there was silence. Yea, a hush so deep,
Breathless and terror-stricken, that the lip
Blanched in its trance.
    "Thou hast a little harp,—
How sweetly would it swell the angels' hymn!
Yield me that harp."
    There rose a shuddering sob,
As if the bosom by some hidden sword
Was cleft in twain.

> Morn came—a blight had found
> The crimson velvet of the unfolding bud,
> The harp-strings rang a thrilling strain, and broke—
> And that young mother lay upon the earth
> In childless agony. Again the voice
> That stirred her vision:
>   "He who asked of thee,
> Loveth a cheerful giver." So she raised
> Her gushing eyes, and, ere the tear-drop dried
> Upon its fringes, smiled—and that meek smile
> Like Abraham's faith, was counted righteousness.[26]

God asks a mother to give up her child. This was not an unfamiliar idea among actual mothers: when Josephine Butler's son Stanley fell ill with diphtheria shortly after the death of her daughter, she "wondered whether God meant to ask us to give up another child so soon."[27] But when the idea is worked out as fully as it is in this poem, the result is startling: for something very like malice is being attributed to God. The mother asks what she can render God to show her gratitude for blessings; and the answer comes as if from the Spirit Ironic—to render the blessing itself, the one gift that would remove the original motive of gratitude. There could even be a wordplay here on *render*, used by the mother in its common meaning of *hand over*, but picked up by God in its more basic etymological meaning of *give back*.

But not only malice: there is also bad faith in this God, as emerges in the use of the verbs: "send," "yield" and "give" (implied by "giver"). The death of the child is brought about by God, not by the mother: God is not persuading her to kill the child; he is telling her that the child will die, and "giving" is precisely what she is not doing. Sigourney did not, of course, intend to write an indignantly anti-Christian poem; her God is orthodox, and the episode has a happy ending, as the mother smiles and is forgiven by God for any untoward thoughts she has had. And the last line points out the parallel with Abraham's sacrifice of Isaac. But this makes the poem more, not less, interesting as a cultural document. A poem which raises and then resolves a moral issue can never be in complete control of the reader's response. To raise a protest and then reply to it presents the author with an obvious dilemma: if the protest is not strong enough, the whole thing will look like a put-up job, but if it is strong and effective we may not be satisfied by the reply. Such dissatisfaction can come primarily from the reader, who may not share the poet's orthodoxy and is therefore harder to convince, or from the text itself, which may offer a more disturbing version of the protest than the poet had intended.

So this poem too can be read as a duck-rabbit. It is completely orthodox, but, if we read it while blinking at certain elements of familiarity, we can see it as subversive, leaving us with a malicious and tricky God, and silencing protest. The parallel with Abraham will, to the orthodox reader, remove all doubts; but to the skeptical or still grieving reader, it may suggest that the story of Abraham is yet another example of God's trickery.

William Shelley

My lost William, thou in whom
    Some bright spirit lived, and did
That decaying robe consume
    Which its lustre faintly hid,—
Here its ashes find a tomb,
    But beneath this pyramid
Thou art not—if a thing divine
Like thee can die, thy funeral shrine
Is thy mother's grief and mine

Where art thou, my gentle child?
    Let me think thy spirit feeds,
With its life intense and mild,
    The love of living leaves and weeds
Among these tombs and ruins wild;—
    Let me think that through low seeds
Of sweet flowers and sunny grass
Into their hues and scents may pass
A portion. . . .[28]

"Where art thou?" Shelley here addresses the question to which the Hemans and the Sigourney poems answer, "He is an angel." Angels are important in this connexion and will be discussed at length in the next chapter. For the moment, I remark that this child, who when alive was a bright spirit in a decaying robe, can be seen in either Christian or Platonist terms. This intense conviction of the life of the spirit, along with a refusal to tie this to theological or philosophical terminology, is very Shelleyan; and when the second stanza provides some sort of answer, this is in pantheistic terms. The child is now a portion of the loveliness which Shelley has made more lovely.

Since I have suggested that Christian consolation may be glib (don't grieve, the child is better dead), I will here add that there is pantheistic glibness too:

> What do you think has become of the young and old men
> And what do you think has become of the women and children? . . .
> They are alive and well somewhere,
> The smallest sprout shows there is really no death.[29]

Whitman's *Song of Myself* is not about the death of anyone in particular, so the assertion "there is really no death" can be taken as delighted acceptance, not as insensitive denial; but the possibility of parody is looming. In Shelley's poem it could be argued that the repeated use of "let me" expresses doubt, or at least reveals how urgent is the poet's *need* to accept this pantheistic vision; but here the vision is complacently asserted.

Pantheism has no theology: trinity, grace, atonement, judgment—these concepts are far too specific for an inarticulate world-spirit to concern itself with. Hence its poetic appeal—at any rate, its appeal to Romantic poetry, where a resistance to conceptualizing is central to the poetic enterprise. Christianity provides for the dead child a category into which it can be fitted and which serves as assurance that it is now better off; but categories and assurances do not belong with the direct expression of emotion, and a Romantic poem on a dead child may therefore convey the urgency of the question, Where and what are you now? without providing an answer. Indeed, the absence of an answer may be a way of insisting that any answer would be false to experience. That, I believe, is what Shelley does.

Shelley wrote another, even shorter poem to William:

> Thy little footsteps on the sands
>   Of a remote and lonely shore;
> The twinkling of thine infant hands,
>   Where now the worm will feed no more;
> Thy mingled look of love and glee
> When we returned to gaze on thee—

These images hover between literal and metaphoric. Is this a memory of William playing on the beach, or an image of William confronting eternity? (The latter would be common enough in Romantic poetry, Wordsworth's *Immortality* ode providing the best known example). The fourth line seems to make it clear that William is now dead. Referring to the present and future, it acts as a corrective to those living twinkling hands, which belong to the past, when William was still alive. The final couplet too could describe the dead infant but sounds much more like a living child, delighted to see its parents. We cannot settle any of this because the sentence is never finished, and this uncertainty fits with the absence of any clear structure of belief.

Both these poems are fragments; and Shelley has left us more fragments than any of the other Romantics. This may be due in part to the thoroughness with which his widow published his work or, in part, to his restless and impatient fluency in composing, but it is possible to see the *List der Vernunft*, the Hegelian cunning of history, at work here. His poems hover between Christian, Platonic, pantheistic, and atheistic thought, exploiting, sometimes to rich effect, the uncertainty of their conceptual status: their unfinished nature enables them to hover and provides an appropriate form for their intellectual indecisiveness.

Shelley was writing about his own children. William died on 7 June 1819, less than a year after the Shelleys' daughter Clara had died. Shelley's letters tell of his distress and make it even more clear that Mary was reduced to something like despair. If we now read the poems with a biographer's eye, especially a feminist biographer's, we can hardly avoid comparing Mary Shelley and Sara Coleridge, the wives who sat at home and watched their children die while their husbands traveled, in body and in spirit, leaving them at home or dragging them round Italy (which was worse?), assuring the world, and themselves, that though the death was cause for grief, grief could be comforted. Can Shelley's restless traveling and restless questioning be seen as an evasion of despair—and did Mary feel that it was easy enough for him to cope? When Coleridge sent Sara his beautiful piece of wordplay, "Be rather than be called a child of God," did she find comfort in it? How did she feel when told that it was not even about Berkeley? "A few weeks ago," Coleridge wrote, "an Englishman desired me to write an epitaph on an infant who had died before its Christening. While I wrote it, my heart with a deep misgiving turned my thoughts homeward."[30]

With Shelley as with Coleridge, turning to consider the poet's own children changes the context—and once again requires us to ask about relating poem to poet. Is such biographical criticism a healthy reminder of the human situation, or is it merely a way of being Philistine and dismissing the poetry? Coleridge's epitaph, once written, is "about" whatever grief the reader applies it to. Whether it is evidence that he did or did not feel grief about his own child (a question that is probably unanswerable) is a biographer's question, not a question about poetry.

Another Shelley fragment addresses these questions almost explicitly, especially if we hinge our reading of it on a single, crucial line.

> My dearest Mary, wherefore hast thou gone,
> And left me in this dreary world alone?
> Thy form is here indeed—a lovely one—
> But thou art fled, gone down the dreary road,
> That leads to Sorrow's most obscure abode;
> Thou sittest on the hearth of pale despair,
> Where
> For thine own sake I cannot follow thee.

This appears to start like a poem to the dead: leaving him in the dreary world alone, being separated from one's outward form—these sound like circumlocutions for dying. Even the last line could describe the survivor's feeling that he needs to live on, to protect the interests or the children or the reputation of the deceased. The only line that clearly indicates that Mary is alive is "Thou sittest on the hearth of pale despair." Not only does this seem to me the most powerful line in the poem, it transforms the lines around it. The hearth is a commonplace enough metaphor, but it gains a shock value from its function: instead of a lament for the dead under the guise of reproach—a rhetorical strategy that goes back at least to Shakespeare ("noblest of men, woo't die?")—it turns out to be an actual reproach, or at least a struggle not to reproach her for surrendering to grief. The last line, then, could be read as an attempt to convince himself that not following her into despair is a sign of his concern for her, not an inability to feel so deeply. This in turn could be related to gender: either "women indulge in the luxury of grief, men have to keep the world going," or "women grieve, men tell them to snap out of it."

Lyrical Ballads

The poet who, it may be felt, lies behind most of these poems has, so far, virtually not been mentioned. All these poets were steeped in Wordsworth, who more than anyone introduced children into English poetry and whose poems are full of dead children.

The most conventional of these poems is probably "The Childless Father," an account of how Timothy adjusts to his daughter's death, concluding with a sentimental glimpse of the tear on the old man's cheek. Its final stanza actualizes the fact of her death by opening with an everyday detail:

> Perhaps to himself at that moment he said
> "The key I must take, for my Ellen is dead."[31]

Timothy resumes his life by joining in the village hunt, and speaks "not a word" of Ellen's death. Acceptance is the theme of this poem, as it is of the others Wordsworth wrote on the subject. In "The Two April Mornings," Matthew remembers how he accepted his daughter's death at the moment when, turning from her grave, he met "A blooming girl, whose hair was wet, / With points of morning dew:

> There came from me a sigh of pain
>   Which I could ill confine;
> I looked at her, and looked again:
>   And did not wish her mine!

In "We are Seven," the best known of the group, the poet attempts in vain to persuade the little cottage girl that there is a difference between the brothers and sisters who dwell at Conway or have gone to sea, and those who "in the churchyard lie," but the child, with splendid obstinacy, refuses to accept this:

> "But they are dead; those two are dead!
> Their spirits are in heaven!"
> Twas throwing words away; for still
> The little Maid would have her will
> And said, "Nay, we are seven!"

"Lucy Gray" is the story of a child who sets out to light her mother home through the snow and is caught by a storm. Her parents search all night, and as they give up in despair at daybreak, they see her footsteps leading to the bridge only a furlong from their door:

> They followed from the snowy bank
> Those footmarks, one by one,
> Into the middle of the plank;
> And further there were none!
>
> —Yet some maintain that to this day
> She is a living child;
> That you may see sweet Lucy Gray
> Upon the lonesome wild
>
> O'er rough and smooth she trips along,
> And never looks behind;
> And sings a solitary song
> That whistles in the wind.

If we examine the narrative details, it is easy to find this poem silly: why did the mother not take her lantern with her when she went, like any sensible woman? Why did the father send his daughter out alone into such danger? How did the mother get home so easily, if the child was caught by the weather? If we read it as a ghost story, then of course we can dismiss these prosaic objections, and the poem seems carefully uncertain whether it wishes to be taken that way. The subtitle, "Lucy Gray; or, Solitude," could be telling us that she is a symbol; and Wordsworth's comments on the poem include the ambiguous reference (deliberately or accidentally ambiguous?) to "the spiritualizing of the character."

The opening too could be seen as ambiguous:

> Oft had I heard of Lucy Gray:
> And when I crossed the wild,
> I chanced to see at break of day
> The solitary child.

The obvious way to read this is that he saw the child before her death—in which case the preterit ("I chanced to see") is probably iterative: each time he crossed the wild. But in the light of the ending we can entertain the

reading that once, crossing the wild, he chanced (this verb is now important) to see the spirit of the wide moor, a child who died, perhaps, long ago,
but whom you "may see" still upon the wild moor if you have good
"chance." The best evidence that it is a ghost story is a crucial omission:
the Fenwick note has her footsteps disappearing halfway across the bridge
(originally the lock of a canal), and then adds that "the body however was
found in the canal."[32] Lucy's body is never found: does that mean she died
no ordinary death?

Yet what a matter-of-fact ghost story it would be: with no sense of mystery, except what arises, without comment, from the stark narrative details.
All these poems have the curious matter-of-factness of *Lyrical Ballads*,
retelling in simple language their incidents of common and rustic life and
refusing conventional poetic ornament. They avoid all mention of religious
belief (perhaps implying that the rural culture they depict is really pagan),
and they avoid explicit consolation and abstract nouns. They render acceptance with Wordsworthian quirkiness, by mentioning some detail from
everyday life and leaving the reader to draw the conclusion. In comparison
with this, the later poets who so admired Wordsworth sound not only sentimental but labored.

Most of these later poets did not derive their Wordsworthian pathos
from the *Lyrical Ballads*; one who did, once, was, surprisingly, Shelley. His
ballad was written soon after the Peterloo massacre but was never published nor even properly finished, and it has no title; it was not even
included by Mary Shelley in the posthumous poems and is still not to be
found in his works. Most of the poem consists of an appeal from a starving
mother and child for bread, addressed to "Young Parson Richards":

> Give me a piece of that fine white bread—
>   I would give you some blood for it—
> Before I faint and my infant is dead!
>   O give me a little bit! . . .
>
> Give me bread—my hot bowels gnaw—
>   I'll tear down the garden gate—
> I'll fight with the dog,—I'll tear from his maw
>   The crust which he just has ate—

The "man of God" does not reply and walks on to look at the woman and
child:

> The child lay stiff as a frozen straw
>> In the woman's white cold breast—
> And the parson in its dead features saw
>> His own to the truth expressed!
> He turned from the bosom whose heart was broke—
>> Once it pillowed him as he slept—
> He turned from the lips that no longer spoke,
>> From the eyes that no longer wept.[33]

This is quite different from Shelley's poems about his own dead child, and indeed different from most of his poetry. It was written shortly after the Peterloo Massacre and comes from the same heated anger that produced *The Masque of Anarchy* and the song "To the Men of England"; it is in what Mary Shelley called his "popular, rude and unfinished" tone, but even in that tone he produced only this one ballad. Richard Holmes praises the poem for its directness, "as if the message of man's inhumanity to man had become so overwhelming in Shelley's mind that every intervening form— politics, satire, even the decorum of poetry, had eventually to fall back before the simple, agonizing, human speech of suffering and need."[34] This description would fit some of the Lyrical Ballads, or the death of Margaret in the first book of *The Excursion* (especially in its earliest and bleakest version), and it seems to belong with the indignant politics of Shelley's *Address to the People on the Death of the Princess Charlotte*, which was quoted in the first chapter. But although the ballad is not only unpolished but also unfinished, it is not true that the decorum of poetry has fallen back before the simple agonizing human speech of suffering and need: the twist by which the dying woman's lament is addressed to her own seducer (a fact of which she seems to be unaware) gives the poem an ironic ending appropriate to a ballad but not to simple agonizing human speech. What was important about the hungry years that led up to Peterloo was that the hunger was a social phenomenon: children suffered not because they were the illegitimate offspring of a callous young gentleman but simply because they were poor. The irony with which the ballad ends singles out that mother and child as exceptional, and their suffering as individually caused, and so gives us a neater ballad by weakening the social statement. Too much plot, even too much irony, can be bad for political poetry.

Catharine

A ballad—even perhaps a lyrical ballad—implies no personal involvement by the poet. It is a story which is allowed to tell itself. The Wordsworth of *Lyrical Ballads* is not the self-centered lyrical and introspective poet who cast such a long shadow over the ensuing century, and these poems invite no biographical context. But one poem does.

The Wordsworths had five children, who in effect had three parents, since William's sister Dorothy lived with them all through their married life. In 1812 the third and fourth children died within a few months of each other, Catharine (aged four) in June, and Thomas (aged six and a half) in December. There is no reason to doubt that all three parents were heartbroken, but their sorrow is very differently documented. Mary has left no written statements, but according to Dorothy she was plunged into depression by the loss. For four days after learning of Catharine's death (she was not present when it happened) she did not eat a quarter of a pound of food; after Thomas's death she seemed almost to give herself up to sadness:

> She is as thin as it is possible to be except when the body is worn out by slow disease, and the dejection of her countenance is afflicting; . . . I feel that it knits about the heart strings and will wear her away if there is not a turn in her feelings. . . . The day through she is dejected—weeps bitterly at times, and at night and morning sheds floods of tears. . . . All this I could bear to see in another—I should trust to time, . . . but in her case it must be struggled against or it will destroy her.[35]

As we read of this mute despair, unable to get behind Dorothy's letters and listen to Mary's own voice, we seem to be in the same position as Dorothy herself, struggling to penetrate the veil of depression and make contact with the person. Dorothy herself, the energetic correspondent of the family, is eloquent and moving. She loved both children, especially Thomas, of whom she wrote:

> Thomas was a darling in a garden, our best helper, steady to his work, always pleased. God bless his memory. I see him wherever I turn, beautiful innocent that he was. He had a slow heavenly up-turning of his large blue eyes that is never to be forgotten.[36]

She has no hesitation about accepting childhood innocence, and if Thomas is now an angel, she believes that is simple fulfillment of his angelic nature: "he was destined for a better world; that divine sweetness in his counte-nance marked him our as a chosen Spirit." Sitting down to write about him was, at times, too much for her:

> Forgive me my dear Friend, for having been so long silent. My spirits have at times been weak, and I shrank from the thoughts of writing, persuading myself that tomorrow or the next day I should be more fit for it. . . . The image of him, his very self, is so vivid in my mind—it is with me like a perpetual presence; and at certain moments the anguish of tender recollections is more than I can bear—followed by that one thought—I shall never see him more"![37]

As with Catherine Tait, as with all the bereaved parents, we have only Dorothy's words: we can only pursue the elusive signified of her suffering through our knowledge that texts refer to experience (though of course they can refer to fictions too). Even her statements that she has had to put down her pen and pause before she could go on writing are statements from her pen. Until, that is, we come upon:

> I have laid down the pen for some minutes, and I can write upon other matters less deeply interesting. Yet once more—blessings be on his grave—that turf upon which his pure feet so oft have trod—Oh![38]

—and the editor adds a footnote telling us, "The MS is here blotted with a tear stain." With a shock we seem to confront the grief itself, free from all words.

But of course we do not. The blot on the page needs interpreting, just as words do: even assuming that de Selincourt is right, that it was a tear stain and not a drop of water, there is the possibility that Dorothy held the letter so that it would fall just at the right spot, or at least did not brush it away. The blot, like words, is writing: moving as it is, it requires the same act of faith in the reality of the signified on our part. The whole of this book is such an act of faith.

And William? Placed next to Dorothy's, his references to the deaths are brief and formal. Apologizing to Samuel Rogers for putting off a business matter he writes, "I am obliged to defer it, and by a cause which you will be most sorry to hear, viz., the recent death of my dear and amiable son,

Thomas."[39] To Basil Montagu he writes "two or three words only—but words of the heaviest sorrow. My sweet little Thomas is no more."[40] Reading these laconic statements next to Dorothy's outpourings (far more extensive than I have quoted), we see afresh that there are two ways of deriving emotions from texts. As fellow human beings, we know that genuineness of feeling does not depend on eloquence, that Wordsworth's tight reticence may conceal a grief as strong as Dorothy's moving prose reveals. But for us as literary readers, language is the expression of emotion, and where the language is barren the reader will be less moved. Dorothy's letters *contain* a grief that William's only refer to. We respect him but we weep with her.

As literary readers? Not Dorothy but William is the poet. That more delayed, oblique, and, finally, more profound form of expression that is a poem came not from the effusive sister but from the reticent brother. But only once: Wordsworth who wrote so much, and so much about himself, left only one poem on the deaths of his children.

> Surprised by joy—impatient as the Wind
> I turned to share the transport—Oh! with whom
> But Thee, deep buried in the silent tomb,
> That spot which no vicissitude can find?
> Love, faithful love, recalled thee to my mind—
> But how could I forget thee? Through what power
> Even for the least division of an hour,
> Have I been so beguiled as to be blind
> To my most grievous loss!—That thought's return
> Was the worst pang that sorrow ever bore,
> Save one, one only, when I stood forlorn,
> Knowing my heart's best treasure was no more;
> That neither present time, nor years unborn
> Could to my sight that heavenly face restore.[41]

So there are not two ways of deriving emotion from words, but three: the dutiful admission that the (male) writer of a stiff letter may be deeply moved; the immediacy with which the female's emotion rises from her intense and moving letters; and a different way in which emotion rises from a poem like this. We can even entertain the thought that little Catharine's death was worth while if it produced so splendid a poem as this (after all, we can add limply, she would by now be dead anyway).

Yet is this wonderful poem about Catharine? Wordsworth told Isabella Fenwick in old age that it "was suggested by my daughter Catharine, long after her death."[42] Lyric poems, we see very clearly here, are about emotions, not about people. (The anonymity of those hundreds of beloved women does not detract from the poetic value of the love sonnets which so many men addressed to them, since the sonnets were about the love, not the women.) This poem, as clearly as any lyric poem I know, imitates the action of an emotion. Two moments of intense feeling are compared, the pang that some other person is not there to share his moment of sudden joy and the remembered pang of first realizing that the person was dead. No attention is wasted on filling in details, such as what the joy was, or whether that earlier moment was the deathbed or the graveside. The poem sets out to do nothing except map the particularities of a specific grief. That being the case, it does not matter whom it is addressed to. It does not even matter that almost every reader, ignorant of the Fenwick note, would assume it to be addressed to a wife or sweetheart. The difference between writing about sexual love and about parental love is simply irrelevant to the expression of this emotion.

To recover emotions from texts: that is what we do to construct history as human happening, and that is what this book has tried to do. As we have frequently observed, this involves theoretical complications: these must not be underestimated, but they must not cause us to abandon the task. One of the complications is that recovering emotion from a poem is very like, and also very unlike, recovering it from a letter. Poems are like letters in that they derive from experience; they are unlike letters in that they turn the experience to a permanent, self-sufficient form that has led some schools of criticism to claim (mistakenly but understandably) that they are purely verbal constructs, pointing to no signified.

And finally, a word on gender. This instance confirms, but also complicates, the conclusions suggested in the cases of Coleridge and Shelley: women suffer, men write poems. Some versions of feminist criticism might wish (mistakenly but understandably) to maintain this oversimplification. It is (I trust) no less feminist for me to state the position as follows. In the case of Coleridge, the male poet poured his feelings effusively into letters and wrote some short, packed poems not explicitly referring to his own loss; the female had silence imposed on her, tried to keep it, but could not always. In the case of Shelley, the male wrote effusive, fragmentary poems of grief and loss; the female grieved in silence. In the case of Wordsworth, the two females split the feminine response: one grieved and despaired, like Mary Shelley, and the other wrote warm-hearted outbursts of grief, blotted with tears (these are the two traditional feminine responses); while the male poet, showing tight-lipped restraint in his letter, wrote one controlled and polished expression of grief, formal and deeply moving—both less and more moving than his sister's heartbroken letters.

A *True Poem*

Here the chapter should end, but there is a postscript. For Wordsworth wrote one more poem about the death of a child, a poem which has little relation to the rest of this chapter but that it is impossible to omit.

> There was a Boy: ye knew him well, ye cliffs
> And islands of Winander!—many a time
> At evening, when the earliest stars began
> To move along the edges of the hills,
> Rising or setting, would he stand alone
> Beneath the trees or by the glimmering lake,
> And there, with fingers interwoven, both hands
> Pressed closely palm to palm, and to his mouth
> Uplifted, he, as through an instrument,
> Blew mimic hootings to the silent owls,
> That they might answer him; and they would shout
> Across the watery vale, and shout again,
> Responsive to his call, with quivering peals,
> And long halloos and screams, and echoes loud,
> Redoubled and redoubled, concourse wild
> Of jocund din; and, when a lengthened pause
> Of silence came and baffled his best skill,
> Then sometimes, in that silence while he hung
> Listening, a gentle shock of mild surprise
> Has carried far into his heart the voice
> Of mountain torrents; or the visible scene
> Would enter unawares into his mind,
> With all its solemn imagery, its rocks,
> Its woods, and that uncertain heaven, received
> Into the bosom of the steady lake.

> This Boy was taken from his mates, and died
> In childhood, ere he was full twelve years old.
> Fair is the spot, most beautiful the vale
> Where he was born; the grassy churchyard hangs
> Upon a slope above the village school,
> And through that churchyard when my way has led
> On summer evenings, I believe that there
> A long half-hour together I have stood
> Mute, looking at the grave in which he lies![43]

Perhaps the best starting point for discussing this poem will be Francis Jeffrey's stern remarks in the *Edinburgh Review*:

> The sports of childhood and the untimely death of promising youth, is also a common topic of poetry. Mr Wordsworth has made some blank verse about it; but, instead of the delightful and picturesque sketches with which so many authors of moderate talents have presented us on this inviting subject, all that he is pleased to communicate of the rustic child, is, that he used to amuse himself with shouting to the owls, and hearing them answer. To make amends for this brevity, the process of his mimicry is most accurately described (Jeffrey then quotes "And there, with fingers interwoven . . . answer him.") This is all we hear of him; and for the sake of this one accomplishment, we are told, that the author has frequently stood mute, and gazed on his grave for half an hour together![44]

This influential representative of pre-Romantic taste clearly had definite expectations of how this subject should be handled: what are they? What are the "delightful and picturesque sketches with which so many authors of moderate talents have presented us?" Looking through the likely authors—Goldsmith, Cowper, Crabbe, Mary Robinson—I have found that it was not quite so common a topic as Jeffrey suggests. Because his remarks come in a review of Crabbe's *Poems* of 1807, that would seem the obvious place to look (even though Jeffrey might not have been willing to relegate Crabbe to the ranks of "moderate talents"), and there is indeed an infant death in Part III of the *Parish Register*, which Jeffrey mentions in passing, but he does not link it with Wordsworth, and indeed it has nothing in common:

> But why thus lent, if thus recall'd again,
> To cause and feel, to live and die in, pain?"
> Or rather say, Why grievous these appear,
> If all it pays for Heaven's eternal year;
> If these sad sobs and piteous sighs secure
> Delights that live, when worlds no more endure?[45]

These contorted lines are a kind of desperate theology: what interpretation of the death, they ask, best fits our picture of God's purposes? The debate continues with a brief account of "the common ills of life" and the burden of having to wait a whole lifetime until the sad spirit attains rest, followed by a counterassertion that it is nonetheless better to live out one's life, since otherwise we'd be forced to believe that

> Love Divine in vain
> Send[s] all the burthens weary men sustain.

Crabbe was, after all, a clergyman, and his poem dutifully addresses the need to demonstrate that living must be better than dying; otherwise, no theodicy would be possible.

This is not a delightful and picturesque sketch; indeed, it is not a sketch at all, since the infant did not survive long enough to become a subject. The sort of poem Jeffrey is referring to will be marked by pathos, and as an example of what he is thinking of I suggest "Childhood," by Henry Kirk White. Kirk White was an infant prodigy who died in 1806 at the age of twenty-one and who clearly owed his fame to his success in emulating the taste and catering to the expectations of what was still, for conventional readers, the Age of Sensibility. "Childhood" has two parts: an account of the poet's "beloved age of innocence and smiles" in a Goldsmithian village, and a reminiscence of his childhood friend George (who apparently became a sailor), now no doubt dead in foreign lands:

> Where art thou laid—on What untrodden shore,
> Where nought is heard save Ocean's sullen roar?[46]

The reminiscence of childhood is drenched in very explicit nostalgia, evoked by contrast with the evils of the present:

> Here once again, remote from human noise,
> I sit me down to think of former joys;
> Pause on each scene, each treasured scene, once more,
> And once again each infant walk explore:
> While as each grove and lawn I recognise,
> My melted soul suffuses in my eyes.

This writing is emotive in the most immediate sense: "Pause on each scene, each treasured scene" is directly mimetic of the breath being caught in a sob. Sobs and sighs are prominent:

> Yet e'en round Childhood's heart, a thoughtless shrine,
> Affection's little thread will ever twine;
> And though but frail may seem each tender tie,
> The soul foregoes them but with many a sigh

The religious terminology in these passages, as all through the poem, is not religious in function. The soul, conceived theologically, cannot melt; but here it signifies the faculty of being moved by tender emotion, just as the "shrine" of childhood's heart has no otherworldly purpose. However much we may be assured of Kirk White's piety (the memoirs are deferentially insistent on this), there is nothing Christian in this writing. Neither is death otherworldly:

> For thou art gone, and I am left below
> Alone to struggle through this world of woe.

The ambiguity of "gone" is wholly appropriate: it does not really matter whether George is dead or merely absent—his companionship has been lost. The possible deaths for George with which the poem toys ("Methinks I see thee struggling with the wave," "Forlorn and sad thou bendst thy weary way," etc.) are aestheticized possibilities, brief scenes unfolded not for their possible truth but so that the melted soul will suffuse in the eyes. George's death, in other words, has nothing to do with George: attention is not on the fact that he is saved from the world but on the world deprived of him—or rather, of the generalized idea of him. Poems, as I remarked earlier, are not about people.

Kirk White's talents were certainly moderate, and he has here written a conventionally touching poem. I have little doubt that this poem is the sort of thing Jeffrey wanted when he read "There was a boy." He clearly found Wordsworth's poem trivial; yet there seems to be a reluctant admiration wrung from him by the description of the mimicry. If we compare his comments to Coleridge's more famous response—in which he picked out the "Uncertain heaven received / Into the bosom of the steady lake" and wrote, "had I met these lines running wild in the deserts of Arabia, I should have instantly screamed out 'Wordsworth!'"[47]—we can see that although Coleridge's enthusiasm contrasts strongly with Jeffrey's coolness, there is no great difference in their perception of what the poem is doing. It is not really a poem about childhood; it is a poem about the relation between subjective experience and the external world. After participating in the boy's awareness of the world around him, it moves to the curious act of concentration when, listening for one thing, he perceives another with heightened awareness. Wordsworth's own note, in the 1815 Preface, explains why the poem was chosen to stand first among the Poems of the Imagination: "Guided by one of my own primary consciousnesses, I have presented a commutation and transfer of internal feelings, co-operating with external accidents, to plant, for immortality, images of sound and sight, in the celestial soil of the Imagination." The phrase "primary consciousnesses" must be an echo of Coleridge's primary imagination, and may well derive from their conversations (*Biographia Literaria* had not yet been published); both expressions refer to sense perception, and both suggest that an understanding of sense perception provides the basis for understanding the imagination.

"For the sake of this one accomplishment," writes Jeffrey contemptuously; the opposite critical response is found in De Quincey's comment on these lines:

> Then sometimes, in that silence, while he hung
> Listening, a gentle shock of mild surprise
> Has carried far into his heart the voice
> Of mountain torrents.

I have often asked readers of the poem to pick out the one word in these lines that gives the clearest indication of Wordsworth's genius. The answers always show that Jeffrey is still riding. In general, they are surprised that these lines should be singled out, for are they not just a straightforward description of a childish accomplishment; and their choice of words ("hung," "shock," "torrents") is usually half-hearted, revealing a (correct) impression that there is no obvious verbal felicity in the lines. Or not till De Quincey reads them:

> The very expression "far" by which space and its infinities are attributed to the human heart, and its capacities of re-echoing the sublimities of nature, has always struck me as with a flash of sublime revelation.[48]

This is, surely, one of those rare critical observations that seem a creative act equal to, perhaps even surpassing, the poet's own: it registers an awareness that a central concern to Wordsworth's poetry is to give to the inner world the same quality of extension that the outer world possesses—or, in other words, it presents Wordsworth as the poet of the primary imagination.[49]

And death? A lively critical discussion is possible about why the child has to die, which can be attached to the milder scholarly discussion of who the child was. The fact that in a manuscript draft the passage is in the first person may make it clear that Wordsworth is drawing on personal memory here (though it is always possible that a skill he had admired in William Rainock or John Vickers—the possible originals for the boy—had been transposed into the first person). Another verbal trace of the fact that the child is assumed to be still alive is the use of the present perfect tense, "has carried" (it would have been easy enough to write "would carry"). When the poem was first published in *Lyrical Ballads*, it ended with the boy's death and Wordsworth standing by his grave. How far this was intended as an inevitable outcome and how far as a justification for treating the episode as an entire poem, we cannot know. When placed in, or restored to, *The Prelude*, it keeps the death, but the context it now belongs with is that of education and the superiority of natural growth over intellectual training; and what is education for if not for life? Its placement in *The Prelude* has the effect of suggesting that the truly important link is not with death but with childhood, and not childhood in its association with loss and absence but childhood as a time of intense concentration. Of course the ingenious critic will always manage to find justifications for making alternative connexions: the two themes, Nature's influence and death, are so resonant that it is unimaginable that they should not overlap. But if death is appropriate, it will be for reasons very different from Kirk White's.[50]

Is Wordsworth himself claiming that the death is appropriate when, in his 1815 note, he asserts that transfer of inward feelings plants the images in the Imagination "for immortality"? This is a puzzling phrase: is it a Proustian idea, that the imagination exists in a realm outside time, or a Christian idea, that the life of the imagination is a preparation for (an anticipation of) immortal life, or is it simply a rhetorical assertion of how important sense experience is for imagination?

The death also enables the poem to conclude with its account of the poet at the boy's grave, where he presents himself as incapable of saying anything. Since this is Wordsworth, that may mean that his thoughts lie too deep for tears, but it may also mean that there is, simply, nothing to say, that the death is a conventional ending, that regrets, lamentation, or praise would all be out of place. As if to underline the fact that silence is the only response, the sentence ends with an exclamation mark—as did Jeffrey's! The contrast between the two exclamation marks is striking. Wordsworth's is that of awe, Jeffrey's like a snort. Imagine standing for half an hour at the grave of a boy who had no claim on your feelings except this "one accomplishment"! The accomplishment of the boy corresponds to the accomplishment of the poem—shifting attention from the familiar subject of child death to a concern with the nature of sense experience and our relation to the physical world. This child is not an angel but simply an absence, and Wordsworth has written a poem about a pervading absence whose trace suffuses our perceptions. Suffuses and, possibly, sharpens, so enabling him to introduce something new into English poetry, and enabling us to speculate that the truest poetry is built on absence.

$$3$$

The Life and Death of Paul Dombey, and Other Child Deaths in Dickens

T he argument of this chapter is complicated. There is more child death in Dickens than in any other novelist, and exploring it will take us in several directions. The Dickensian child leads a lively existence before dying, though that life is always touched (even enlivened) by the thought of death; so it will be necessary to relate such a child (Paul Dombey is the main example) to traditions of the representation of childhood. When the child dies—and here we move from Paul to Nell—it is represented above all as an angel, and the discussion of the nature and function of belief in angels uses a comparison with Goethe, who turns out to be more skeptical than Dickens. A brief excursus into the biographical origins of Little Nell leads to a discussion of the uncertainty of the boundary between child and adult, and how that relates to both sexuality and death. Finally, the chapter turns to the nature of pathos and how it is achieved, relating it first to Dickens's well-known theatricality and then to political anger.

Since Paul Dombey enters the world as he enters the novel, we can begin with his birth:

> Dombey sat in the corner of the darkened room in the great arm-chair by the bedside, and Son lay tucked up warm in a little basket bedstead, carefully disposed on a low settee immediately in front of the fire and close to it, as if his

constitution were analogous to that of a muffin, and it was essential to toast him brown while he was very new.

Dombey was about eight-and-forty years of age. Son about eight-and-forty minutes. Dombey was rather bald, rather red, and though a handsome well-made man, too stern and pompous in appearance, to be prepossessing. Son was very bald, and very red, and though (of course) an undeniably fine infant, somewhat crushed and spotty in his general effect, as yet.[1]

Why is it funny that the baby is so close to the fire? Because it is being used not as an invitation to ask if the little dear is too hot or too cold but as an opportunity to turn him into a muffin. We know about muffins: they're not important, but they are familiar, and so they can tell us something about that totally baffling object, a baby. Those who treat babies as human, as potential people, are dismissed with condescending patience ("and though of course an undeniably fine infant"); those with eyes to see (it is like a parody of Tennyson's claim that he could look at his own child with the eyes of an artist, "a man who has eyes and can judge from seeing")[2] do not understand babies in the conventional way, and on them the baby makes an almost meaningless impression: "somewhat crushed and spotty in his general effect as yet." This is a world in which human beings are best understood (should we rather say "understood"?) by being compared to inanimate objects—a world in which the inanimate objects have a tendency to be more alive than the people. It is the world of Dickens.

At what point does this strange object fade into the light of common day and turn out to be that dull thing, a human being? If he dies young enough, the answer could be, Never:

> To five little stone lozenges, each about a foot and a half long, which were arranged in a neat row beside their grave, and were sacred to the memory of five little brothers of mine—who gave up trying to get a living exceedingly early in that universal struggle—I am indebted for a belief I religiously entertained that they had all been born on their backs with their hands in their trousers-pockets, and had never taken them out in this state of existence.

The stone lozenges are not only the most alive presence in the opening paragraphs of *Great Expectations,* they also bestow some of their vitality on the dead brothers, who, like the forty-eight-minute Paul, are animated not by breath but by their participation in the inimitable Dickensian style.

But these brothers do not reappear in the novel: they need have no other than a stylistic existence. Little Paul, however, is to be a central character and cannot be confined to the surface brilliance, the purely and ostentatiously verbal existence, that makes the minor characters in Dickens so memorable. Paul has a life to lead, albeit a brief one, and must enter the world of motives and affections, of hopes and disappointments—the world, in short, of personages with a biography.

So, now, a short biography. Paul Dombey, second child and only son of a rich city fellow (as Cousin Feenix calls him) lost his mother at birth: poor dear Fanny, as her sister-in-law remarked sadly, just did not make an effort. Paul was nursed by Polly Toodle, the mother of an almost unlimited number of babies; he was fussed over by his aunt and friends; he was worshipped with a stiff dynastic love by his stiff, reserved Papa; and he was loved by, and passionately loved in return, his older sister Florence. He was sent to Brighton for his health, where he (and Florence, whom he could not bear to be without) lived with Mrs. Pipchin, a highly respectable widow, whose husband broke his heart in pumping water out of the Peruvian mines ("Not being a Pumper himself of course"). Then at the age of six he was sent to Dr. Blimber's Academy, where he made little progress with Latin grammar, but was a universal favorite, his fellow-students and teachers realizing, along with the reader, that he was not long for this world. He left the academy in a whirl of affection and delirium, and went back to the Dombey mansion to die, leaving his sister and father heartbroken, and plunging, as Forster said in his life of Dickens, a whole nation into mourning—with nearly three quarters of the novel yet to run.

The sister and the father, though both heart-broken, do not grieve in the same way. No one in the novel is as shattered by Paul's death as his father, yet, though Mr. Dombey feels most intensely the sorrow that the death is designed to arouse in the reader, he does not feel it as he should. This naturally produces in the reader an ambivalent response to his response, both sharing and repudiating his love for Paul, since it was love for the idea of Dombey-and-Son rather than for the actual old-fashioned child whom Florence loved so devotedly and maternally. Yet Florence in her turn showed little response to Paul's quirky individuality (which will be discussed below): her protective love saw him only as pitiable and weak. So it is only the reader who responds with an appreciation of little Paul's full complexity.

Mr. Dombey's stiff repudiation of comfort ("Louisa, have the goodness to leave me. I want nothing. I am better by myself") tells us that his grief is not authentic, that he would be better if he did want something—his daughter's affection: dynastic grief is less human than paternal grief. Yet dynastic grief can be real too: what, I wonder, would Dickens have said to Josiah Conder, who after losing his only son described that young life as "the strongest root which fastened a man to the world,"[3] an expression which men did not usually use about their daughters? Certainly this dynastic sounding sentiment contrasts with the way Joseph Gibbins wrote about the death of his daughter:

> I am so overwhelmed with the sudden loss of my precious child, that I scarcely know how to write. . . . She is constantly before me in every movement I take, remembering how joyfully she met me upon my return from Town in the omnibus, was the first to open the door, and come to meet me—indeed it seemed to her a pleasure in every way to anticipate my wishes, that I cannot express the sorrow it has brought over my mind[4]

This clearly is how Mr. Dombey should have felt: he should have loved his son as fathers love their daughters.

A child leads a richly imaginative life, for the world around him has not yet settled into humdrum convention, and he keeps seeing it new. A child is endlessly entertaining, for he says the unexpected, misses the obvious, and juxtaposes the diverse. A child moves us easily to tears, especially if he suffers, and most especially if he is likely to die. This gives us three elements in the portrayal of Paul, fantasy, humor, and pathos, which exist both separately and in combination. The pathos always derives from Paul, and the fantasy usually does; but the comedy may be supplied by others, Dr. Blimber or his assistants, above all by Toots, the "weak-eyed young man with the first faint streaks or early dawn of a grin on his countenance":

> "It was a beautiful night. When I had listened to the water for a long time, I got up and looked out. There was a boat over there, in the full light of the moon; a boat with a sail." The child looked at him so steadfastly, and spoke so earnestly, that Mr Toots, feeling himself called upon to say something about this boat, said "Smugglers." But with an impartial remembrance of there being two sides to every question, he added, "or Preventive." (Chapter 12)

The more pathetic Paul grows, the more valuable, for the total effect, is the presence of Toots—unless, as with the deathbed scene, the effect desired is pure pathos, and then Toots is not admitted.

But before coming to that too-famous deathbed, it will be useful to move outside the novel and place Paul in a context. *Dombey and Son* is inimitably Dickensian, but it does not derive from Dickens alone: behind the author lies, as with all texts, a tradition—that is, a set of practices—or rather, in this case, two traditions: one, which associates children with wisdom, is very old; the other, which associates them with pathos, is much more recent.

The Wise Child

The wise child, in one of its forms, goes back to the New Testament. When Jesus was twelve years old and had waxed strong in spirit and been filled with wisdom and the grace of God was upon him, his parents went up to Jerusalem, and as they returned

> the child Jesus tarried behind in Jerusalem; and Joseph and his mother knew not of it. . . . And when they found him not, they turned back again to Jerusalem, seeking him. And it came to pass, that after three days they found him in the temple, sitting in the midst of the doctors, both hearing them and asking them questions. And all that heard him were astonished at his understanding and answers. And when they saw him they were amazed; and his mother said unto him, Son, why hast thou thus dealt with us? behold, thy father and I have sought thee sorrowing. And he said unto them, How is it that ye sought me? wist ye not that I must be about my Father's business? (Luke 2: 43–49)

Here the child Jesus is wise beyond his years, able to astonish the doctors and the listeners. He is the *puer senex*, the child with an adult's wisdom. In the apocryphal gospels, the Gospel of St. Thomas, and the Pseudo-Matthew, there is a whole series of stories about the magic powers and the wonderful knowledge of the infant Jesus, who causes other children to drop down dead or come back to life, expounds the mystic meanings of the letters of the alphabet, or stretches a beam of timber that is too short. But if the *puer senex* has an adult's wisdom, if the point about him is (as Jesus says in pseudo-Matthew) "Fear not, neither conceive that I am a child, for I always was and am a perfect man," then he is not very interesting as a version of childhood—how could he be, if he is not really a child? The most interesting moments in the Gospel of Thomas are the moment when Jesus carries home water in his cloak—"And when his mother saw the miracle that Jesus did, she kissed him and said 'Lord hearken unto me and save my son'"—and the moment when they visit a dyer and the child Jesus, for no apparent reason except naughtiness, pushes all the clothes into the black dye.[5] The first seems to embody both the mother's awareness of how weird the childhood miracle is and her maternal fear that such powers will, somehow, prove fatal to the child; the second seems pure childish naughtiness. The wise child, in short, is most interesting not when he is really an adult, but when he has the kind of quirky wisdom that a child might have and an adult could not. In the story from Luke, if we are meant to see a connection between the naughtiness of the child who runs off without telling his parents and the insight that astonishes the doctors, then we can say that the uncanny wisdom of childhood is the basis of the mysterious wisdom of the Son of God. The best place to look for that tradition may not be in saints' lives, or even the gospels, but in folklore, and nowhere better than in the tale of the Emperor's new clothes, where it takes the child's bluntness to say what the timid conventionality of the adults pretends not to notice.

The wise child is not common in English literature before Dickens, but like so much else he does turn up in Shakespeare. Lady Macduff's bitterness at what she sees as her husband's desertion, when he runs off to England, leads her to say to her to her sprightly son, "Sirrah, your father's dead. And what will you do now? How will you live?" It is a brilliant example of female resentment: she is moved by pity for her son, abandoned along with her, but at the same time some of her resentment can be taken out on him by unfairly thrusting onto him a responsibility that she knows to be premature (he'll have to fend for himself now, serve him right, he's a male). The son puts up some stout resistance ("My father is not dead, for all your saying"), but his main response is to turn his mother's cynicism back on her:

> Yes, he is dead: how wilt thou do for a father?
> Nay, how will you do for a husband?
> Why I can buy me twenty at any market.
> Then you'll buy 'em to sell again. . . .
> Now God help thee, poor monkey: But how wilt thou do for a father?
> If he were dead you'd weep for him: if you would not, it were a good sign, that I should quickly have a new father. (Macbeth IV, ii, 38ff)

A precocious lad, who can show his mother that sauce for the gander is sauce for the goose too; shrewd to observe and privileged to speak. There may not be many such children in English literature, but their number will be increased if we include the fools. The fool, too, is shrewd to observe and privileged to speak, and his shrewdness, like the child's, is not of the ordinary sensible kind. Paul when alive belongs in this tradition: he is the comic child with a touch of fantasy and more than a touch of bluntness, who functions as naive satirist, his satiric themes being money, education, and childhood. Sitting with Mrs. Pipchin in front of the fire, he is very like the child who sees that the emperor is naked:

> Once she asked him, when they were alone, what he was thinking about.
> "You," said Paul, without the least reserve.
> "And what are you thinking about me?" asked Mrs Pipchin.
> "I'm thinking how old you must be," said Paul.
> "You mustn't say such things as that, young gentleman," returned the dame. "That'll never do."
> "Why not?" asked Paul.
> "Because it's not polite," said Mrs Pipchin, snappishly.

"Because it's not polite": besides Paul's bluntness, this injunction is exposed in all its superficiality and evasiveness: even Mrs. Pipchin knows this—that is why she is snappish. When she tries to tell him a moral tale, it does not work:

> "Never you mind, sir," retorted Mrs Pipchin. "Remember the story of the little boy who was gored to death by a mad bull for asking questions."
> "If the bull was mad," said Paul, "how did he know the boy had asked questions? Nobody can go and whisper secrets to a mad bull. I don't believe that story." (Chapter 8)

Just as Young Macduff turns his mother's cynicism back at her, so Paul inspects Mrs. Pipchin's story and gives it back as a dud. Simply by calling him "sir," as, earlier, "young gentleman," she shows that she is going to lose; if Paul really were a young gentleman he would accept arguments like "it's not polite," but he isn't: he is a child.

Old-fashioned Children

When Paul is serving the function of wise child, he is described as "old-fashioned" with such regularity that the word could be called a stock epithet or a label: in the first half of chapter 14 he is called "old-fashioned" by Mrs. Blimber, Miss Blimber, the apothecary, and the clock-maker, and the boys of the school "all agreed that Dombey was old-fashioned." The meaning (still, we are told, current in Scotland) is no. 3 in the *OED*: "having the ways of a grown-up person," or "precocious, knowing": this meaning is not well documented in the *OED* itself, but the English Dialect Dictionary gives some excellent examples (some under the variant form "old-farrand"), such as "a three-year old child whom he saw smoking as awd-farrantly as a man of threescore" (it is easy to imagine little Paul Dombey smoking a pipe) or—even closer to Paul—"she's an aud-farrand little lassie! She's like a lahtle grandmother."[6] "Old" here is, of course, the opposite not of new but of young; and sometimes when Paul is functioning as *puer senex* he is referred to simply as "old": "those old, old moods of his," or "Heaven and Earth, how old his face was as he turned it up again towards his father's." Of course, this is not the *puer senex* of hagiography, in which the fact of childhood is impatiently brushed aside, but the *puer senex* of folktale, in which we are aware of the grotesqueness.

There are other strangely grown-up children in Victorian fiction, such as Paulina Home in *Villette*, who is not associated with death, but who has her own frailty—an emotional vulnerability, covered over by stiffly formal and self-defensive manners. Like Paul she is compared to a grown-up, even to an old woman, and has something not altogether human about her: "whenever, opening a room door, I found her seated in a corner alone, her head in her pygmy hand, that room seemed to me not inhabited, but haunted" (chapter 2). Paulina is not, however, referred to as "old-fashioned": the only other explicitly old-fashioned child I have come across in Victorian fiction is in *Sara Crewe, or What Happened at Miss Minchin's*, a story by Frances Hodgson Burnett. Sara is "a queer little child, with old-fashioned ways and strong feelings." She is left at Miss Minchin's Select Seminary for Young Ladies by a father who then loses his money and dies; Miss Minchin tells her she must now work for her keep and asks, "Don't you intend to thank me for my kindness?" to which Sara replies "in a strange unchildish voice, 'You are not kind.'" The story then describes Sara's desolate life, her ill-treatment by Miss Minchin, and her unpopularity with the other pupils: "Sara, with her elfish cleverness . . . and her odd habit of fixing her eyes upon them and staring them out of countenance, was too much for them." Her one companion is her doll, Emily, until she makes friends with a slow-witted girl who is sent difficult books by her intellectual father and expected to read them; Sara reads the books and describes them to her friend, who is delighted and tells her that she makes the French revolution "seem like a story." With what today would seem like narratological sophistication, Sara replies: "They are all stories. Everything is a story—everything in the world. You are a story—I am a story—Miss Minchin is a story."[7]

Miss Minchin is disconcerted when she finds "the odd unchildish eyes fixed upon her with something like a proud smile in them." Once she boxes Sara's ears for laughing and asks what she was laughing at. "I was thinking," Sara explains. Ordered to apologize, she replies, "I will beg your pardon for laughing if it was rude, but I won't beg your pardon for thinking." The other girls are fascinated: "it always interested them when Miss Minchin flew at Sara, because Sara always said something queer, and never seemed in the least frightened."

Regrettably, Sara grows less interesting as the story proceeds and she grows good, giving her buns to a beggar girl after an exemplary moral struggle; and less interesting still when she meets the man who had ruined her father and is presented with an implausible happy ending. But for the first part of the book she is very like Paul.

Paul is called "old-fashioned" and "old," Sara "unchildish," and these expressions mean much the same. *Unchildish*, of course, really means *childish*: unlike other children, to be sure, but with the vivid imagination and quirky wisdom that we do not expect in adults. When young, Sara fits, and enriches, the meaning of "old-fashioned" and would be at home in the Dickens world.

What the Waves Were Saying

Paul too loses his old-fashionedness, not through a happy ending but through death (which is presented as strenuously happy). There is a touch of pathos to the old-fashioned child, but in death Paul becomes pathos and nothing else. He dies in one of the great cultural set pieces of Victorian England, the chapter entitled "What the Waves Were Always Saying." As a child on Brighton beach, he had listened continually to the waves. That is not in itself unusual for a child: before Paul was (in either sense) conceived, Emily Shore was taken to the seaside at the age of twelve and found it fascinating:

> None of us have ever seen the sea before, and therefore I at least was much delighted with it. It is a great pleasure to me to sit on the sands and watch the boats. . . . I think it is also extremely amusing to watch a wave rolling on, gradually increasing in bulk, and at last breaking into foam.[8]

We could not, even in this slightly archaic sense, use the word "amusing" to describe Paul's obsession with the waves; he uses them simply as a trigger for his morbid fantasy: "'I want to know what it says,' he answered, looking steadily in her face. 'The sea, Floy, what is it that it keeps on saying?'" (chapter 8). Whereas Emily stared intently at the wave that so interested her, Paul stares at his sister, thinking only of his question. And in the end, of course, he learns the answer.

> Whereto answering, the sea,
> Delaying not, hurrying not,
> Whisper'd me through the night, and very plainly before daybreak,
> Lisp'd to me the low and delicious word death,
> And again death, death, death, death,
> Hissing melodious, neither like the bird nor like my arous'd child's heart,
> But edging near as privately for me rustling at my feet,
> Creeping thence steadily up to my ears and laving me softly all over,
> Death, death, death, death, death.[9]

Whitman's poem is almost contemporary with *Dombey and Son*, and its effect is both like and unlike Paul's death. Suppose we inserted those repetitions into Dickens's prose: "What were the wild waves saying? Death, death, death, death, death." We could hardly resist the temptation to read them with a weary sigh (Yes, yes, I *see*), not with the soothing restfulness they carry in the poem. Only in a lyric poem, where we are offered a single consciousness unsullied by other voices, can the lulling rhythm produce this kind of auto-hypnosis, this Romantic death wish. In the novel there are other consciousnesses besides Paul, and the reader stands outside looking on: this eliminates the hypnosis and enables the pathos. Pity is only possible when we are detached from the pathetic object.

Verbal effects alone will not direct us to the most important elements in Paul's deathbed. Its enormous impact as a cultural document derives mainly from three strands: the absence of physical distress, the ubiquitous goodwill, and the religiosity.

The first of these resembles, but can be distinguished from, the lyric death wish. A good deal of Romantic poetry longs to cease upon the midnight with no pain, to sit down like a tired child till death like sleep might steal on me—representing death as longed for, as offering the pleasant torpor of falling asleep. If we ask why this should seem so attractive, one answer is obvious: if sleep is like death, then death is like sleep. If as we fall asleep we wish to imagine we are dying, then we are telling ourselves that as we die it will be like something pleasantly familiar. The death wish is a protection against the fear of death.

But only an adult will feel this way: a child has no need to fear death or to devise a mechanism for evading the fear. We are spectators when Paul dies, not invited to identify with him, so that when the unpleasantness is eliminated from the process it is not so that as readers we can accept our own death, but so that we shall not be too distressed for the child. Paul therefore, like almost all children who die in Victorian novels, does not feel pain or scream or cough agonizingly or even grumble. It is not possible, of course, to claim that illness is actually enjoyable, but presenting it as weakness and mild delirium makes it the fascinating occasion for fantasy:

> Mr Toots's head had the appearance of being at once bigger and farther off than was quite natural: and when he took Paul in his arms, to carry him upstairs, Paul observed with astonishment that the door was in quite a different place from that in which he had expected to find it, and almost thought, at first, that Mr Toots was going to walk straight up the chimney. (Chapter 14)

Illness brings out the charm of childhood—even perhaps our own wish to return to a magical world where doors do not keep still and where people change into one another.

As Paul falls ill, everyone is kind to him. The process begins when he is still at Dr. Blimber's Academy:

> They were so kind, too, even the strangers, of whom there were soon a great many, that they came and spoke to him every now and then, and asked him how he was, and if his head ached, and whether he was tired. He was very much obliged to them for all their kindness and attention. (Chapter 14)

The voice in that last sentence is Paul's rather than the author's, whereas the first sentence seems to belong to both. The effect is to combine a sentimental reassurance from author to reader about human kindness with the child's surprise that people should take so much notice of him.

In the deathbed scene itself there is nothing but goodwill. Mrs. Pipchin has lost her sharpness; Mr. Dombey has lost his sternness and sends for the old nurse, whom he had dismissed, and for Walter, whom he dislikes, simply because Paul asks for them. Clearly there is a parallel between the smoothing of the illness and the smoothing of the people: a sick child makes everyone better natured, and as a kind of reward this mollifies, even removes, the pangs of sickness.

This is even more true of a child death that is seldom noticed, that of Lucie Manette's son in *A Tale of Two Cities.* That boy lives for only one paragraph and is never named:

> Even when golden hair, like her own, lay in a halo on a pillow round the worn face of a little boy, and he said, with a radiant smile, "Dear papa and mamma, I am very sorry to leave you both, and to leave my pretty sister; but I am called, and I must go!" those were not tears all of agony that wetted his young mother's cheek, as the spirit departed from her embrace that had been entrusted to it. (Chapter 21)

Here there is not even any sharpness to be smoothed away. This child is born only to excuse himself with well-bred politeness, and die.

Nothing here to make the reader weep, only consolation, thrust upon us before there is anything to console us for. The one detail that is striking, when we pause to notice it, is the syntactic hiccup in the last sentence. We would expect "that" to refer to the spirit, and this was no doubt Dickens's intention: the boy, for his brief sojourn on earth, was entrusted to his mother's embrace. But it is, grammatically, more natural to attach "that" to its immediate antecedent, in which case the mother's embrace is entrusted to the boy, who briefly accepted the embrace, and then abandoned her. For all the reassurance, then, the angel did betray her—by dying.

Syntactic effects like this are the main concern of Garrett Stewart's extraordinary book *Death Sentences*, a structuralist study of "styles of dying in British fiction." Stewart describes Paul's waves as "a lulling signifier without a signified," and the fact that what they are saying is obviously death is, for him, less important than the fact that we are never told this: the answer is "elided out entirely, referred away to the unavailable in the

consoling monotone of mere recurrence" (of course that could be a definition of death, too). This stimulating—and correct—account of the verbal
strategy is followed by an analysis of the death of Jo in *Bleak House* and the
use made there of incomplete utterance:

> "Jo, can you say what I say?"
> "I"ll say anythink as you say, sir, for I knows it's good."
> "OUR FATHER"
> "Our father!—yes, that's wery good,sir."
> "WHICH ART IN HEAVEN."
> "Art in heaven—is the light a-comin, sir?"
> "It is close at hand. HALLOWED BE THY NAME!"
> "Hallowed be—thy—"
> The light is come upon the dark benighted way. Dead! (Chapter 47)

What is crucial here for Stewart is Jo's inability to manage the repetition,
and he points out both the importance of the typography ("Jo's feeble,
lower-case response") and the fact that Dickens originally intended the
sentence to be completed, then (in proof) deleted the last word. The cor-
respondences between the subject matter (death) and the process of writing leads to the kind of symbiosis, even identity, between the two that
structuralist and post-structuralist criticism so often asserts: "Death is again
defined by the interface between private radiance and narrative perora-
tion."[10]

The death of Jo is much more explicitly Christian than anything in
Dombey and Son; and Victorian deathbeds, as a whole, seldom find it possible to exclude all religious elements.[11] In order, now, to discuss the relation
of Dickens's death scenes to Christianity, it will be necessary to look at the
one other child death that is as famous as Paul's.

Little Nell

Six years before *Dombey and Son*, Dickens had scored an equally
resounding success with the death of Little Nell in *The Old Curiosity Shop*.
Again, let us begin with a short biography, which in this case lends itself to
very simple summary. Her only relative is her grandfather, to whom she is
totally, even pathologically devoted. He loves her, but his weakness for
gambling (which he tells himself is for her benefit) makes him utterly unre-

liable as a protector, and she has to take on the role of looking after him, even to the extent of having to prevent him from stealing her money. Because of his gambling debts, the old curiosity shop, which he owns, falls into the hands of Quilp, Dickens's most brilliant grotesque villain, whose hideous vitality forms an ongoing counterpart to Nell's frail purity: Steven Marcus even suggests that the reason Nell has to die is because in order to distinguish her from Quilp she cannot be associated with life and energy.[12] Nell and her grandfather run away and spend much of the novel wandering aimlessly through a mainly pastoral England, until Nell finally dies in a wintry but idyllic village setting.

Her actual death does not form a set piece but is mentioned in passing as part of the description of the already dead body and its setting; in this earlier, more static novel, the emotional effect derives from iconographic, pictorial elements and from the accumulating, pervasive atmosphere that leads us to think about death almost all through the book. As early as chapter 9, before she and her grandfather have started on their travels, she sits at her window watching the people passing along the street: "She would perhaps see a man passing with a coffin on his back, and two or three others silently following him to a house where somebody lay dead." During their wanderings they stop for a while with a village schoolmaster whose favorite pupil dies (this is a kind of rehearsal for the ending); when the schoolmaster later shows Nell the house he has obtained for her and her grandfather, describing it as "a peaceful place to live in, don't you think so?" she replies, clasping her hands earnestly, "Oh yes, a quiet happy place—a place to live and learn to die in!" (chapter 52). And when she has been sitting in the church reading her Bible, the spot "awakens thoughts of death"—but what of it: "Die who would, it would still remain the same; these sights and sounds would still go on, as happily as ever. It would be no pain to sleep amidst them." She then climbs the tower and looks out. "Oh the glory of the sudden burst of light. . . . It was like passing from death to life; it was drawing nearer Heaven" (chapter 53). But the image of drawing nearer heaven might more easily suggest passing from life to death. Life— the life of rustic England that she sees from the top of the tower—is impregnated with death.

If life is suffused with the idea of death, will not the reverse be true: that death is perceived as not very different from life? So the long-standing Christian assertion (not dead but sleeping) can be used to soften and sentimentalize the harshness. In the novel, this is used to show us that Nell's grandfather, insisting that "she is still asleep," has begun to lose his wits; but the same refusal to accept the reality of death is insisted on by the novel itself:

> She was dead. No sleep so beautiful and calm, so free from trace of pain, so fair to look upon. She seemed a creature fresh from the hand of God, and waiting for the breath of life; not one who has lived and suffered death. (Chapter 71)

Is this a description of a dead body or a refusal to describe it? Contemporary readers might have been uncomfortable with putting the question this way, but they would have had one great advantage over us if they had tried to answer it: that they had seen dead bodies, and quite possibly dead children. Today the cosmetic skill of the mortician, and all the other apparatus of avoidance, keeps us away from the dead; so for comparison I will turn to a contemporary description of a dead child:

> From the gorgeous sunlight I turned round to the corpse. There lay the sweet childish figure; there the angel face; and, as people usually fancy, it was said in the house that no features had suffered any change. Had they not? The forehead, indeed—the serene and noble forehead—*that* might be the same; but the frozen eyelids, the darkness that seemed to steal from beneath them, the marble lips, the stiffening hands, laid palm to palm, as if repeating the supplications of closing anguish—could these be mistaken for life?[13]

Thomas De Quincey lost his nine-year-old sister when he was six, that is in 1791, but he wrote this account at about the same time Dickens wrote *The Old Curiosity Shop*: this is an adult writing, though attempting to recall a child's perception. It could almost be a commentary on the description of the dead Nell, beginning (except for the use of the term "corpse," which Dickens avoids) with two clauses in the same mode as the novel, then asking in a more matter-of-fact way whether what "people usually fancy" (and, we could add, what novelists usually write) corresponds to what we actually see.

The emblems associated with the dead Nell are those we might expect: snow and, more generally, winter; churchyards and the interior of churches; and birds. Kit brings the dying Nell her bird in a cage; the birds that she used to feed, obedient to the pathetic fallacy, die when she does, "that they may not wake her"; her caged bird outlives her, but only just: it is "a poor slight thing the pressure of a finger would have crushed" (chapter 71).

And above all, there are the angels: these pervade *The Old Curiosity Shop*. Nell dreams of the "little scholar" who dies in chapter 25 "not coffined and covered up, but mingling with angels and smiling happily." Kit explains to Barbara that he has been used to talk and think of Nell almost as if she was an angel. And a child comes to Nell in tears (inevitably, in the churchyard) and clasps "his little arms passionately about her neck":

> "She is not one yet!" cried the boy, embracing her still more closely. "No, no. Not yet."
>
> She looked at him wonderingly, and putting his hair back from his face, and kissing him, asked what he meant.
>
> "You must not be one, dear Nell," cried the boy. "We can't see them. They never come to play with us, or talk to us. Be what you are. You are better so."
>
> "I do not understand you," said the child. "Tell me what you mean."
>
> "Why, they say," replied the boy, looking up into her face, "that you will be an Angel, before the birds sing again. But you won't be, will you? Don't leave us, Nell, though the sky is bright. Do not leave us." (Chapter 55).

Mrs. Tait, who also thought of the deaths of her children as their becoming angels, was reading to the dying Catty, from a book that the child herself chose, until

> I could hardly read it; it was some story about a little child telling of the death of his brother, and it said "God wanted another angel to be in heaven, and so he called my brother, and I have had to play alone since then." I soon stopped, saying, "Darling, it is not good for you to have so much reading at a time."

Clearly she felt the same resistance to the child becoming an angel as did Nell's little friend, though she kept it to herself, avoiding the subject with the usual evasive tact of grown-ups.

Mignon

"Are ye for ever to your skies departed?" wrote Felicia Hemans. "Oh! will ye visit this dim world no more?" She need not have worried. Belief in angels—even in sentimentalized angels—did not die with the nineteenth century. Angels are all around us today, if we are to believe Professor Michel Serres, or Dr. William Bloom, or Ms. Jane Howard, who represent three peaks of modern angelology: the first a distinguished French academic who identifies angels with radio waves, with airplanes (and their passengers), and with the Internet; the second a psychologist who runs workshops entitled "Devas, Fairies and Angels: A Practical Approach"; and the third an agony aunt who pours out sugared reassurances to her clients, telling them all (in person, by telephone, in best-selling books) that they are in the peaceful embrace of their divine guardian angel. Modern anxieties, like Victorian certainties, can be fed into a popular culture of sentimentalized reassurances.[14]

And, obviously, such belief is much older than the nineteenth century; for an earlier example of the association of children with angels, I turn to Goethe, whose career, spanning almost sixty years, seems to contain within itself most of the literary history of his time—eighteenth century Enlightenment, Sturm und Drang, German Romanticism. Within *Wilhelm Meisters Lehrjahre*, begun in 1777 and rewritten in 1794–1796, we can find traces of all these—and even of Gothic melodrama. Early in the story Wilhelm rescues and adopts a girl who is being beaten by the leader of the troop of acrobats she belongs to. The girl, known only as Mignon, is a mysterious figure, of whom nothing is known: only at her funeral is she recognized by an Italian marchese as his niece, and he then reveals that she was the child of an incestuous union between his brother and sister. While Mignon is alive, however, we know nothing of her origin; and the funeral oration delivered by the otherwise all-knowing Abbé says of her: "Von dem Kinde, das wir hier bestatten, wissen wir wenig zu sagen. Noch ist es unbekannt, woher es kam, seine Eltern kennen wir nicht, und die Zahl seiner Lebensjahren vermuten wir nur." (*Wilhelm Meister* 8:8). (Little is known about the child we are here burying. We do not know where she came from, or who her parents were, and we can only guess at her age.) Goethe cleared up the first two mysteries for us, but not the last, which is the most interesting, for whereas Mignon's origins belong to the Gothic mystery that forms what to us must seem a very dated layer of the novel, her age is a piece of information that would enter more immediately into our reading. We need to know her age in order to know whether she has reached puberty and, so, to understand more about her intense and intimate devotion to Wilhelm: does she regard him as a father figure or as a potential lover? The doctor who treats Mignon when she is in Natalie's care manages to learn more about her than Wilhelm ever could and passes the knowledge on to him, but this does not resolve the sexual ambiguity.

In Book V, on the night after the performance of *Hamlet*, Wilhelm receives a secret visit from a woman who came into his bed and left without revealing her identity (we later learn that this was the impulsive Philina), and Mignon confesses to the doctor that she had seen this and that it had led to an agony of jealousy that almost killed her. The episode is a strange blend of sexual desire and innocence:

> Durch leichtsinnige Reden Philinens und der anderen Mädchen, durch ein gewisses Liedchen aufmerksam gemacht, war ihr der Gedanke so reizend geworden, eine Nacht bei dem Geliebten zuzubringen, ohne das sie dabei etwas weiter als ein vertrauliche, glückliche Ruhe zu denken wusste. . . . Schon war sie vorausgelaufen, um sich in der unverschlossenen Stube zu verbergen, allein als sie eben die Treppe hinaufgekommen war, hörte sie ein Geräusch, sie verbarg sich, und sah ein weisses, weibliches Wesen in Ihr Zimmer schleichen. . . . Mignon empfand unerhörte Qual, alle die heftigen Empfindungen einer leidenschaftlichen Eifersucht mischten sich zu dem unerkannten Verlangen einer dunklen Begierde und griffen die halb entwickelte Natur gewaltsam an. Ihr Herz, das bisher vor Sehnsucht and Erwartung lebhaft geschlagen hatte, fing auf einmal an, zu stocken. (8:3)

> Her attention was roused through frivolous remarks by Philina and the other young women, together with a certain song, so that the thought of spending a night with her beloved took on a charm for her, without her having any other idea than an intimate and happy rest. . . . She had already run on ahead in order to hide herself in your unlocked room, and just as she reached the top of the stairs she heard a noise, hid herself, and saw a white female form slip into your room. . . . Mignon felt a pang she had never before experienced, all the violent feeling of passionate jealousy mingled with the unrecognised demands of dark desire, and seized hold of the half-developed nature. Her heart, that up to then had beaten violently with longing and expectation, suddenly began to fail her.
> . . .

Mignon may be the same age as Nell, but a passage like this reminds us how completely Nell is still a child. Poised on an uncertain frontier between childhood and womanhood, Mignon is consumed by a passion somewhere between filial devotion and sexual obsession; the assurances that she does not know what spending a night with her beloved really means accompany what looks very like a determination to yield up her virginity, and the doctor does not hesitate to describe the intruding female figure as a "rival" (Nebenbühlerin). The description of her jealous spasm makes it sound almost fatal (she finds that she cannot breathe), and suggests that her sudden death a few chapters later may be caused by jealousy.

This death is prompted by the greeting between Wilhelm and Theresa. Theresa throws herself into his arms with the words "My friend! My beloved! My husband! Yes, I am yours for ever," and kisses him warmly ("Mein Freund! mein Geliebter! mein Gatte! ja, auf ewig die Deine! rief sie unter den lebhaftsten Küssen" [8:5]). A moment later, Mignon falls with a cry at Natalie's feet, and all attempts to revive her fail. The circumstantial evidence points unquestionably to jealousy—and the fact that Wilhelm is not in love with Theresa no doubt lends the moment an extra irony; but apart from the fact that jealousy seems implausible as the immediate cause of death in this way, the girl is now protected by the language from any suggestion of sexuality: she is referred to as the dear creature (das liebe Geschöpf), and Wilhelm now calls her a departed angel.

Although she becomes an angel by dying, there is none of the elaborate angelic imagery and none of the long-drawn-out pathos of Dickens: the death of the child is not yet a site for sentimentality on the scale that was to come later. But this is not the first time that Mignon is an angel: a few chapters earlier she dressed up as one, a performance arranged by Natalie as part of an educational program;

> Schon seit einiger Zeit hatten meine Mädchen aus dem Munde der Bauernkinder gar manches von Engel, vom Knechte Ruprecht, vom heiligen Christe vernommen, die zu gewissen Zeiten in Personen erscheinen, gute Kinder beschenken und unartige bestrafen sollten. Sie hatten eine Vermutung, dass es verkleidete Personen sein müssten, worin ich sie denn auch bestärkte und, ohne mich viel auf Deutungen einzulassen, mir vornahm, ihnen bei der ersten Gelegenheit ein solches Schauspiel zu geben. . . . Ich hatte mir Mignon zu dieser Rolle ausgesucht, und sie ward an dem bestimmten Tage in ein langes, leichtes, weisses Gewand anständing gekleidet. . . . Anfangs wollte ich die Flügel weglassen, doch bestanden die Frauenzimmer, die sie anputzten, auf ein Paar grosse goldene Schwingen, an denen sie recht ihre Kunst zeigen wollten. (8:2)

My girls had for some time been hearing from the peasant children about angels, about the knight Rupert and about the holy Christ, who appeared in person at certain times, and were supposed to give presents to good children and punish the naughty. They had an idea that they were people in disguise, an idea which I encouraged, and without going too much into explanations I decided to lay on such a performance for them at the first opportunity.... I had selected Mignon for this role (that of an angel), and when the day came she was suitably dressed in a long light white robe.... I wanted at first to leave out the wings, but the women who were getting her ready insisted on a pair of large golden pinions in order to show off their skill.

Though written in the eighteenth century, this sounds like religion after Feuerbach. Christian myths are valued as a set of images to represent human feelings and relationships; they should not be believed in, but put to good use. Supernatural trappings, like wings, should preferably be omitted, but can be retained if they mean a lot to those taking part. Natalie's agnostic respect for religion would have appealed to George Eliot.

The angel, when it appears, interprets itself to the children in agnostic terms:

Bist du ein Engel, fragte das eine Kind.
Ich wollte, ich wär' es, versetzte Mignon.
Warum trägst Du eine Lilie?
So rein und offen sollte mein Herz sein, dann wär' ich glücklich.

"Are you an angel?" asked one of the children.
"I"d like to be," declared Mignon.
"Why are you carrying a lily?"
"My heart should be as pure and open as it is; then I"d be happy."

The angels of *The Old Curiosity Shop*, too, are not always inhabitants of heaven. The schoolmaster explains to Nell that "there is not an angel added to the Host of Heaven but does its blessed work on earth in those that loved it here" (chapter 52): here "angel" is little more than a term to suggest, without obvious unorthodoxy, that immortality consists in becoming your admirers, in a continued life in the memory of the living. And when we are told that it is by means of the "mild lovely look" of the dead

Nell that we shall know the angels in their majesty, after death, we can reverse the sequence and read it as telling us that "angel" is a figure for bestowing status on the loveliness of the dead child.

Does this mean that the Dickensian angel has broken free of the Christian belief from which it originated? This is the view of Nina Auerbach, who, aware that we have lost sympathy with the "numinous element" of Victorian novels, attempts to recuperate some of the force of these angels for the modern reader by seeing them as "emanations of an intensely felt and thoroughly non-Christian religion that Dickens shared with many of his most brilliant contemporaries".[15] Whether this replacement of direct value judgment by cultural history can be used to change the value judgment is a question I shall address in the last chapter; here I pause for a moment on the assertion that these angels belong to a thoroughly non-Christian religion. That angels are a traditional part of Christian belief is not, of course, in doubt. Medieval theology elaborated a series of propositions about the angelic orders which had the appearance of rigorous system; it left its traces in *Paradise Lost*, where the angels are ranked as "Thrones, dominations, virtues, princes, powers," but this is probably one of the details that made *Paradise Lost* old-fashioned; it faded from Protestantism, and the angels who are so prominent in nineteenth century imagery are no longer ranked in ternions and classes: such a system is by then seen as "a fruitful theme for those who have exhibited perhaps more ingenuity and subtlety than humility and reverence." For Mrs. Stone, author of this remark, graves are the footprints of angels. Angels have now become symbols of the emotional life, above all of grief and hope; and belief (perhaps we should say "belief") in angels has taken a new lease of life.[16]

The almost imperceptible detachment of angels from other-worldliness permeates *The Old Curiosity Shop* and is found elsewhere in Dickens—in *A Child's Dream of a Star*, for instance, another tale of child death, which ends with a vignette of heaven seen as a kind of family reunion:

> My daughter's head is on my sister's bosom, and her arm is around my mother's neck, and at her feet there is the baby of old time, and I can bear the parting from her, GOD be praised.

This does not look like the heaven where there is no marrying or giving in marriage, but it is very like the heaven whose gates are ajar and in which we shall recognize our friends.[17] It illustrates perfectly Ariès' claim that the heavenly home, in the nineteenth century, becomes "the earthly home saved from the menace of time" (though not, surely, his further claim that "when God is dead, the cult of the dead becomes the only authentic religion," because this family seems so very much alive.)[18] In the mid-nineteenth century, before the death of God has been announced, Christianity has already begun to turn into religiosity.

Aries' point is very like Auerbach's, though whether we call it "thoroughly non-Christian" will depend on whether we equate Christianity with Christian theology. And in a curious way the point is also made by Dickens himself. At the moment of Paul Dombey's death, the term "old-fashioned," with which the novel has made such play, is reintroduced, in order to speak of "the old, old fashion—Death!.." Immediately after that comes the final paragraph:

> Oh thank God, all who see it, for that older fashion yet, of Immortality! And look upon us, angels of young children, with regards not quite estranged, when the swift river bears us to the ocean! (Chapter 16)

One reason for the enormous emotional impact this had on contemporaries may be its ambivalence about Christianity. It does not actually profess belief in immortality: by calling it, so lovingly, a "fashion," the writing offers it as a beneficent invention, a doctrine devised to help us bear the pain of death. Yet this Feuerbachian claim is uttered not critically, not even sceptically, but with gratitude. And so the angels of young children could be seen as a human invention, a way we have taught ourselves to speak of dead children, and all the finer for that. What weakens the theology strengthens the consolation.

Christianity, with the prominence given to sin, is not a sentimental religion, but it can be sentimentalized. When Paul is ill, and still at Dr. Blimber's, he thinks frequently of an uplifting religious picture:

> He had much to think of in association with a print that hung up in another place, where, in the centre of a wondering group, one figure that he knew, a figure with a light about its head—benignant, mild, and merciful—stood pointing upward. (*Dombey and Son*, chapter 14)

Here is Jesus Christ without any theological content: not the son of God, not divine, certainly not crucified, not even supernatural: simply an emblem of goodwill. Except that it is the center of a wondering group, we could take the figure to be Florence rather than Jesus.

To describe this as religiosity is to see it as the "spilt religion" that Irving Babbitt attributed to Romanticism, as that which lays claim to the emotional effect of religion with none of the doctrinal content—and not even to all the emotional content, but only to that which is reassuring: not judgment, not even self-sacrificing love, but benevolence (benevolence costs nothing, love may cost a great deal). There are even better candidates than Florence if we are, mischievously, to seek a Dickensian identity for that figure pointing upwards—Mr. Pickwick perhaps, or even Pecksniff, saying, "There is no deception, ladies and gentlemen, all is peace, a holy calm pervades me."

So when at the moment of death Paul enters heaven, it is a heaven that may have no existence except its effect on earth. "Tell them that the print upon the stairs at school is not divine enough. The light about the head is shining on me as I go." What is intended is clearly that Paul is seeing Christ in glory, but it is tempting to claim that he is actually looking into a mirror, so placed as to send the light down to us. That he should say all this himself might be acceptable to the Christian reader if Paul were in fact entering heaven, and perhaps to the agnostic reader if he is willing to suspend his disbelief; but if Paul is a living child still, and the mouthpiece of his author, then the comparison with Pecksniff may not be merely mischievous.

Nell, Dickens, and Mary

Death permeates *The Old Curiosity Shop* but not until the second half of the book is it clearly attached to Nell herself, and even then one cannot be sure that her association with images of death means that she is ill herself. The first suggestion that she is likely to die comes in chapter 45, and from then on it strengthens her attractiveness to everyone she meets: "Even careless strangers . . . —even they saw it—even they pitied her—even they bade him [the grandfather] good day compassionately, and whispered as they passed." We are often told that we treat death today with the embarrassed evasiveness with which the Victorians treated sex: this is true, but we see here that they had some of our embarrassment too.

If Nell is to die, why are we so far into the novel before she is clearly identified as Death's victim? The delay may not need explaining: plot and rhetorical strategy may prefer that she does not fall ill too soon. But it may also be because Dickens had not yet decided on the outcome. In a letter to Thomas Latimer, Dickens claimed that he had "the design and purpose" of the story "distinctly marked in my mind from its commencement," and that he intended "to stamp upon it from the first the shadow of that early death."[19] But Forster claimed in his *Life* that it was he who suggested to Dickens that Nell should die, even quoting a letter in which Dickens thanks him for his "valued suggestion."

> He had not thought of killing her when, about half-way through, I asked him to consider whether it did not necessarily belong even to his own conception, after taking so mere a child through such a tragedy of sorrow, to lift her also out of the commonplace of ordinary happy endings, so that the gentle pure little figure and form should never change to the fancy.[20]

We cannot know the truth; but we can observe a different, but parallel, issue about how early the death of Paul is implied. When Dickens had finished the first number of *Dombey and Son*, he read it to his circle of English acquaintances at Lausanne; and "old Mrs Marcet, who is devilish cute, guessed directly (but I didn't tell her she was right) that little Paul would die."[21] Did Mrs. Marcet feel that an old-fashioned child should not grow up, because that would remove the basis for his quaint wisdom, or did she detect the incipient pathos that would eventually kill Paul? She plays the same role as Forster did with Nell, the difference being that Dickens is now in charge: he does not need anyone to detect the resonances of his text; he is aware of them, has even planned them, and decides not to tell.

Before leaving little Nell we ought to relate her death to its biographical context—which is, after all, what Dickens himself did. He and Kate did lose a daughter, Dora, who died in infancy in 1851, but that was after both *The Old Curiosity Shop* and *Dombey and Son* were finished and published; the death that he believed lay behind Nell's was that of Mary Hogarth, and this view was accepted, and enlarged on, by Edmund Wilson, the first truly modern and post-Freudian of Dickens's critics.[22] The death of Mary is one of the most intense, and famous, episodes in Dickens's life. After his marriage to Catherine Hogarth in 1836, her younger sister Mary came to live with them, and on 7 May 1837 she was taken suddenly ill after a visit to the theater and died the next day, in Dickens's arms (a point he mentions almost every time he tells the story). Dickens's letters on the subject express overwhelming grief. "Since our marriage," he wrote,

> she has been the grace and life of our home—the admired of all, for her beauty and excellence—I could have better spared a much nearer relation or an older friend, for she has been to us what we can never replace, and has left a blank which no one who ever knew her can have the faintest hope of seeing supplied.[23]

He writes here—and in several other letters—in the plural, but in the more intensely grief-stricken passages he moves from "our sufferings" to saying "I have lost the dearest friend I ever had. Words cannot describe the pride I felt in her, and the devoted attachment I bore her." He loved her "more deeply and fervently than anyone on earth," sometimes (by no means always) adding, "after my wife."[24] For months after her death he dreamed of her every night. He even set his heart on being buried with her and was almost frantic with distress when, four years later, her young brother George died and was buried with her instead. Needless to say, this has fascinated Dickens's biographers, and not only those inclined to psycho-analyzing their subject. Dickens never wrote about his wife with such passion, not even in the early, happy days of their marriage. It seems a classic instance of splitting, the sexual attraction felt towards Kate and the idealization bestowed on Mary. And if we add the third sister, Georgina, who later came to live with them and remained with Dickens to look after the children after the marriage broke up, we can postulate a threefold split: Georgina the practical housewife and child-rearer, Kate the sexual partner and focus of domestic resentments, Mary the idealized angel-figure. That one man should find three sisters among whom to divide his affections in this way seems like a story invented to fulfil male fantasies.

In January 1841 Dickens wrote to Forster:

> This part of the story is not to be galloped over, I can tell you. . . . It is such a very painful thing to me, that I really cannot express my sorrow. . . . Dear Mary died yesterday, when I think of this sad story.[25]

The death of Little Nell predates all the fictional child deaths discussed in this and the next chapter and is the cause as much as the result of literary conventions; so it is natural that we should look for an extra-literary—that is, a biographical—source for it. But Mary was a young woman, Nell is a child. How important is this difference?

To answer this, it will be best to look first at a similar liminal case in the fiction.

"Come up and be Dead"

The most important link between childhood and death in *Our Mutual Friend* is purely metaphoric. "Come up and be dead," Jenny Wren calls to Riah, the kindly old Jew who has befriended her. Sitting on the roof, far from the squalor by which she is normally surrounded, Jenny sees "the clouds rushing on above the narrow streets," and "the golden arrows pointing at the mountains in the sky from which the wind comes, and you feel as if you were dead" (book 2 chapter 5). Jenny is a pathetic child, crippled, poor, and with a drunken father to support. She does not die, but Mrs. Marcet would have been forgiven for expecting her to, for death seems ever lurking when she appears. She sees her father die, she retreats to a kind of heaven on the roof and refers to it as "being dead," and she is surrounded with the icons of death, especially with flowers and angels. She describes to Eugene how she keeps smelling flowers, though she has seen very few flowers indeed, in her life:

> As I sit at work, I smell miles of flowers. I smell roses till I think I see the rose-leaves lying in heaps, bushels, on the floor. I smell fallen leaves till I put down my hand—so—and expect to make them rustle.

And, as well as flowers, children: but not the children she meets and is mocked by:

> They were not chilled, anxious, ragged or beaten; they were never in pain. . . . Such numbers of them, too! All in white dresses, and with something shining on the borders, and on their heads. . . . They used to come down in long bright slanting rows and say all together, "Who is this in pain?" (*Our Mutual Friend* 2:2).

These children are easy enough to identify; and although Jenny does not die, I have no hesitation in adding her to the company of Nell and Paul, as an example of how inextricably child pathos is associated with death. When she first appears in the novel, Lizzie Hexam describes her with the traditional attributes of the suffering orphan—

> the Mother is dead. This poor ailing little creature has come to be what she is surrounded by drunken people from her cradle—if she ever had one—

and the chapter ends with exclamatory pathos:

> Poor little dolls' dressmaker! How often dragged down by hands that should have raised her up; how often so misdirected when losing her way on the eternal road, and asking guidance! Poor, poor little dolls' dressmaker (2:2).

This is familiar enough, and there are occasional reminders, as the novel proceeds, that there was "no querulous complaining in [her] words, but they were not the less touching for that"; and like Little Nell she is a natural nurse, as emerges when she sits at the bedside of the injured Eugene and anticipates his slightest need. But this direct pathos is marginalized in the full portrait of Jenny: though a suffering child, she is a variant of the pattern.

The fact that Jenny does not die is both crucial and unimportant. Once again we can turn to Garrett Stewart for some illuminating remarks (though once again they need to be treated with caution) about the contrast between actual death and the luxury of "being dead":

> The predication "be dead" is. . . . an exonerating oxymoron, reminding us that we are in the presence . . . not of death and non-being, but of rebirth. . . . You can come up and be dead as often as you like, but one day body will catch up with soul, and then no one, not even yourself, will be able to bring you down and back.[26]

This is true; but we could claim that the opposite is true of Nell, whose body has caught up with her soul, but in a way that transforms ordinary death into something very like "come up and be dead." The real oxymoron comes when we juxtapose Jenny and Nell: the character pretending to be dead as a way of coping with the pain of living and the author "pretending" that, turned to an angel, the young girl is not really dead.

Jenny differs from Nell in other ways too. She has, in the first place, much more of the wise child about her. She sees through Eugene's supercilious air, realizing that he is both better and worse than he presents himself. When he claims that he is a man to be doubted because he is a bad idle dog, she replies "Then why don't you reform and be a good dog." Her directness when talking to adults could remind us of Paul, but although, like him, she is disconcerting to talk to, it is not, in her case, the sharpness of innocence.

And second, there is the liminality. She belongs not to childhood but to a borderline state that overlaps with adulthood. "Child or woman?" asks Miss Abbey in a whisper when she first meets her. Jenny is thirteen, perhaps fourteen, no older (after all) than Little Nell, but there is never any doubt that Nell is a child. In Jenny's case, however, almost every detail suggests ambivalence. She is a doll's dressmaker. (Those who make dolls for sale usually buy the wax or china figure that they then clothe, so the expression is accurate, but it also holds the suggestion of not being a real dressmaker, of having and not having a real adult trade.) Then there is her handling of her father. She is not the only Dickens heroine who mothers her father (there are Agnes Wickfield, Amy Dorrit, and, of course, Nell looking after her grandfather); but Jenny is the only one who has devised a myth to draw attention to the reversal. She speaks to him as if she were the one in authority (to which he submits), and even reproaches herself after his death for not bringing him up properly.

Then there is the obliquity of her name: she is really called Fanny Cleaver but is known as Jenny Wren by her own choice, and even prints this on her cards. "Miss Jenny Wren," the card runs, "'Dolls' Dressmaker. Dolls attended at their own residences." It is a parody of a visiting card. And when she sings at her work, "trolling in a small sweet voice a mournful little song, which might have been the song of the doll she was dressing, bemoaning the brittleness and meltability of wax" (4:8), it is hard to say if this is pathos, or a parody of pathos. (That is after all common enough in Dickens. The comic parts of *Nicolas Nickleby* read very like parodies of its melodrama and pathos, and Alexander Welsh has discovered in Mrs. Gamp an uproarious parody of most of the commonplaces of pathetic death.)[27] Jenny's song belongs both to real humanity and to the doll world: the pathos is a joke (not flesh but wax is grass) without ceasing to be sad. And her appearance is equally ambivalent: she is small and looks like a child, but she is small because crippled, and she has an abundance of long golden hair, as if to cast a glow of sexuality over the shrunken, virginal, undeveloped body. This is taken up in the imaginary figure of "Him," the fantasy husband she looks forward to marrying—and keeping in order, as she has never succeeded in keeping her father in order. Again, it is unreal—a child's joking way of looking forward to adulthood and marriage—and deeply real—a young woman's sexual nervousness and resentment, her dependence on a man accompanied with an impatient sense that she should not need him because she can do everything better than he can.

Henry James did not care for *Our Mutual Friend*. His unfavorable review reveals a strong preference for the early Dickens over the later and, so, belongs very much to its time: this is James the Victorian not James the proto-modern. Times have changed, and there is no need to hold that preference against him; but when it comes to Jenny, James makes a crucial mistake that can illuminate a good deal for us. He describes her, correctly enough, as "a poor little dwarf, afflicted, as she constantly reiterates, with a 'bad back' and 'queer legs'," forever assuring those she speaks to "that she knows their tricks and their manners"; but then he continues:

> Like all Mr Dickens' pathetic characters, she is a little monster; she is deformed, unhealthy, unnatural; she belongs to the troop of hunchbacks, imbeciles and precocious children who have carried on the sentimental business in all Mr Dickens' novels; the little Nells, the Smikes, the Paul Dombeys.[28]

Here is one of those cases where adverse criticism seems to hover on the edge of lively appreciation: we would only need to change "carried on the sentimental business" to, say, "shown the ambivalence of pathos and parody." And the mistake is, of course, that Little Nell is not grotesque: she hasn't enough corporeal existence for that. Jenny differs from Nell precisely in the lively grotesqueness of her imagination. "If you were treated as you ought to be," she says to her father,

> you'd be fed upon the skewers of cats' meat; only the skewers, after the cats had had the meat. As it is, go to bed. (2:2)

This is hardly the way we expect a pathetic young creature to talk; and worse is to come. Turning from the father whom she calls her child, to the "Him" she pictures herself marrying, she speculates on what she would do if he turned out a drunkard:

> I tell you what I think I'd do. When he was asleep, I'd make a spoon red hot, and I'd have some boiling liquor bubbling in a saucepan, and I'd take it out

hissing, and I'd open his mouth with the other hand—or perhaps he'd sleep with his mouth ready open—and I'd pour it down his throat, and blister it and choke him. (2:2)

We have met this before. Daniel Quilp heated up his liquor till it boiled and drank it direct from the red-hot saucepan: Jenny's fantasies are Quilp's acts. Dickens has here incorporated the antiself into the figure of the innocent girl. Hence the cruelty that has distressed—and delighted—so many readers of *Our Mutual Friend*. After the grasping hypocrite Fledgeby has been attacked and savagely beaten by one of his victims, he is found by Jenny rolling about in agony on the floor of his apartment. Jenny, as we know, is a good nurse, and she dresses his wounds; he asks if vinegar and brown paper is the sort of application, and she replies, with a silent chuckle, "It looks as if it ought to be Pickled." This little verbal sting is followed by a very nonverbal act: before applying the plasters, she gets down the pepper pot and sprinkles them liberally. Mr. Fledgeby, not surprisingly, utters "a sharp howl as each was put in its place" (4:8). This is pure Quilp: Jenny is not Nelly now, she is Nelly's antiself. What Henry James should have written is: "Unlike all Mr Dickens' pathetic characters, she is a little monster."

"Dear Mary died yesterday when I think of this sad story." Returning now to Mary Hogarth, we can see that when Dickens identified her with Nell, and so shifted her from woman to child, he revealed a typical ambivalence about what we would now call a teenager. The difference between child and young woman is, obviously, determined by puberty, and the consequent possibility of being seen sexually. Puberty is a physiological fact that can be established objectively: the age of menarch in the nineteenth century was higher than today, and no doubt lay somewhere between fourteen (Nell and Jenny) and seventeen (Mary Hogarth). Sexual availability, on the other hand, depends on perception by the observer as well as the condition of the subject, and since the conventions of representation of the young female in the nineteenth century are carefully designed to disguise sex, it is not easy to say just how a virgin of sixteen is being presented: the absence of explicit sexuality can be attributed either to the evasivness of the representation or to her being still a child. Even the manner in which the young heroine's age is stated has a liminal quality about it. Rose Maylie is "not past seventeen"; Kate Nickleby is "about seventeen"; Mary Hogarth died, according to the epitaph Dickens wrote for her, "at the early age of seventeen"—on the threshold of sexual maturity. She was actually slightly under seventeen.

Even the denial of sexuality must mention it and, so, raise the possibility that what is being denied is actually there. Am I then justified in treating the child as a nonsexual being, as I have been doing? The strongest assertion to the contrary that I know is that of James Kincaid. Paul Dombey, in Kincaid's view, is "a pedophile pin-up," "laid before us from the very first as a tidily arranged bundle of morbid childish eroticism," capable, like Peter Pan, of "pumping up enormous gushers of desire in onlookers," and he describes Nell's blissful death as "a model of perfect eros." The "child-loving" that provides the title of Kincaid's book is quite explicitly erotic: as we read about Nell we are "driven by desire." If one asks why Kincaid believes that these children are erotic creatures whom the reader sees in erotic terms, the answer seems to be that he assumes it because he believes that all children are seen erotically.[29] A discussion of that must become a psycho-analytic discussion, taking in Freud's claims on infantile sexuality; and this book is written from a position that is highly sceptical about psycho-analysis. If we are to operate with the possibility of distinguishing an erotic from an innocent view of childhood, a more useful starting point is provided by Robert Polhemus, who observes: "it seems crucial that Nell die a virgin, unpolluted by sexuality, but sexual vulnerability and peril are very much a part of her story and destiny."[30] This invites us to ask what elements in the book present Nell as pre-sexual and what elements eroticize her, and once we do that the answer is obvious. It is Quilp.

Many critics have realized that Nell and Quilp are not in the same novel by accident. Her purity and devotion, his violent energy; her ethereal spirituality, his vividly portrayed bodily existence; her passivity, his leering, sadistic eloquence, spreading fear and horrified fascination all around him—all this makes Quilp her antiself. She is angel, he is devil. The offensiveness of Quilp's constant references—to Nell "going to bed in her own little room," the invitation to "come to sit upon Quilp's knee" or to be his "number two . . . my second; my Mrs Quilp"–depends on the fact that our view of her is so different from his; but we could shrug them off more easily if they did not strike a chord in the reader, either because we are all incipient pedophiles (Kincaid's view) or because we are aware that she is on the threshold of adulthood (the view that makes liminality central).

One more Dickens heroine, now, to show the importance, and the complexity, of liminality. Amy Dorrit is twenty years old, and so technically is an adult, but she is small, and she keeps the nickname "little." She looks after the half-witted Maggie, who is younger than she is, but much bigger.

On the night when she is locked out of the Marshalsea, she and Maggie wander the streets together. Occasional voices call out, when they meet prowlers, to "let the woman and the child go by." They meet a prostitute who says to Maggie, "What are you doing with the child?," then to Amy, "Kiss a poor lost creature, dear, and tell me where she's taking you." With a shock, she realizes that Amy is a woman, and Amy's compassion then can do nothing for her: "I should never have touched you, but I thought you were a child" (*Little Dorritt*, book 1, chapter 14).

The ironies are quite complicated here. Neither of them is literally a child, but retarded Maggie is a kind of big overgrown child. The prostitute, calling out to Maggie, "What are you doing with the child?" was wrong but also, if we reverse the figures, right. And when she refuses Amy's help and compassion ("You are kind and innocent; but can't look at me out of a child's eyes") she is quite right: childhood is the cure for sex, and Amy can no longer help the sexual offender, for she is past puberty.

I can now suggest a way of relating the death of Mary to the young girls and women in the novels. Dickens joined Mary to Nell because both figures were liminal: child and young woman blend, as I have suggested, through the process of idealizing desexualization. But Nell, like Rose Maylie, like Kate Nickleby and Madeline Bray, is never seen sexually, and the ambivalence results only in a vague idealized blur—though Madeline, like Nell, *is* seen sexually—by the villain: Gride's gloating references to "having that dainty chick for my wife" bracket off the sexualizing of the virginal heroine as coming only from a desiccated, elderly villain; but even as they bracket it off, they allow it, like Quilp's view of Nell, to enter the book. Amy, in this scene from *Little Dorritt*, and Jenny throughout, are not simply presexual children but are more interesting, for in them the liminality is explicit. The psychological complexity that is excluded from the usual Dickens heroine, and from the presentation of the real life Mary, becomes a controlling principle in the case of the doll's dressmaker.

The Theatricality of Pathos

Pathos is central to the dying Dickens child, and to see the basic recipe for it we can look at little Dick, who dies midway through *Oliver Twist*. He has no identity except that of the helpless sufferer awaiting death. "How pale you are," Oliver remarks to him, and he replies, "I heard the doctor tell them I was dying." He knows the doctor must be right, because "I dream

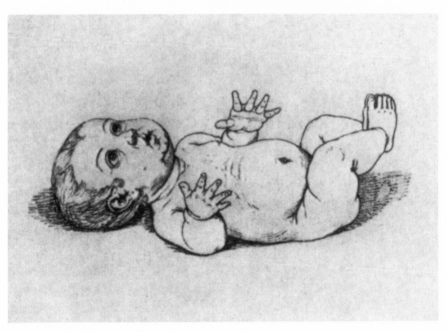

"The Child," by Otto Runge.

LIFE AND DEATH

Otto Runge's drawing of a child (1809) suggests vitality, energy, and entrance into life; its hands are open to receive the world.

Charles Wilson Peale's portrait of his dead daughter (1785) contrasts in every way: the child is clothed, no doubt in the clothes she will be buried in, she not only lies stiff, with her arms rigid at her sides, she even has the arms bound, and she is accompanied by the very conventionalized figure of the grieving mother. When the picture hung in Peale's studio it was concealed by a curtain, on which was written: "Before you draw this curtain, consider whether you will affect a Mother or Father who has lost a child."

In contrast to the self-sufficiency of the lively infant, bereavement is seen as a family event.

"Rachel Weeping," by Charles Wilson Peale. Courtesy of The Philadelphia Museum of Art.

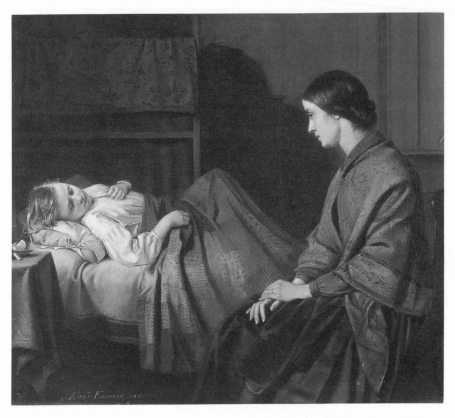

"An Anxious Hour," by Alexander Farmer. Courtesy of Victoria and Albert Museum.

AT THE BEDSIDE

Almost all we know about sick or dying children comes, of course, from those who watched and waited. Alexander Farmer's "An Anxious Hour" (1865) shows us the grieving, helpless mother: it could be Catherine Tait or Margaret Oliphant.

Luke Fildes' picture of "The Doctor" (1891) was one of the most popular of all Victorian paintings. Grief and fear are here replaced by the suggestion of expertise: the doctor has sat by many such bedsides and knows what to look for—but, as chapter 1 makes clear, there is little he can do.

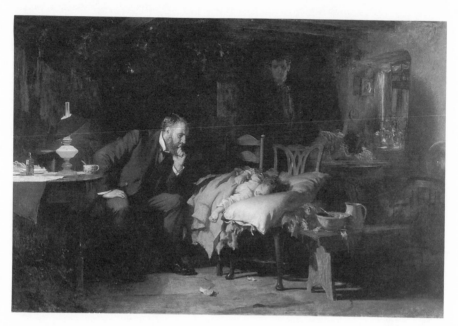

"The Doctor," by Luke Fildes. Courtesy of The Tate Gallery, London.

"Angel faces smile," by Elizabeth Hawkins

ANGELS AND ABSENCES

The two themes of this book are juxtaposed in these two images. "Angel faces smile" is a sculpture by Elizabeth Hawkins in Highgate Cemetery, London: the group of angel faces seems to have been a standard pattern for children's graves in the late nineteenth and early twentieth centuries.

A sentimentalized dog grieves over "The Empty Cradle" in the picture by W. Archer (1839–1935) of the dead child as an absence.

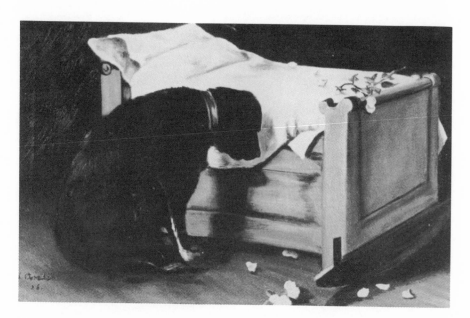

"The Empty Cradle," by W. Archer

"Little Nell," by George Cattermole for first edition of *The Old Curiosity Shop*.

LITTLE NELL: NOT DEAD BUT SLEEPING

The Old Curiosity Shop was illustrated by Hablot Browne ("Phiz"), who was Dickens's main illustrator, and by George Cattermole, who did these two pictures. "The child in her gentle slumber," near the beginning of the story, lies surrounded by contrasting grotesque images, their untidy menace kept at bay by her air of innocence (and a few religious icons): Quilp is not present here, but in other, similar illustrations he lurks as a constant threat. Nell herself looks angelic enough to be thought dead rather than asleep, unless we say that her arms lying on top of her body is a sign of life—in contrast with her arms at her side, clutching a book (presumably a Bible) when she is finally dead, in Cattermole's picture for the conclusion of the story—this time surrounded only by uplifting, not at all by grotesque, images. "No sleep so beautiful and calm," says the text, "so free from traces of pain, so fair to look upon."

"Little Nell," another version by George Cattermole.

"Kit's First Writing Lesson," by Robert Martineau, The Tate Gallery, London.

Robert Martineau's painting (1852), based on *The Old Curiosity Shop*, does not associate Nell with death at all and has none of the pathetic images so prominent in the illustrations to the novel. His version of Nell is competent and matter-of-fact, sewing as she supervises Kit's education; and the contents of the curiosity shop are neither grotesque nor frightening. Quilp has no place in this world.

"Felix Grundy Eakin," by John Wood Dodge. Courtesy of Cheekwood Museum, Nashville.

Felix Grundy Eakin was already dead, at the age of three, when this portrait was painted for the parents by John Wood Dodge in 1846; he is shown as if alive, only the urn possibly suggesting death.

"Paul and Mrs. Pipchin," by Hablot Browne, from the first
edition of *Dombey and Son*.

TWO VERSIONS OF PAUL DOMBEY

Paul looking up at Mrs. Pipchin in wide-eyed wonder is a more
"authentic" version than C. W. Nicholls's tinted lithograph of Paul
on Brighton beach, since it is one of the original illustrations by
Phiz, with whom Dickens worked very closely—though it should be
added that this is one of the few drawings Dickens was dissatisfied
with. It does, however, capture the solemnity of the old-fashioned
child, who "was not fond of Mrs. Pipchin; he was not afraid of her;
but in these old, old moods of his, she seemed to have a grotesque
attraction for him."

Nicholls's very bland version of Paul shows him at the point when,
having slept by the seaside, he wakes up and asks Florence, "The
sea, Floy, what is it that it keeps on saying?"

"What Are the Wild Waves Saying," tinted lithograph by C. W. Nicholls in the possession of the Brighton Art Gallery and Museum.

so much of Heaven and Angels, and kind faces that I never see when I am awake" (chapter 7). Having uttered the necessary pieties, Dick kisses Oliver and is left behind, to make one more appearance, ten chapters later, for the purpose of sending a message to Oliver and to produce a further variant on why it is best to die young: "for perhaps if I had lived to be a man, and had grown old, my little sister who is in Heaven might forget me, or be unlike me; and it would be so much happier if we were both children there together" (chapter 17). Since *Oliver Twist* is an attack on the work-houses set up under the New Poor Law, we are then nudged into indignation by the remarks of the beadle and the baby-farmer: "I never see such a hardened little wretch." Hard-heartedness from the authorities is, of course, a signal for tears from the reader.

The most famous use of hard-heartedness to offset child pathos is of course *A Christmas Carol*: who can imagine Tiny Tim without Scrooge? Tiny Tim, like Dick, is pure pathos all through. In a tale intended as a modern morality, to show the spirit of Christmas overcoming meanness, we should perhaps expect nothing else, and certainly we get nothing else. Bob Cratchit, Scrooge's clerk, has a large family to keep on his fifteen shillings a week ("Bob had but fifteen 'Bob' a week himself; he pocketed on Saturdays but fifteen copies of his Christian name"), but to suggest that it was improvident to beget so many children would savor of the Malthusian spirit of calculation that the tale sets out to refute—well, not to refute, for it uses no arguments, but to show the meanness of. There appear to be six children (but who—except Scrooge—counts in this tale?), and the youngest is crippled and dying. He comes in on Bob's shoulder carrying his crutch (inevitably, his "little crutch"), his limbs supported by an iron frame, having been at church where, Bob tells us, his imagination has indulged in an ecstasy of unselfishness:

> "He told me coming home that he hoped the people saw him in the church, because he was a cripple, and it might be pleasant to them to remember upon Christmas Day, who made lame beggars walk, and blind men see." Bob's voice was tremulous when he told them this, and trembled more when he said that Tiny Tim was growing strong and hearty. (Stave 3)

The trembling announces to readers much less cute than Mrs. Marcet that Tiny Tim is going to die, and die he does—temporarily. This glimpse of the Cratchits at home is shown to Scrooge by the Ghost of Christmas Present, and the Ghost of Christmas Yet To Come shows a sadder scene, though Bob and his wife are doing their best to cheer each other up. Mrs. Cratchit has to lay her sewing aside because the color hurts her eyes; Bob "walks a little slower than he used," a detail noticed by Peter, the eldest son, who now acts as guide to the reader's emotions. When Bob comes in he has been to see Tiny Tim's grave, and as he speaks of it his effort to be cheerful collapses:

> It would have done you good to see how green a place it is. But you'll see it often. I promised him that I would walk there on a Sunday. My little, little child!" cried Bob. "My little child!"
>
> He broke down all at once. He couldn't help it. If he could have helped it, he and his child would have been farther apart than they were. (Stave 4)

The memory of Tiny Tim will live on, wrapped in a plethora of "littles" and exerting a moral influence on the family:

> "And I know," said Bob, "I know, my dears, that when we recollect how patient and how mild he was; although he was a little, little child; we shall not quarrel easily among ourselves, and forget poor Tiny Tim in doing it." "No, never, father," they all cried again. (Stave 4)

But because this is a ghost story, nothing is final, not even pathos as fulsome as this. The Ghost of Christmas Yet To Come, it turns out, is the spirit only of a conditional future—of what will come if Scrooge does not mend his ways. When he repents, gives up meanness for charity, and becomes "as good a friend, as good a master, and as good a man, as the good old city knew, or any other good old city, town, or borough, in the good old golden world," we are offered an alternative ending (for this supposedly modernist device belongs with very traditional forms of narrative, as long as they are nonrealistic), in which Scrooge raises Bob's salary and becomes a second father to Tiny Tim, "who did NOT die." The capitalized NOT is a device that belongs to writing, but when Dickens adapted the story for reading it turned out to belong far more triumphantly to oral delivery, for on one occasion, at this point, the whole audience, "rising spontaneously, greeted the renowned and popular author with a tremendous burst of cheering."[31]

In this nonrealist world we need not expect plausibility; but it is still worth remarking that if Tiny Tim had died, it would not have been because

Scrooge was unkind. Whatever his ailment (we are not told, nor even whether it is connected with his lameness), it needed modern medical science rather than kindness, or even money, from Scrooge. His cure is as much of a miracle as Scrooge's reform.

A Christmas Carol was one of the great successes of Dickens's public readings: clearly there is great theatrical potential in child pathos. It is not surprising, then, to find another child death among the reading successes, one in which theatricality is quite explicit. *Dr Marigold's Prescriptions* is the story of a cheap jack, or travelling seller of job lots, whose patter provides much of the vocabulary of his narrative. Near the beginning of the tale his daughter dies in his arms while he is holding one of his auctions.

> "Now, you country boobies," says I, feeling as if my heart was a heavy weight at the end of a broken sash-line . . . "now let's know what you want tonight, and you shall have it. But first of all, shall I tell you why I have got this little girl round my neck? You don't want to know? Then you shall. She belongs to the Fairies. She is a Fortune-teller. She can tell me about you in a whisper, and can put me up to whether you're a going to buy a lot or leave it. Now do you want a saw? No, she says you don't, because you're too clumsy to use one. . . . So I went on in my Cheap-Jack style till . . . I felt her lift herself a little on my shoulder, to look across the dark street. "What troubles you, darling?" "Nothing troubles me, father. I am not at all troubled. But don't I see a pretty churchyard over there?" "Yes, my dear." "Kiss me twice, dear father, and lay me down to rest upon that churchyard grass so soft and green." I staggers back into the cart with her head dropped on my shoulder, and I says to her mother, "Quick, shut the door! Don't let these laughing people see!"[32]

This is in every sense a theatrical death: it happens on a stage, and for maximum effect it should be enacted on a stage. The story was published in *All the Year Round* in 1865, and a few months later he included it in his new series of readings, simplifying the title to *Dr Marigold* (the "prescriptions" were the stories Marigold told to make his daughter "laugh in a pleasant way—or to make her cry in a pleasant way," and it therefore can be said to refer to Dickens's own story, which has the same double purpose). This double effect in performance is described in rather ponderous language by the *Staffordshire Sentinel*: the opening moments had the audience "primed for cacchinatory exercise," but soon Marigold's pathetic description of his child's death "rendered humid the majority of the eyes in the room."[33]

Though some of the notices of the reading were critical, this compound effect was enormously successful with most of the audience, showing not only how compatible the humor and the pathos are but also how both are central to Dickens's success as a popular entertainer. Laughter is a public act, so it is not surprising that the comic scenes went down well at readings; but it is equally the case that tears are more readily stimulated in public than in private, so that the pathos of a death scene gains enormously from being read aloud. Gained then and gains now: for a modern public reader of Dickens has assured me that when he read the death of little Dombey to a teachers' conference (hard-headed late twentieth century teachers!) the chairman was reduced to tears so overwhelming that he couldn't give the vote of thanks.[34]

Theatricality obviously presupposes an audience—or a reader—whose emotions are worked on by the mountebank-author. For a curious parody of that reader, I turn to *The Wreck of the Golden Mary*, a strangely inconclusive story of a shipwreck, narrated first by the captain, then when he collapses, by the first mate, two heroic figures. The Golden Mary strikes an iceberg near Cape Horn, passengers and crew get off in two boats, and at the end they are left unrescued, so that we do not know if they survive, unless we take the fact that captain and mate are telling the story as evidence. Among the passengers is a young mother with a three-year-old child, who is nicknamed the Golden Lucy, to correspond to the boat, and "a sordid selfish old gentleman" called Mr. Rarx, who becomes obsessed with the child's safety, but only, we are later told, "because of the influence he superstitiously hoped she might have in preserving him." Lucy and Rarx are the only two characters who die, and the child's death is accompanied by a harsh counterpoint from the old man:

> For days past the child had been declining, and that was the great cause of his wildness. He had been over and over again shrieking out to me to give her all the remaining meat, to give her all the remaining rum, to save her at any cost, or we should all be ruined. At this time, she lay in her mother's arms at my feet. One of her little hands was almost always creeping about her mother's neck or chin. I had watched the wasting of the little hand, and I knew it was nearly over.
>
> The old man's cries were so discordant with the mother love and submission, that I called out to him in an angry voice, unless he held his peace on the instant, I would order him to be knocked on the head and thrown overboard. He was mute then, until the child died, very peacefully, an hour afterwards.[35]

Lucy dies, no doubt, of exposure; but she also dies of the story's need for pathos. We can be left in suspense about the other passengers, but here is a clear-cut emotional effect that cannot be passed over. But why is Mr. Rarx there? I suggest he is a kind of parody of the reader, obsessively fixated on the child and convinced that his own well-being is somehow involved with her survival. When he dies shortly afterwards, we realize that he was right.

The Unmentioned

We have, surely, seen enough to accept Fitzjames Stephen's unkind remark, that an interesting child in Dickens's novels "runs as much risk as any of the troops who stormed the Redan,"[36] and to wonder whether there is some deep-seated association, in Dickens's fiction, perhaps in the Victorian mind, between children and death. We have seen how children who do not die are nonetheless associated with death—even a child who survives to heal rifts and continue the race, like Florence. After the death of her mother, Florence asks, "What have they done with my mama?" and Polly Toodle, who is after all performing the life-enhancing task of nursing her baby brother, tells her a "story" about a very good lady "who, when God thought it right that it should be so, was taken ill and died. . . . Never to be seen again by any one on earth, and was buried in the ground where the trees grow." To this Florence, "shuddering," responds, "the cold ground": she knows what death is, after all, and Polly comforts her in a series of images that resolutely have it both ways:

> "No! The warm ground," returned Polly, seizing her advantage, "where the ugly little seeds turn into beautiful flowers, and into grass, and corn, and I don't know what all besides. Where good people turn into bright angels, and fly away to Heaven!" (Chapter 3)

Where good people turn into bright angels? This does not happen in the ground (unless we are to take the resurrection of the body very literally indeed), but Polly's comfort seeks to blend the advantage of pagan comfort ("le don de vivre est passé dans les fleurs") and Christian afterlife. Perhaps this is because Polly is uneducated and knows no better; more probably it is the novel itself that seeks to console in every way possible, never mind the inconsistencies.

For a stronger example, there is Florence's encounter with the wid-
owed father. Still grieving over Paul, Florence meets a "very poor man, who
seemed to have no regular employment," whose function in the book is to
love his daughter, thus providing a foil to Mr. Dombey. The daughter is
sick and cross, in contrast to the angelic Florence; in fact, she is not only
sick but dying, and the father is pleased to get even an impatient gesture
out of her, "because the day'll come, and has been coming a long while . .
. when to get half as much from that unfort'nate child of mine . . . would be
to raise the dead."

The effect of this on Florence is that she imagines herself ill: "if she
were to fall ill, if she were to fade like her dear brother, would he then
know that she had loved him; would she then grow dear to him?" After one
paragraph of imagined illness, the next begins: "Yes, she thought if she
were dying, he would relent," and in the scene of reconciliaton she imagines she says, "It is too late for anything but this; I never could be happier,
dear father!" and dies (chapter 24).

Not only does she die: she is then absorbed into the imagery that came
to dominate Paul's death, the golden water on the wall, the dark river, and
all the mournful apparatus that she now looks on "with awful wonder but
not terror." There is no open mention of the self-pity that we would
assume to be the normal state for imagining oneself dead: Florence's pity
must come from us.

Even Florence, then, must "die." Is the image of childhood inextricably bound up with death? The usual association with children is, after all,
the continuance of life: they carry on our existence after we die. Before
leaving Dickens, I will ask briefly if there is any trace of this in *Dombey and
Son*. The direct opposite of the Dombey family would be a family in which
children are constantly being born—would be, in fact, the Toodles.

Polly Toodle, Paul's "old nurse" is married to a stoker on the new railway. We know that Dickens intended to point the comparison between
Dombey and Toodle as fathers: in a deleted passage, Toodle tells Mr.
Dombey that he means to bring up his eldest son, little Biler, to his own
occupation.[37] But such parallels are superficial compared to the enormous
contrast between the two families. Every time we see the Toodles there are
"numbers of new babies." There is an endless supply and a constant
vagueness about the actual numbers (you would have to be a Scrooge to
count them): "'Polly, my gal,' said Mr. Toodle, with a young Toodle on each

knee, and two more making tea for him, and plenty more scattered about—
Mr. Toodle was never out of children, but always kept a good supply on
hand . . ." (chapter 38).

Children are seen almost as one sees food; there is no shortage of either
in the Toodle household, which exudes an air of contentment, Mr. Toodle
having "made over all his own inheritance of fuming and fretting to the
engines with which he was connected." Two things are striking in the representation of this family. First, the husband is there for stud purposes only.
It is not, of course, put like this, because of the convention of sexual reticence, but it is hard to see that he serves any other necessary function. Not
even his financial support is mentioned. The women (Polly and her sister)
run the family; the husband, when he is home, enjoys the pleasure of
domestic life in a purely passive way.

And second, as well as sex, pregnancy is not mentioned. Despite the
vast number of children, we never see Mrs. Toodle pregnant, nor is there
the slightest hint of the physical burden of bearing them. They appear by
magic, in this very masculine view of family life. The one character who is
always described as being "in an interesting condition" is Mrs. Perch, wife
of the messenger at Dombey's office, and the treatment of that is purely
comic.

There is one other numerous family in the novel, that of Mrs. Mac-
Stinger. She has only three children, but they take up enough space for
thirteen. There is no father, nor any mention of what happened to him. He
cannot have been long dead, since the baby is so small, but there is no sign
of grief; and though there is not the slightest hint of either sexual desire or
domestic bliss associated with her, she is nonetheless on the hunt for a new
man—as Bunsby discovers. Nineteenth century conventions of reticence
extend beyond sex to include a great deal of bodily function. Not death,
but, as we have seen, illness, if conceived of as a physical experience, and
likewise pregnancy, which the masculine imagination is too frightened of to
take seriously. Is it going too far to say that one reason Dickens associated
children with death is that he was embarrassed at associating them too
openly with life?

Pathos into Anger

One further variant of the pathetic-child death in Dickens, on which
this chapter will conclude, is the political. Here we need to consider the

social standing of the children who die; they virtually all fall within the
social range of Dickens's readership. Dickens was read, as all Victorian novelists were read, overwhelmingly by the middle classes; and in his pages,
no aristocratic children die, and hardly any of the children we have so far
looked at belong to the proletariat. Nell is poor, but she has come down in
the world; culturally she quite obviously belongs to the middle class. The
Cratchits are shabby genteel, near the bottom, socially, of Dickens's readership. Little Dick is perhaps the only case who falls quite clearly below it.
The introduction of the Bumbles, after Dick has died, adds to the pathos a
touch of anger at the workings of the Poor Law, for when it comes to the
death of proletarian children pathos may not be the only ingredient: it can
be supplemented, even replaced, by indignation. This can be seen in *Bleak
House*, where there are two deaths of poor children, very different from
each other. Jo the crossing sweeper is poor, ignorant, and a pure victim. He
is connected with the plot by a number of ingenious links, but essentially
he is there to be told to move on, to declare that he "never knowd
nothink," to catch smallpox, recover from that, and die of the need for
pathos. But his death is also part of the political message of the book:

> Dead, your Majesty. Dead, my lords and gentlemen. Dead, Right Reverends
> and Wrong Reverends of every order. Dead, men and women, born with Heav-
> enly compassion in your hearts. And dying thus around us every day.

Jo is not only a victim but also a moral touchstone: good characters are kind
to him, bad characters bully him. He dies in the company of Allan Woodcourt, the good young doctor, and Mr. Snagsby the law-stationer, and dying
he has, for the first time, a good deal to say for himself.

> "Jo! Did you ever know a prayer?"
> "Never knowd nothink, sir."
> "Not so much as one short prayer?"

> "No, sir. Nothink at all. Mr Chadbands he wos a-prayin' wunst at Mr
> Sangsby's, and I heerd him, but he sounded as if he wos a-speakin to hisself,
> and not to me. He prayed a lot, but *I* couldn't make out nothink on it. Differ-
> ent times, there wos other genlmen come down Tom-all-Alones a-prayin, but
> they all mostly sed as the t'other wuns prayed wrong, and all mostly sounded to
> be a-talkin to theirselves, or a-passin blame on the t'others, and not a-talkin to
> us. *We* never knowd nothink. I never knowd what it wos all about." (Chapter 47)

The ignorance of laboring children in Victorian England was almost total, and deeply shocking to those who read the reports of the Children's Employment Commission (one of those who read them was Marx):

> Four times four is 8; 4 fours are 16. A king is him that has all the money and gold. We have a King (told it is a Queen), they call her the Princess Alexandra. . . . Have heard say that God made the world, and that all the people was drownded but one; heard say that one was a little bird. . . . God made man, man made woman. . . . Had been to chapel, but missed a good many times lately. One name that they preached about was Jesus Christ, but I cannot say any others, and I cannot tell anything about him. He was not killed but died like other people. . . . The devil is a good person. I don't know where he lives. . . . Christ was a wicked man. . . .[38]

One wonders if there is a kind of twisted intelligence at work in some of this, but it is very different from Jo, though Jo is surely meant to be one of their company. Jo is, in fact, very articulate: his carefully limited solecisms (Sangsby for Snagsby, nothink for nothing—even some touches of misspelling that do not indicate the slightest mispronouncing like "wos" or "wuns") cannot disguise the lucidity and complexity of his thinking. He has perceived that sectarian disputes interfere with piety and shares Dickens's own dislike of evangelicals. When Allan Woodcourt teaches him a prayer to die with, he is a ready pupil and appreciates what is being done for him: "I'll say anythink as you say, sir, fur I knows it's good." He repeats the words and dies saying, "Hallowed be—thy—." His death is not as different from Paul's as we might at first think, and is not meant to be.

The death of little Johnny in *Our Mutual Friend* contains the same indignation, and the same address to "my lords and gentlemen and honourable boards" (the last expression is put in because the protest here is not simply about neglect but about the workings of the New Poor Law). Johnny does not die in such complete ignorance as Jo, and has more of Dick and Nell about him when he gives his toys to the poor child in the next bed; and he is more interesting because of Sloppy, his grandmother's "mangler," who speaks in Dickenspeak, turning the description of Johnny's illness into a splendid paragraph of colorful evasiveness:

> Mr Sloppy . . . proceeded to remark that he thought Johnny "must have took 'em from the Minders." Being asked what he meant, he answered, them that

come out upon him and partickler his chest. Being requested to explain himself, he stated that there was some of 'em wot you couldn't kiver with a six-
pence. (2:9)

We do not know what Johnny dies of, and in Sloppy's mouth our ignorance
of the ailment is swallowed up by the comic style:

> "He called it something as wos wery long for spots." Rokesmith suggested
> measles. "No," said Sloppy, with confidence, "ever so much longer than them,
> sir."

As with Dr. Marigold's daughter, humor and pathos are combined; but in
this case, each belongs to a different personage.

The other poor child who dies in *Bleak House* is Jenny's baby. Jenny is
the wife of a drunken brickmaker, and she and her friend Liz also have a
peripheral connexion with the plot. Their husbands beat them, and they
have to slip off secretly to do their good deeds. Jenny's baby dies, and she
attaches herself to Liz's as a substitute: neither the dead nor the living baby
is given a name, and neither mother has much identity. The one person
who has an identity is Jenny's husband, when he rounds on Mrs. Pardiggle
for her charitable visiting:

> I wants a end of these liberties took with my place. . . . Now you're a-going to
> poll-pry and question according to custom—I know what you're a-going to be
> up to. Well! You haven't got no occasion to be up to it. I'll save you the trou-
> ble. . . . A'nt my place dirty? Yes, it is dirty, it's nat'rally dirty, and it's nat'rally
> onwholesome; and we've had five dirty and onwholesome children, as is all
> dead infants, and so much the better for them, and for us besides. . . . How have
> I been conducting of myself? Why, I've been drunk for three days; and I'd a
> been drunk four, if I'd a had the money." (Chapter 8)

This voice sounds with an authenticity seldom heard in Victorian bourgeois
fiction: it assaults the condescension of Mrs. Pardiggle and the pious exhortations of the pamphlets she distributes ("It's a book fit for a babby, and I'm
not a babby"). It assaults every touch of sentimentality: there is to be no
glossing over the nastiness of the life or the casualness of the children's
deaths. It assaults the reader's expectations as they were raised by the portrait of Jo. Jenny's child, without even a name, belongs to the world uncov-

ered by the great Blue Books. The two women are tempted by, and the man defiantly expresses, the view that it is better dead—and not for any otherworldly reason. There is nothing radical about pathos; but at moments like this, we can almost accept the claim that Dickens was a radical.

The world of the Blue Books: let us conclude with a child who was one of their statistics: a real child, who was better dead.

Henry Mayhew's interviews with the London underworld (at almost exactly the same time as *Bleak House* was being written) include one very moving encounter with a prostitute who had lost a child. Deserted by her seducer and left to look after the child, she did "machine-work" until bad times left her unemployed, and then

> She saw her child dying by inches before her face, and this girl, with tears in her eyes assured me she thanked God for it. "I swear," she added, "I starved myself to nourish it, until I was nothing but skin and bone, and little enough of that; I knew, from the first, the child must die, if things didn't improve, and I felt they wouldn't. When I looked at my little darling I knew well enough he was doomed, but he was not destined to drag on a weary existence as I was, and I was glad of it.

Gone are the commonplaces of pious poetry, that the child taken from the temptations of this world into the presence of God is better off as a result: this child is rescued not from sin but from hunger.

The interview concludes with an account of the effect of the child's death on the mother:

> It may seem strange to you, but while my boy lived, I couldn't go into the streets to save his life or my own—I couldn't do it. If there had been a foundling hospital, I mean as I heard there is in foreign parts, I would have placed him there, and worked somehow, but there wasn't, and a crying shame it is too. Well, he died at last, and it was all over. I was half mad and three parts drunk after the parish burying, and I went into the streets at last; I rose in the world—(here she smiled sarcastically)—and I've lived in this house for years, but I swear to God I haven't had a moment's happiness since the child died, except when I've been dead drunk or maudlin."[39]

It was not the effect of the child's death, and the thought of being watched over by an angel, that exerted a moral influence on this woman, but the literal presence of the child when alive: this seems to invest the uplifting poems of Hemans and Sigourney with a peculiar unreality.

But moral influence? That she did not feel able to work as a prostitute when her child was alive is understandable, even admirable, but it killed the child. After his narrative, Mayhew adds a paragraph of commentary whose severity may surprise us:

> Although this woman did not look upon the death of her child as a crime com-
> mitted by herself, it was in reality none the less her doing: she shunned the
> workhouse, which might have done something for her, and saved the life, at all
> events, of her child.

He thought she should have gone to the workhouse, though he can understand why, like Betty Higden, she wouldn't. Mayhew was too conventional—or too reluctant to offend his readers—to suggest that she should have become a prostitute, but that would probably have saved the child's life. There is clearly a sense in which he was right to hold her responsible for the death; and it may well be an awareness of this that lies behind the intense and painful bitterness with which she regards her "rise" in the world.

Dickens's novels are by far the most celebrated examples of child pathos; but the subject is everywhere in nineteenth century fiction, and I turn now to the others.[40]

4

Heaven Claims Its Own:
Child Deaths in Nineteenth Century Fiction
—and After

Muriel

She was dead. No sleep so beautiful and calm, so free from trace of pain, so fair to look upon. One could almost fancy the little maid had just been said "good-night" to, and left to dream the childish dreams on her nursery pillow, where the small head rested so peacefully. She seemed a creature fresh from the hand of God, and waiting for the breath of life.

The pathetic description of little Nell on her death bed not only stirred the hearts of thousands of readers, it activated the pens of a good number of imitative novelists—as can be seen from the quotation above, which blends the description of Nell with that of little Muriel Halifax, in Dinah Mulock's *John Halifax Gentleman*,[1] into a seamless web of cliché. Though the death of Muriel was not as sensationally successful as that of Nell, it must have drawn plenty of early Victorian tears and illustrates most of the regular devices for eliciting pathos.

Muriel is born blind, so from the outset she is an object of pity: she is her father's first and favorite child, bears her affliction without complaint, and is a cheerful and loving daughter. The first hint of her death comes in chapter 25:

"Is Muriel anxious to be grown up? Is she not satisfied with being my little daughter always?" "Always."

Her father drew her to him, and kissed her soft, shut, blind eyes.

The difficulty of accepting that children grow up and leave the nest is treated in later chapters, when the sons fall in love and quarrel, and the point implied in this exchange is, of course, that dying young is the only way to remain a child.

In order to lose no opportunity for pathos, Muriel is in effect given two deaths: first she catches smallpox, then is kicked by a horse. She recovers from the first and dies of the second, but I have little doubt that contemporary readers, as soon as she caught smallpox, expected her to die. The novelist who puts her trust in careful plotting does not let anything happen by accident; it would not be enough to tell us that smallpox broke out in the village and Muriel caught it, since that would be accident. Her exposure to the disease must in some sense be self-caused, and this point is made doubly. First, John Halifax allows the families of his workmen to come to his house when they are evicted by the wicked aristocratic landlord, and one woman brings her sick child, who (she knows but does not say) has smallpox, thus repaying the kindness by bringing infection into the Halifax household; and then, to underline self-causation even more, Muriel, very curious about death, steals into the room where the dead child is lying and touches the body. From the first moment when the father is told that she has sickened ("it seemed to him almost like the stroke of death. 'Oh, my God! not her! Any but her!'"), all seems set up for a deathbed scene, with tears from the family and the reader alike. But only half a page later we learn that God "brought us safely through our time of anguish: He left us every one of our little ones."

Why is Muriel saved? "I trust in God," says her father when she sickens. "This trouble came upon us while we were doing right; let us do right still, and we need not fear." In a Christian context, child death obviously raises the question of trust in God's love, and relying on that trust to bring the child through must, since children do die—and frequently—result in naiveté or irony. In this novel the trust appears to be rewarded, and the shrewd reader might then guess that Muriel is, after all, going to die.

Her death is caused by Lord Luxmore's horse. He is the wicked landlord who plagues the Halifax family and who tries to ruin John by diverting the stream that runs his mill; when John Halifax installs a steam engine his lordship rides up to watch and sneer, and when told "your cutting off the water-course has been to me one of the greatest advantages I ever had in my life; for which, whether meant or not, allow me to thank you" (chapter 27), he loses his temper and spurs his horse violently. The blind and help-less Muriel is standing in the horse's path and is knocked down. Once again, the plot leaves nothing to chance.

After the kick, "Muriel lay day after day on her little bed in an upper chamber, or was carried softly down in the middle of the day by her father, never complaining, but never attempting to move or talk." When she sobs out that she cannot walk, the narrator (who is John Halifax's great friend) tells us, "I think in that moment [John] too saw, glittering and bare, the long-veiled Hand which, for this year past, I had seen stretched out of the immutable heavens, claiming that which was its own" [chapter 28]. This time there is to be no escape, and Muriel dies before the chapter is over, as sadly and splendidly as little Nell, with the extra touch that the climactic sentence is able to say, "She saw, now."

And what does she see? "Dim conceptions of white-robed thousands wandering in the golden Jerusalem, by the jasper sea."[2] The Book of Rev-elation, shorn of its paranoiac and vindictive elements, provides much of the stock imagery for glimpses of heaven, as in this sentence from *Misun-derstood*, a forgotten novel by Florence Montgomery (1869). Little Humphrey, who is here dying, had been a boisterous lad, constantly lead-ing his little brother Miles into mischief, and his boyishness is used to sen-timental effect when he makes his "will":

> I leave my knife with the two blades to Miles. One of the blades is broken, but the other is quite good. . . . I've got twopence somewhere: I don't exactly know where, but give them to lame Tom in the village. . . . (277)

Humphrey is motherless, and this has the advantage, as it had for Paul Dombey, that there is someone familiar to welcome him into heaven: "Not strange to him that throng of angels, for foremost among them all, more beautiful than any, is the figure of his mother, standing as in the picture, looking down upon him with a smile." The Victorian imagination, as we saw in chapter 2, preferred a heaven that was familiar.

Better Dead?

The child deathbed is what literary historians call a topos—a widely used theme, accompanied with a more or less fixed set of details. Once a topos has established itself, it recurs from author to author with remarkably little change; and literary history, if conscientiously done, can therefore grow very repetitive. This chapter will not be concerned with literary history, strictly speaking: it will not treat the novels in chronological order and will not seek to establish which authors had read which others (though there can be little doubt of the enormous influence of Dickens). My concern will rather be with the methods by which pathos is aroused and the reasons for its popularity, and with the religious and political significance of the topos. Most of the novels we shall look at were extremely popular, though not always for quite the same reasons. The stern evangelicalism of Mary Sherwood's *The Fairchild Family*, for instance, must have appealed to a rather different public from the pathos of Nell and Muriel, but it probably has more child deaths than any other novel of the century.

Part i of *The Fairchild Family* was published in 1818, followed by two further parts in the 1840s. It was an enormously popular improving story in its day; subsequently, it has enjoyed a mild notoriety as a document of stern and repressive Calvinism. The first of its child deaths comes about one-seventh of the way through, when Augusta Noble, daughter of the local landowner, is burnt to death. She "had a custom of playing with fire, and carrying candles about, though Lady Noble had often warned her of the danger."[3] Her disobedience results in her dying in agony, and the episode is headed "Fatal Effects of Disobedience to Parents." Eighty pages later little Charles Trueman dies with exemplary Christian patience. The pain about his heart is sometimes so bad that he cannot help crying out; but he asks God to give him grace to bear it with patience and to cry, "Thy will be done." He explains that he wishes to die because he knows himself to be a grievous sinner, and he tells little Henry Fairchild not to cry because he is happy now. The clergyman who is present asks Charles to explain to them why he is happy, "that we may all here present lay fast hold of the same hope, which is able to make a dying bed so easy." Charles turns his dying eyes towards him and quotes Job: "I know that my redeemer liveth; and though after my skin worms destroy my body, yet in my flesh shall I see God" (pages 160–169). This section is called "A Happy Death." Two-thirds of the way through, the children's grandmother talks of the death of her childhood friend Evelyn Vaughan. It is preceded by the sudden death of Evelyn's favorite little friend Francis Barr, aged four, who is playing in the road when a carriage comes along at full gallop, killing him on the spot. Evelyn, aged ten, saw "her little loved one cold, yet beautiful, in death, having one small hand closed upon a lily, and the other on a rose," then "uttered a wild shriek, and fell senseless to the floor." Because her constitution is "naturally delicate," she never recovers from this shock, and in the next chapter she slowly wastes away and dies. Her death is also exemplary: her last night is one "which, no doubt, she will remember through all eternity as the most blessed of her existence." God opens her heart: she was "enabled to see and to receive Him as the beginning and end, the author and finisher of her salvation," and "from that happy moment the dying Evelyn remained in a state, not only of perfect peace, but sometimes of joy inconceivable; not one dark cloud seemed to pass over her mind (pp. 384–392). Near the end little Annie Kelly, daughter of a ne'er-do-well family, steals into a concert where her neighbor is singing, is enraptured by the sacred music, but "as might be expected, the poor child, from over-mental anxiety, long watching, and sleeping in the cold, awoke next morning with all the symptoms of fever." Her kindly neighbors take her in so that she can die in good hands ("by the wise and merciful dispensation of Providence, the bad father of Annie just at this time, while from home, met with an accident"—which results in his continued absence and that of his wife, so that Annie and her brother can conveniently move next door: thus "it was arranged that the work of grace should be allowed to have full liberty for operating"). She dies in Christian faith and humility, and also—with some difficulty—persuades her unregenerate brother to be baptized along with her (something their bad parents had failed to do earlier). Her actual death is theatrically perfect:

> She then murmured a few words, of which some only were heard: "Home—
> light—redemption—blest redemption there." After which her eyelids
> dropped—one gentle sigh escaped, and . . . the redeemed dove had passed the
> portals of the gates of everlasting glory. (522)

As well as these sustained episodes, there are at least three other child deaths mentioned: that of little Theodore, son of the Marchioness of Roseville in the valley of the Waldenses (this story illustrates the wickedness of Roman Catholics); and that of the Fairchilds' two cousins, Emily and Ellen (Emily, dying first, comforts Ellen by saying "do not cry, gentle sister, we shall not be parted long"). Sherwood children, we see, have a life expectancy no better than those of Dickens.

The Fairchild Family is Calvinist in theology and rigidly conservative in politics. Its most important lesson is that the human heart is utterly wicked and that no good deed or even good thought is possible without the direct intervention of God's grace, made possible by the sacrifice of Jesus Christ. This lesson is continually drummed into the children:

> "You know, my dear," said Mrs Fairchild, "that our hearts are all by nature wicked?"
> "Oh yes! mamma, I know that," answered Lucy. (128)

Asked for a biblical reference, Lucy eagerly quotes Mark 7: 21–23:

> From within, out of the hearts of men, proceed evil thoughts, adulteries, fornications, murders, thefts, covetousness, lasciviousness, an evil eye, blasphemy, pride, foolishness: all these evil things come from within, and defile the man.

And when Evelyn is dying, she asks that Mrs. Harris should not visit her, "because she tells me what is not true":

> She tells me I am good; she has always told me so, and I once believed her, and that made it worse when I found out that I was not good. (387)

There is an awkward problem attached to the doctrine of total depravity accompanied by justification by faith alone, especially when predestination is added in: if good deeds can play no part in salvation, since that depends only on grace, then the sinner chosen by God will be saved, the good man who relies on the light of nature will be damned. This can lead, by a small further step, to the antinomian heresy, the claim that the elect *ought* to commit adulteries, fornications, murder, thefts, in order to show that abstaining from these is of no avail in the eyes of God.

This worthy children's book does not, of course, intend to suggest that, but it comes alarmingly close through the character of Bessy, the lively, thoughtless, good-natured girl whose "low practical jests . . . often produce more mischief than more decided acts of hostility." In a discussion on the

uselessness of good works, Bessy is given what is perhaps the most interesting theological statement in the book:

> I am not expecting to do well after death on account of any good work I can
> do. I know that I never have, and never shall deserve heaven by any of my
> good doings. But, surely, if I thought that the only way of escaping the fear of
> death is by doing such good works, I should be even more silly than I am now,
> if I did not resolve to try to do some of them when frightened as you now are,
> though I know that I should forget my good resolutions the very first time I
> got into merry company. But unhappily, as my aunt often says, "they that talk
> most of being saved by good works are those who commonly do the fewest."
> (481).

The logic of these ifs and nots has proved too tricky even for the author.
Bessy the scapegrace produces here an impeccably orthodox statement. *If*
she believed in good works, she would be silly; *since* she is so unreliable
when it comes to good behavior, she is in no danger of relying on it for her
salvation; and so she can range herself with her admirable aunt in a final
sentence that sounds very like a defense of the mischievousness that is
elsewhere so sternly condemned, but that need not damn her if salvation
depends only on God's decree.

Mrs. Sherwood's principles of child-rearing are based on the doctrine of
depravity. Misbehavior and disobedience are signs of original sin and must
be firmly chastized. The Fairchild children, therefore, are not always
depicted as models of good behavior, so that we can study their faults; and
even when they commit no faults, they must be reminded of their natural
wickedness. So when Lucy remarks that they seem to be better than they
used to be, because they have not been punished for a long time, her
mother tells her not to boast or think well of herself:

> If you have not done any very naughty thing lately, it is not because there is
> any goodness or wisdom in you, but because your papa and I have been always
> with you, carefully watching and guiding you from morning to night. (43)

A real child made the answer that Lucy is not allowed to make. Elizabeth Fry's daughter Betsy, who died, aged four, in 1815, declared to her
mother:

"Mamma, I love everybody better than myself, and I love thee better than
everybody, and I love Almighty much better than thee, and I hope thee loves
Almighty much better than me." I believe my answer was, "I hope or believe
I do," which she took up and said, "I hope thee does, if not, thee are wicked."
Afterwards I appeared to satisfy her that it was so.[4]

The Frys were not Calvinist, but Betsy has internalized the idea of depravity, perhaps even of a natural depravity needing to be transformed by the
love of God (whom she charmingly calls "Almighty," as if it was a name)—
though she takes this, un-Calvinistically, to mean her love for God, not
God's for her. And then she takes the step that no Fairchild child would
ever dream of taking, suggesting the possibility that her mother, if she gets
the hierarchy of loving wrong, might be wicked. She takes this step lovingly, and her mother can accept it, for this real situation is one of deep natural affection. But the normal situation of the fictitious Fairchilds is one of
conflict, and if the children were allowed to think their parents wicked it
would be an accusation.

But, of course, parents are sinners too: a theological point that Mrs.
Sherwood glosses over. A system of child rearing that gives total responsibility to parents must assume that they at any rate have some goodness or
wisdom—indeed, Mrs. Fairchild even remarks on the sad plight of those
poor children "who have not good fathers and mothers to take care of
them." This comes out most sharply in the episode of Henry's refusal to
learn Latin. Mr. Fairchild tells him plainly that he will need to work hard,
and Henry responds with passive resistance, refusing to learn or even to
answer his father when rebuked. All he says is "I don't want to learn
Latin." This produces a stern speech and a sterner punishment from his
father, who announces that he will speak to Henry no more, neither will his
mamma or sisters, and he will be given only bread and water. His sisters,
forbidden to speak to him, run away when he addresses them, his mother
and the servants will only tell him how wicked he has been, and this, of
course, soon breaks his spirit, and he gives in, thus justifying his father's
strictness—and his father's goodness. The thought that Mr. Fairchild's
treatment of his son is a sign of his own wicked heart is not for a moment
entertained, and when he says to Henry, "I stand in the place of God to
you," there is not a hint of irony. The point is even more striking because
of the issue—learning Latin. Children did not learn Latin in the nine-

teenth century for directly Christian reasons: the Bible is, after all, written in Hebrew and Greek. They learned Latin because it was an accomplishment of gentlemen, that is, for very secular reasons.

This leads us to politics. *The Fairchild Family* is totally single-minded in its acceptance of the status quo and does not distinguish between, on the one hand, growing up as a good Christian and, on other hand, growing up as a young lady or gentleman. It is important that the children play only with the right companions:

> "Why Henry," interrupted Mrs Fairchild, "What is this I hear? Bill Rogers and Sykes! They are not fit companions for you, my dear boy. How came you acquainted with them? (437)"

Evil communications corrupt good manners: are Bill Rogers and Sykes unfit companions because they will lead Henry into sin, or because they will teach him to enjoy ungentlemanly pursuits? Mrs. Fairchild does not draw the distinction, but we can; and we can notice her saying that "no gentleman by birth is a *real* gentleman who loves the stable-yard, and the company of uneducated grooms and keepers of dogs," or, even more explicitly, explaining that "all the conditions of the children of God on earth are appointed by Him; some being placed in low degrees, some in middling, and some in higher."

I have gone into the theology of *The Fairchild Family* not only because it governs the way child death is represented, but also because the implied author we meet in its pages invites comparison with another famous child story. We know that this novel was written by Mary Sherwood; but how easy to imagine it being by Mr. Brocklehurst. The Reverend Carus Wilson, headmaster of the school that Charlotte Brontë attended, is usually considered the "original" of Mr. Brocklehurst, the tyrannical schoolmaster in *Jane Eyre*; Wilson was editor of *The Children's Friend*, a pious evangelical paper, though whether he was specifically a Calvinist is disputed. Both Mr. Wilson himself and Mr. Brocklehurst base their treatment of children on the premise of the child's sinful nature. Mr. Brocklehurst's mission "is to mortify in these girls the lusts of the flesh, to teach them to clothe themselves with shamefacedness and sobriety, not with braided hair and costly apparel." He orders Julia Severn's hair to be cut off, and when told that Julia's hair curls naturally he replies, "But we are not to conform with nature. I wish these children to be the children of Grace."[5] His punishment of Jane for "lying" has considerable resemblance to Mr. Fairchild's punishment of Henry: "let no-one speak to her during the remainder of the day." Henry, it is true, does not have to stand on a stool in front of everyone, but he is sent to Coventry for much longer, indeed indefinitely: only after he has come to his father to beg his pardon are others allowed to speak to him.

But there are of course two important differences between the novels. In the first place, Mr. Brocklehurst is a hypocrite: his own daughters are elaborately and expensively dressed, their tresses are artificially curled, and his wife "was enveloped in a costly velvet shawl, trimmed with ermine, and she wore a false front of French curls." There can be no doubt that this weakens the book: an attack on Puritan strictness, if the Puritan turns out to transgress his own precepts so flagrantly, is not an attack on Puritanism at all. Hypocrisy is always an easy target and diverts the satire from its true object.

The representation of hypocrisy, too, is always problematic. Explicit authorial assurance of hypocrisy instructs us to listen with distrust and therefore preprograms our response—thus distracting us from genuinely listening and from the more interesting question, whether we would know, just by hearing or reading it, that a speech was hypocritical. Would we, for instance, know that Goneril is putting on an act when she insists, in the first scene of *King Lear*, "Sir, I love you more than words can wield the matter, / Dearer than eyesight, space or liberty"? To "wield the matter": does this suggest a labored effort and, so, imply that she does not mean it? and even if it does, could we not say that this is the inevitable consequence of being asked to make a public declaration of a private feeling, so that even if she did love her father, it would sound like an act?

Mr. Brocklehurst's speeches do not offer that degree of verbal subtlety, but the issue is still raised. There is a hypocrite in *The Fairchild Family* too, the children's cousin Louisa, a worldly, selfish girl, who, when she is given a lecture (her word) by Mrs. Fairchild, thinks "that her aunt required some answer, and that the shortest way to close the lecture would be to seem to agree with what she said," and so replies:

> Dear aunt, how can I be grateful enough for the pains you have taken to explain these things to me? I only wish that since I came here I had paid more atten-tion to the instructions which you and my kind uncle give in the family. (499)

Mrs. Fairchild hears this answer "with a sigh," yet when her own daughter Lucy says to Mrs. Colvin, "Oh ma'am, you are very, very kind; and will you please, today, to tell us everything we do wrong, as mamma would? We wish to behave well, but sometimes we do not"—we are meant to accept this as genuine. The representation of hypocrisy as hypocrisy is clearly beyond Mrs. Sherwood's powers (it might almost be beyond Shakespeare's), and we need authorial assurance to tell us that we are to believe Lucy and disbelieve Louisa. If then we ignore Mr. Brocklehurst's wife and daughters (whose appearance constitutes a kind of authorial assurance), we could be forgiven for perceiving him as a version of Mr. Fairchild.

Mr. Fairchild's disciplinary method succeeds with Henry, but Mr. Brocklehurst's fails with Jane, who does not repent, as Henry does, but is filled with resentment, rather like Louisa. What enables her to bear the punishment is the glance she gets from her friend Helen Burns:

> What an extraordinary sensation that ray sent through me! How the new feeling bore me up! It was as if a martyr, a hero, had passed a slave or victim, and imparted strength in the transit. (Chapter 7)

Helen it is who dies an edifying death, and this glance of love is our first preparation for it. Her compassion is a Christian virtue, and at this moment she is almost a type of Christ, but her influence on Jane would draw no approval from Mrs. Sherwood or Mr. Brocklehurst, for it brings no awakening to a sense of sin. Jane is moved by Helen's loving glance but not to a recognition of her own wicked heart—indeed, she is never moved to this, no more than Louisa is. Louisa's response to death could belong to the late twentieth century: it is to think about something else:

> Louisa shuddered, for she had within the last few days permitted her watch to go down, that she might not hear its measured tickings when she lay awake in the silent hours of night; . . . she exclaimed: "What, then, if such is our miserable condition—if we must always live with the fear of death preying on our inmost hearts—what must we do—what can we do? Nothing seems to me to be left for us, for me at least, but to fill my mind with other things; and I must try to do so." (498)

Of course this is meant to be thoroughly deplorable, and it unleashes Mrs. Fairchild's "lecture." Yet how it resembles Jane's famous retort to Mr. Brocklehurst. Asked where the wicked go after death, Jane is ready with the orthodox reply, "They go to hell"; asked, then, what she must do to avoid this fate, she is not at all orthodox: "I must keep in good health, and not die" (chapter 4). The only reason we cannot imagine Louisa saying this is because of its succinctness and forcefulness. Her more long-winded reply has not the blunt strength of Jane's shocking sentence, and of course this causes Jane to come to life in a way that Louisa never does (the nearest thing, perhaps, is when she slips in "for me at least"). To the reader, this is an invitation to identify with Jane; if we wish to state it in terms of authorial involvement, it can mean that Brontë is drawn to identify with Jane as Mrs. Sherwood is never drawn to identify with Louisa. This directness of Jane is far more important, in terms of our reading experience, than the moral question of what approval or disapproval the author thrusts at us: it is an effect that could not be undone by any number of assurances of Brontë's orthodoxy.

The death of Helen forms a kind of conclusion to Jane Eyre's childhood. It takes place during an epidemic of typhus, more than half the pupils of Lowood falling ill, and many of them dying; though since none are named, these other deaths function simply as background. Jane escapes infection, and, because of the relaxation of discipline, is allowed to run wild in the countryside; and this serves to make her far more intensely alive. Helen dies not of typhus but of consumption, as befits so ethereal a creature. Her death is both like and unlike the model deaths in *The Fairchild Family*: we would not expect, in this more complex novel, anything so straightforwardly exemplary. She dies in Christian confidence and uses the familiar image that she is going "to my long home—my last home." Jane is deeply moved, but in ways that are subtly different from a Fairchild deathbed. First, her presence at the deathbed is surreptitious. She is told not to go into the sick room and steals there furtively at night: her presence is not an obligatory attendance, in order to be improved, it is stolen by her, as a private experience. Then she trespasses even further by climbing into bed with Helen. Little Miles climbs into bed with the dying Humphrey in *Misunderstood*, to produce a vignette of childhood innocence:

> There in the golden sunset they lay. The sun kissed their little faces, and touched with a lovely hand their curly hair. It lingered lovingly round them, as if it knew that the lambs would be frisking when it rose again. (316)

The pathetic fallacy of the loving sun in this must have drawn warm tears from many a sentimental reader; its conventional innocence contrasts vividly with the strange stolen intimacy between Jane and Helen. Their conversation touches on forbidden subjects: for they talk not about sin or repentance but about belief—and its difficulty:

> "But where are you going to, Helen? Can you see? Do you know?"
>
> "I believe; I have faith: I am going to God."
>
> "Where is God? What is God?". . .
>
> "You are sure, then, Helen, that there is such a place as heaven; and that our souls can get to it when we die?"
>
> "I am sure there is a future state; I believe God is good.". . .
>
> "And shall I see you again, Helen, when I die?"
>
> "You will come to the same region of happiness; be received by the same mighty universal Parent, no doubt, dear Jane."
>
> Again I questioned, but this time only in thought. "Where is that region? Does it exist?" (Chapter 9)

There is an urgency here that is never present in Mrs. Sherwood's deaths. None of her children ever asks "What is God?," or holds on to silent reservations in the way Jane does at the end. None of them conveys the sense of being physically shut out by skepticism as Jane does when she asks whether our souls "can get to it" when we die. The emotional function of the whole deathbed topos has now been brought to the surface: its purpose is consolation, and consolation is not easy, indeed may not succeed. If Helen Burns has an effect on Jane, this will depend not on her virtue but on the possibility of intimacy, even bodily intimacy. This is not a lesson in theology but a search for human comfort, for the warmth of being in bed together. Helen's last question is, "Are you warm, darling?" By the time morning comes, she is dead and offers Jane no warmth.

Conviction of one's own depravity, the doctrine that looms so large in the world of Mrs. Sherwood and Mr. Brocklehurst, means that earthly life is nothing but a series of temptations; and in that case, the sooner one escapes from it the better. It is only a short step from this to wishing the child dead. As Elisabeth Jay has pointed out,[6] children, to the Evangelicals, were no more innocent than the rest of us, so there is no actual advantage in dying early—from the moment one is born, one is plunged into sin. But the idea of childhood innocence dies hard. Perhaps the most famous assertion of it is Traherne's claim, "Certainly Adam in Paradise had not more sweet and curious apprehensions of the world, than I when I was a child," which comes very close to denying the doctrine of original sin:

So that with much ado I was corrupted and made to learn the dirty devices of this world. Which now I unlearn, and become as it were, a little child again that I may enter into the Kingdom of God.[7]

Certainly a Calvinist, almost certainly any other Evangelical, and arguably any orthodox Christian will take issue with this, but the belief seems indestructible—and widespread in the nineteenth century. Thackeray, so deeply of his time even when claiming to resist it, spoke for a central Victorian sentiment when, after the death of his eight-month daughter Jane, he wrote to his mother with highly sentimental religiosity:

O God watch over us too, and as we may think that Your Great heart yearns towards the innocent charms of these little infants, let us try and think that it will have tenderness for us likewise who have been innocent once, and have, in the midst of corruption, some remembrances of good still.[8]

David Grylls draws a useful contrast when he divides nineteenth century attitudes to childhood into the "Puritan" and the "Romantic," the former believing strongly in original sin and the need to break the child's will, the latter believing in the natural goodness of children; he then points out that both schools favored deathbed scenes.[9] And despite the logic of their stern theology, it is the Puritan or Evangelical deaths that tend to assert most strongly that dying early is a blessing, because it enables us to escape the temptations of this world. Little Charles, dying an edifying death in *The Fairchild Family*, comes very close to saying this.

I know myself to be a grievous sinner, and one that cannot live a day without doing that which is evil; therefore, why should I grieve because God is pleased to take me so soon from this state of sin and sorrow? (161)

"So soon": this could of course simply express his impatience to get to heaven, but it is very easy to hear relief as well: the earlier he dies, the surer he is to get there.

And in *Amy Herbert* this is quite explicit. In this improving story by E. M. Sewell, little Rose, the youngest Harrington child, whom everyone adores, is watched on her deathbed by the governess, Emily Morton, for whom Rose's death would be "the severing of her dearest earthly tie," but she cannot bring herself to wish that Rose should live, since death "would be an escape from all the dangers of the world to the enjoyment of rest and peace for ever"; so that to ask for her survival "would be merely a selfish regard to her own feelings, without any reference to considerations of far higher importance." That seems plain enough; but in the next paragraph comes an even more explicit statement:

> To lose her now, would be to feel that she was gone to happiness; to lose her then [i.e., later], might be to dread lest she should have forgotten the promise of her baptism, and departed from the path of holiness in which she had so earnestly endeavoured to lead her.[10]

There is no antinomianism here. The governess can produce a good effect, but there is no knowing how long it will last. A yet uncorrupted child is better dead.

Little Eva

The most famous child death in nineteenth century fiction, outside Dickens, is that of little Eva. Eva St. Clare and Uncle Tom are the two Christian spirits in Harriet Beecher Stowe's *Uncle Tom's Cabin* (1851): the young girl and the old man, the slave-owner's daughter and the slave. Extremes meet to show us that earthly status is of no importance in the judgment of heaven. This is the egalitarianism of other-worldliness, that, by separating out spiritual equality and regarding it as untouched by earthly hierarchy, also protects the status quo, leaving worldly hierarchy safely untouched by spiritual equality. In the other world all are really equal—but not till then.

Eva's death owes a good deal to Nell's. Both are etherealized, never disfigured by suffering, and both end up lying beautiful in their deathbeds, surrounded by emblems of innocence and regeneration. Around Nell there are winter berries and green leaves ("something that has loved the light and had the sky above it always") and her little bird ("a poor slight thing the pressure of a finger would have crushed"—like Nell herself, continually escaping from the finger of Quilp); Eva is "robed in one of the simple white dresses she had been wont to wear when living: the rose-colored light through the curtains cast over the icy coldness of death a warm glow."[11] Both are angels before their time and have a premonition of their end. Nell's premature change into an angel, to the distress of her little friend, was quoted in the last chapter; Eva is more explicit, telling Tom, "I'm going *there*, to the spirits bright, Tom; I'm going *before long*"—this enables the text to tell us explicitly, "It is as if heaven had an especial band of angels, whose office it was to sojourn for a season here, and endear to them the wayward human heart, that they might bear it upwards with them in their homeward flight" (chapter 22). There is even a toying with etymology for the child's name: "O Evangeline! rightly named," her father says, "hath not God made thee an evangel to me?" (chapter 16). "Angel" derives from the Greek word for "messenger," "evangel" and (the older term in English) "evangelist" derive from the Greek for "good news," and the two are connected, because a messenger brings news, but it is doubtful if St. Clare was thinking of that; he was simply leaping at the opportunity to call his child an angel.

As a spiritualized being—a proto-angel—Eva is very like Nell, but there is nothing in *The Old Curiosity Shop* like her public oration just before dying: "'I want to see all our people together. I have some things I *must* say to them,' said Eva." What she must say is, first, that she loves them all and is soon going to leave them; this leads to "bursts of groans, sobs and lamentations," to which she replies, "If you love me, you must not interrupt me so. Listen to what I say." Since it was her announcement that caused the outburst, what we are being shown is a contradiction inherent in such exhortation: the grief which makes it harder to hear her message is also what makes the hearers more receptive to it. The message itself is a simple Christian call to repentance and conversion, in which she becomes so explicitly a Christ figure that the heartbroken slaves "sobbed and prayed and kissed the hem of her garment" (chapter 26).

Uncle Tom's Cabin was Stowe's first novel, but not her last child death; and I will add an example from *The Pearl of Orr's Island* (1862). Strictly speaking, the death of Mara is not a child's death, since the novel is a love story, and she is already engaged to Moses; but when it comes to the deathbed she is no longer seen as nubile, but functions just as a child might; and the elements are taken straight from the tradition that runs through Nell and Eva:

> Mara seemed to rule all around her with calm sweetness and wisdom, speaking unconsciously only the speech of heaven. . . . She seemed like one of the sweet friendly angels one reads of in the Old Testament, so lovingly companionable, walking and talking, eating and drinking, with mortals, yet ready at any unknown moment to ascend with the flames of some sacrifice and be gone.

When the moment comes "when heaven claims its own," the details are almost identical to those surrounding little Eva:

> The bed was then all snowy white, and that soft still sealed face, the parted waves of golden hair, the little hands folded over the white robe, all had a sacred and wonderful calm, a rapture of repose that seemed to say "it is done." (Chapter 43)

He Never Called Me Mother

Grief is a personal experience and may seem essentially private, but it needs the presence of others for its full release: we weep not only to relieve our inner distress but also to obtain comfort. Even when we weep alone, we are partly aware of ourselves as social beings. Grief will therefore be intensified if the weeping has to be suppressed and the comfort is not available. A mother who has to watch her child die without being able to weep openly will give an extra twist to the pathos.

This bright idea occurred to Mrs. Henry Wood, and the result was *East Lynne* (1861), one of the most popular novels of the century, and even more popular as a play. Isabel Carlyle, having by a series of rather improbable coincidences run away from her husband with a melodramatic villain, and then been abandoned and later disfigured in a railway accident in which she is thought to have died, returns incognito to her now remarried husband as governess to her own children and, without being able to reveal her identity, watches the older boy, William, die: "Oh, Willie, my child! dead, dead, dead! and he never knew me, never called me mother!" This, perhaps the most famous line in Victorian melodrama, does not actually occur in the novel, but was added in the stage adaptation by T. A. Palmer in 1874.

Having thought of this device for increasing pathos, Wood then executed it in totally predictable language:

> By the side of William Carlyle's dying bed, knelt the Lady Isabel. The time was at hand, and the boy was quite reconciled to his fate. Merciful indeed is God to dying children! It is astonishing how very readily, where the right means are taken, they may be brought to look with pleasure, rather than fear, upon their unknown journey.

William's vision of heaven belongs in the tradition that stems from Paul Dombey and is very circumstantial in its filling in of the details:

There will be the beautiful city, with its gates of pearl and its shining precious stones, and its streets of gold; and there will be the clear river, and the trees with their fruits and their healing leaves, and the lovely flowers; and there will be harps, and music, and singing; and what else will there be? (Part iii, chapter 20).

"Not much else," it is tempting to reply to a child who has read improving tracts with such thoroughness!

To intensify the pathos, Isabel needs to speak as well as think her grief at having to conceal her identity, and the novel therefore allows her to be recognized at the end, so that when dying she can say to her husband,

Think what it was, to watch William's decaying strength; to be alone with you in his dying hour, and not to be able to say, he is my child as well as yours! (Chapter 23)

The Ironic Deathbed

Isabel's exclusion from full participation in the deathbed is a form of irony (she is mother and not mother); but it is irony as a tactic for intensifying the pathos. There is no hint that conventional pathos is being subverted, there is simply her distress at not being allowed to indulge it. This is stable not radical irony.

For deeper instability we turn naturally to that most ironic of English novelists, Thomas Hardy. A child dies in each of Hardy's last two novels, in scenes that mock the conventional reader's expectations. The death of Tess's infant, though necessary for the plot, is used by Hardy mainly to write a scene of anti-Christian mockery. The child has no real existence except as the cause of Tess's distress that by dying unbaptized it will be "consigned to the nethermost corner of hell, as its double doom for lack of baptism and lack of legitimacy"; the baptism that she carries out herself, waking her brothers and sisters and making them kneel round the washing-stand, "putting their hands together with fingers exactly vertical," is a grim parody of the service itself, transformed, by Tess's urgent love and fear, into something more valuable than the original. Tess's theological notions are crude, even ridiculous ("she saw the arch-fiend tossing it with his three-forked prong, like the one they used for heating the oven on baking days"), but her "ecstasy of faith almost apotheosized her" and she looked to the kneeling children like "a being large, towering, and awful—

a divine personage with whom they had nothing in common." If the pain of child death is smoothed over by sentimental reassurance in conventional Victorian novels, it is hard to know if Tess's intense, ridiculous, and touching distress about damnation intensifies or pushes aside the motherly grief.[12]

That is savage enough; Hardy's most famous child death, the suicide of Little Father Time in *Jude the Obscure*, is more sardonic still, a clear anticipation of modern black comedy. The one form of dying we would never expect for a child is suicide; and double murder followed by suicide seems grotesque to the point of parody. Little Father Time (even his name is not ordinary), the unwanted child who travels by train with his half-ticket stuck in his hat, whose stare "seemed mutely to say, 'All laughing comes from misapprehension. Rightly looked at there is no laughable thing under the sun'," is a child only in years. His suicide note after hanging the two younger children and then himself, "Done because we are too menny," wears its misspelling as the boy wears his small size, as a transparent disguise for the aged pessimist who seems to have been reading Schopenhauer, or at least Hardy. The description of him on his first appearance ("He was Age masquerading as Juvenility, and doing it so badly that his real self showed through crevices") is offered as the author's comment on the character, but how easily it could be a critic's comment on the strained effect achieved by the author.

Little Father Time is the mouthpiece of Hardy's Spirit Ironic, who looms so menacingly over *The Dynasts*; and it would seem obvious that he is not really a child at all, except that Hardy goes out of his way to insist that he is. The doctor who is called when the children die tells Jude that

> "there are such boys springing up amongst us—boys of a sort unknown in the last generation—the outcome of new views of life. They seem to see all its terrors before they are old enough to have staying power to resist them. He says it is the beginning of the coming universal wish not to live." (VI, ii)

We are presumably being invited to share this opinion, but boys of this sort exist only in the pages of Thomas Hardy. It is even tempting to wonder if Hardy speaks only of boys, not of children, out of mere linguistic habit, or if he is signalling to us that girls have the sense to remain uninfected by the "new views of life." We know that such views were not shared by Hardy the man, who liked to declare himself a meliorist rather than a pessimist; and the manifestation of this mad pessimism in children who have not yet learned it through experience looks like the inheritance of acquired characteristics.

The labored, grotesque, yet somehow shocking death of Jude's children seems to announce the end of the pathetic child-death, undermined by a weird irony inherent in the scheme of things; but it had been undermined thirty years earlier across the channel. No one thinks of Flaubert as a sentimental novelist, but *l'Education sentimentale* does contain one child death, and one near death, that brush against conventional effects only to invert them.

Frédéric Moreau, the hero, has worshipped Mme. Arnoux with an idealizing love from the moment he set eyes upon her, on the second page of the novel; when at last they declare their love for each other and arrange a rendezvous, it turns out to be a day of popular demonstrations (it is 1848, and Flaubert's novel is full of the interplay between love and politics). For Frédéric, politics, now as always, must take second place to love: he is determined that the long platonic relationship with Mme. Arnoux shall finally be consummated, hires an apartment and lays elaborate plans, but his own revolution is less successful than the political one: she does not turn up, and only after a detailed account of his long anxious wait do we learn that her son had fallen ill and seems to be dying. The account of his symptoms is vivid and gruesome:

> Eugène tenait sa tête de coté, sur le traversin, en fronçant toujours ses sourcils, en dilatant ses narines; sa pauvre petite figure devenait plus blême que ses draps; et il s'échappait de son larynx un sifflement produit par chaque inspiration, de plus en plus courte, sèche et comme métallique.[13]

> Eugène held his head to one side on the bolster, continually frowning and dilating his nostrils; his poor little face grew paler than the sheets; and from his larynx came a whistling sound with each dry, metallic intake of breath, which came shorter and shorter.

Mme. Arnoux—and probably the reader too—is convinced that the child is dying, and things are made worse by a series of mix-ups over finding the right doctor. When eventually Dr. Colot arrives, Eugène has vomited something strange, looking like a tube of parchment. She imagines that it must be a piece of his intestines, but he now starts breathing freely and regularly, and the doctor tells her that her child is saved. Only then does she remember the appointment with Frédéric.

This broken appointment is crucial in Frédéric's sentimental education, since it throws him finally into the arms of Rosannette, the prostitute. The near death of the child is there for its function in the plot—as was the death of the child in Goethe's *Wahlverwandschaften*, which may have influenced Flaubert.[14] The child in Goethe's novel dies by drowning, an accident which could happen at any time: its death is as anomalous in the nineteenth century as was the real death of Eva Butler.

Goethe has no interest in the child for its own sake. When it is baptized, several people notice that it resembles not its parents but those whom its parents love; and when it drowns, this is taken as a sign that the elective affinities of the title are doomed, and the happy ending that the rearrangement of couples could so easily have brought about is abandoned. In both these books, the child is an instrument of fate: "C'était un avertissement de la Providence," thinks Mme. Arnoux. It is an episode in the lives of the adults, in whom, in these sophisticated novels, we are alone invited to be interested. The child in *Die Wahlverwandschaften* is not even named.

The child who does die in *l'Education sentimentale* is not named either. This is the little son of Frédéric and Rosannette, who delights his mother but leaves his father indifferent: when Frédéric comes to see him just after his birth, he feels no attraction to the "yellowish-red something, extremely wrinkled, which smelled bad and wailed" (quelque chose d'un rouge jaunâtre, extrêmement ridé, qui sentait mauvais et vagissait (part iii, chapter 4), and even has to conceal his repugnance. Since Rosannette, for Frédéric, represents sexual pleasure and dissipation, not maternity or family feeling, the child is of no importance to him and of little importance to the novel until he dies. He is boarded out in the country, and though Frédéric when he sees him has a moment in which he imagines him as a young man and companion, this touch of fatherhood is soon obscured by an "incompréhensible tristesse"—yet sadness is not all that incomprehensible for a child who is both illegitimate and unwanted, and of whom the father thinks that it would have been better if he had not been born.

When the child dies, a dozen pages later, the contrast is striking between the passionate if short-lived grief of Rosannette and the coolness with which Flaubert handles the scene: after she tells Frédéric that the infant is no longer moving, Flaubert introduces the account of her distress with the terse sentence, "In fact, he was dead" (En effet, il était mort). The novelist's ideal of remaining detached from his characters is here carried about as far as it could be. Why does this child die? The question is always ambiguous in the case of fiction: within the world of the novel, the answer will be in medical terms, and when we consider the novel as an artefact, the answer will be in terms of plot devices and authorial intention. The first answer will concern us in a later section; the second takes us very close to the heart of Flaubert's imaginative world.

Rosannette and Frédéric keep a vigil next to the body, which by then is unrecognizable—here follows some of Flaubert's bleak naturalism, reducing a human body to a physical object as, most famously, with the death of Emma Bovary. Even before it died, the child had been reduced to something like vegetable matter: Frédéric is alarmed by

> ces taches bleuâtres, pareilles à de la moississure, comme si la vie, abandonnant déjà ce pauvre petit corps, n'eût laissé qu'une matière où la végétation poussait. (the bluish spots, resembling mildew, as if life, already abandoning the poor little body, had left nothing but matter for vegetation to grow on). (Part iii, chapter 4)

Rosannette keeps opening the curtains to look at the child, seeing images of the future it might have had, while Frédéric sits unmoving in the other chair, thinking about Mme. Arnoux. He is tortured by his ignorance of what she is now doing and tells himself that he is her true husband; this leads to a tearing apart of his whole being, and the tears that had been accumulating all day start to overflow:

> Rosannette s'en aperçut.
> —"Ah! tu pleures comme moi! Tu as du chagrin?"
> —"Oui! oui! j'en ai! . . . "
> Il la serra contre son coeur, et tous deux sanglotaient en se tenant embrassés.
>
> .   .   .   .
>
> Rosanette noticed.
> "Ah! You're crying, like me. Are you miserable?"
> "Yes, yes, I am!"
> He pressed her to his heart, and both of them sobbed, holding each other in an embrace. (Chapter 5)

Tennyson's poem "As through the land at eve we went" tells how the speaker and his wife fell out, and then,

When we came where lies the child
We lost in other years,
There above the little grave,
O there above the little grave,
We kissed again with tears.[15]

So that is the function of child death in Flaubert. Sharing their grief over a dead child, Tennyson tells us, is the way for parents to draw together: he makes the point simply in this very simple poem, not even telling us what the quarrel was about ("We fell out, I know not why"). Flaubert has explored in great detail the growing distance between Frédéric and Rosannette and leads very skilfully up to this moment of reconciliation, perhaps the truest union they ever attain—and based completely on a misunderstanding. It is as if Flaubert set out to mock Tennyson's sentiment by means of a carefully placed irony, a tiny explosion to wreck the perfect pathos. Compared to this destructive neatness, Hardy seems to indulge in a flurry of words.

Destroyed by Opium

Charlotte M. Yonge has not—or not yet—benefited from the revival of interest in dead female novelists, either because she wrote so much or because of her formidable reputation as an Anglo-Catholic of uncompromising piety; but she is not without her interest today, and *The Daisy Chain* (1856) handles child death in a way that partly fits and partly departs from the now familiar stereotypes.

Dr. Richard May is a country physician whose wife dies at the beginning of the book, leaving him with eleven children to bring up. The "daisy chain" is the image he affectionately uses to describe his family, and the novel is an exploration of the complex and shifting emotional relationships within the family, the distribution of responsibilities, the growing up of the children, and the gradual rearrangement of functions. Our concern is with the second daughter, Flora, whose baby dies in part ii, chapter 20. Flora is beautiful, competent, and unsentimental: her one fault as a child had been love of admiration, and as she grows up she finds "temptation in the being everywhere liked and sought after." She marries the stolid and wealthy George Rivers, well-meaning and dull, choosing him out of prudence, not romance, pleased at the thought that she will be influential (her husband gets into Parliament largely through her urging) and that she will be able to help her brothers and sisters. She makes George a good wife and enjoys tactfully organizing his life.

Their daughter, happy and healthy at first, suddenly turns sleepy and fretful. Dr. May rushes to see her, arriving in time to watch her die. It turns out that she has been "destroyed" by a popular preparation called God-frey's cordial, administered freely by the nursemaid, who "had not known that the cordial was injurious, deeming it a panacea against fretfulness, precious to nurses, but against which ladies always had a prejudice, and, therefore, to be kept secret." The death has a shattering effect on the family. George, the father, reacts with anger, insisting that the police should be called and the nurse punished, and his insensitive raging adds to his wife's distress, so that Dr. May has to persuade him to leave her alone. Flora, the mother, reacts with bitter self-reproach, and when her husband declares that the nurse should be turned out of the house at once, she bursts out: "George, turn me out of the house too! If Preston killed her, I did!" and gives a "ghastly laugh." She is convinced that she is to blame for neglecting her child: she had devoted herself too wholeheartedly to her husband's career and to her own social success, leaving the baby too much to the care of the nurse:

> I have never set my heart right. I am not like you nor my sisters. I have seemed to myself, and to you, to be trying to do right, but it was all hollow, for the sake of praise and credit. I know it, now it is too late; and He has let me destroy my child here, lest I should have destroyed her Everlasting Life, like my own.

It is never quite clear how far Flora recovers from this despair. The one duty she throws herself into whole-heartedly is keeping her husband happy, in order to atone for the wrong she feels she has done him:

> For George . . . her attention was always ready, and was perpetually claimed. He was forlorn and at a loss without her, every moment; and, in the sorrow which he too felt most acutely, could not have a minute's peace unless soothed by her presence.

When the funeral takes place, Flora does all that is expected of her but does not derive from the ritual the comfort that it is designed to bring:

> The burial, however, failed to bring any peaceful comfort to the mourning mother. Meta's tears flowed freely, as much for her father as for her little niece;

> and George's sobs were deep and choking; but Flora, externally, only seemed
> absorbed in helping him to go through with it; she, herself, never lost her fixed,
> composed, hopeless look." (Part ii, chapter 20)

We seem to be watching Flora at this funeral with very much the same eyes
with which the public watched Prince Leopold at Charlotte's funeral,
observing outward behavior and speculating on inner feeling. Prince
Leopold's feelings were not directly accessible because a public occasion
does not reveal private grief; Flora's are not available because the novelist
has chosen, for a time at least, to hold us at bay, inviting us to share the
ignorance of the family and wonder just how Flora is reacting, to be slightly
puzzled by her shift of attention from lost child to husband, to suspect that
what this shows is despair.

During this whole episode, Flora is pregnant—a fact that we do not
learn until the end of the novel, for another daughter is born in the penul-
timate chapter. Even the fact is not quite certain, because the passage of
time is not very clearly marked. The disaster seems to have occurred in the
summer, and the new child is born on December 24. With her fierce Victorian reticence, Yonge does not, of course, drop even a hint that Flora's
despair might be the result of her condition—just as there was no hint that
Mrs. May, who produced the daisy chain, might have found eleven preg-
nancies burdensome. The exclusion of pregnancy as an experience limits
the Victorian novel as much as the exclusion of sex—perhaps more, since
there are so many traditional ways of representing sex obliquely.

The new daughter is named Margaret. This is certainly significant,
Margaret being the name both of Flora's beloved eldest sister and of her
affectionate sister-in-law, whereas the dead child had been called after
George's wealthy and rather interfering aunt, whom Flora manages with
great skill. Names are value-coded, and the rather fancy and affected
"Leonora" has now been replaced by a good English forename.

But the new infant "is not nearly so fine and healthy as her sister was,"
and although renewed motherhood brings back some of Flora's energy, she
has not, by the end, ceased her self-reproaches: her passionate insistence
that she will never join her mother in heaven has passed, but she does
claim, immediately after the birth, that she can now die, declaring that
Ethel (her sister) will be the best mother to her child. She gets over that
too, but in the end we realize that

the shock of her child's death had taken away the zest and energy which had rejoiced in her chosen way of life, and opened her eyes to see what Master she had been serving; and the perception of the hollowness of all that had been apparently good in her, had filled her with remorse and despair. (Part ii, chapter 26)

The Daisy Chain has a palpable design on the reader, for Charlotte Yonge is more overtly didactic than most Victorian novelists; but she is also more complex than some, and her handling of this death is more interesting than most of the others that this chapter deals with. It raises, for instance, the question of class.

Godfrey's cordial was a mixture of opium, treacle, and infusion of sassafras. Its use was widespread in the nineteenth century, and there is no doubt that it was responsible for an enormous number of child deaths. In Coventry alone, ten gallons (enough for twelve thousand doses) were sold each week; and Dr. H. Julian Hunter wrote in 1863, "there is not a little village shop in the country that sells anything that does not sell its own Godfrey."[16] Doctors were agreed that narcotics was a principal cause of infant death, caused sometimes through well-meaning ignorance on the part of the mother, sometimes by "wilful neglect with the hope of death—in fact, infanticide"—and of course all the gradations in between. But the children who took Godfrey's cordial were the children of the poor— and (in Victorian terminology) of the undeserving poor; the Floras would never have dreamed of using it. What is shocking in the case of little Leonora is that a procedure which belongs with the lower classes has invaded a respectable family: hence the importance of the nursemaid Preston (calling women by their surname only, now—ironically—a sign of emancipation, was of course a class marker in the nineteenth century). The contrast between George's anger and Dr. May's stern but kind treatment of Preston is not only a moral contrast; it is also about the ways of warding off a threat from below. George thinks of punishment and of calling the police (those protectors of the bourgeoisie), while Dr. May, just as staunch a Tory in theory, tries to use the occasion to teach the nurse. And Flora, when eventually she brings herself to see Preston, turns her away with a gift of money and the assurance, "If you are ever in any distress, I hope you will let me know." Meta, her sister-in-law, is "a little disappointed to see sovereigns instead of a book," and gently suggests that she might, instead, have given her a Bible. "You may give her one if you like," Flora replies. "I could not." This is of course about degrees of forgiveness (the one less involved can forgive more fully); but it is also about the cash nexus as the bond between classes. With an irony she would not have wished, Yonge has shown that the less complete forgiveness has produced what the working-class maid, surely, will value more.

Now this strategy of presenting with shocked horror an occurrence that was common enough among the poor is not unique in the Victorian novel. A parallel would be the treatment of illegitimacy in such novels as *Adam Bede* and *Tess of the D'Urbervilles*. Hetty's disgrace and Tess's shame, along with the emotional intensity of everyone's reaction—condemnation, tact, or compassion—belong to respectable bourgeois society, to the world of the readers rather than to that of the novel.

The ideological implications of this are ambivalent. It can of course be seen as hypocrisy or avoidance: the pretence, conscious or otherwise, that such things do not happen, that all of society can afford to be as scrupulous as the bourgeois reader undoubtedly is. That is the radical reading. But it can also be seen as protest, as a way of showing the outrageousness of the whole process, a way of compelling us to be shocked, not to take refuge in the knowledge that what is widespread in the lower classes will not affect us. These two readings seem to me equally plausible, and no doubt it will be the ideological preference of the critic that will determine the choice between them.

As well as class, there are issues of gender raised by the episode. What are a woman's duties? Flora's despair is caused by deciding she had been a bad mother; but is this not an example of how the conservative imagination stigmatizes progress as wicked? Flora seems to have behaved like a modern professional mother, used child care, and while conscientiously loving and visiting her child regularly, taken care that it did not interfere too much with her own life.

But not quite. The tasks for which Flora had "neglected" Leonora were just as feminine as mothering: she had encouraged her husband to go into Parliament and supported him when there, both socially, as a hostess, and by unobtrusively making sure that he said the right things and gave the right speeches. The choice lies between her duties as a mother and her duties as a wife, with a strong suggestion that "worldly motives" loom larger in the latter: motherhood on the other hand is so sacred a function that the motives in carrying it out can hardly be anything but pure. This

dilemma is explored in a way that is both rigidly conventional and interestingly complex:

> The sorrow that had fallen on the Grange seemed to have changed none of the
> usual habits there—visiting, riding, driving, dinners, and music, went on with
> little check. Flora was sure to be found the animated, attentive lady of the
> house, or else sharing her husband's pursuits, helping him with his business, or
> assisting him in seeking pleasure, spending whole afternoons at the coach-
> maker's, over a carriage that they were building, and, it was reported, playing
> ecarté in the evening. (Part ii, chapter 21)

Does this contrast the selfishness of her grief with the dutiful carrying out
of wifely support, or the profundity of grief with the triviality of the daily
round? No simple didactic point can be folded into this part of the narrative. And Flora's final decision has a similar ambivalence. She has what
seems a cathartic experience at the very end of the book, when she
announces that she wants to give up "dinners and parties, empty talk and
vain show," persuade George to give up his Parliamentary seat, and live in
peace in the country. This has the ring of redemptive self-discovery, but
she is finally persuaded out of it by her wise clerical brother—reinforced by
the bracing sharpness of Ethel's remark: "I don't think it is for his dignity
for you to put him into Parliament to please you, and then take him out to
please you" (chapter 27). The clear choice between self-indulgence and
duty is as muddied here as it is in reality: Flora's future life will continue to
wind its way among moral ambiguities.

And, finally, what of the pathos and uplift that we have come to expect
when a child dies? Does little Leonora become an angel and see the bright
light shining, casting an improving influence on all around? The difference
between child death and infant death is of course important here: an infant
who cannot yet speak is obviously not able to say "the print upon the stairs
at school is not divine enough. The light about the head is shining on me
as I go!" But little Nell had no dying words, and could not the static
vignette of her death be that of an infant? Nell, who dies either of TB or of
the nameless wasting that is unsullied by diagnosis, naturally comes to a
peaceful end, whereas Leonora's death is meant to shock us into awareness
of the abuse; so she must suffer and not die in tranquillity. The "poor little
sufferer" becomes not an angel but a "little corpse."[17]

So devout a novelist as Charlotte Yonge could not avoid emphasizing the religious dimension of the death, but this is diverted into something like an aside. It is Ethel who is given this conventional reflection:

> It had been with a gentle sorrow that Ethel had expected to go and lay in her resting-place the little niece, who had been kept from the evil of the world in a manner of which she had little dreamt. Poor Flora! she must be ennobled, she thought, by having a child where hers is, when she is able to feel anything but the first grief. (Part ii, chapter 20)

The lively Ethel is probably the nearest thing to the heroine of the novel and perhaps the least appropriate character to be given this conventional reflection—not only conventional but also wrong, since, as we have seen, Flora is not ennobled. Nothing is made of this reflection on the infant's own spiritual welfare: though she was "kept from the evil of this world," and therefore has a good chance of heaven, her presence there is no more certain than that of the enskied Mrs. May, a constantly beneficent presence—though she, after bearing eleven children, can hardly be said to have escaped the world and its evils.

Diagnosis—and Nondiagnosis

And what did these fictional children die of? The answer may be even more elusive than in the case of the real children, because in addition to the embarrassment, reticence, and fear that are present in the accounts of real disease, we need to add the effect of vagueness in assisting plot development or character portrayal.

The death of Muriel Halifax is perhaps the clearest case of sacrificing medical plausibility to literary effect. That she dies not of disease but from the kick of a horse is, I suggested, for reasons of plot, but for reasons of pathos she does not die immediately, lingering on for several weeks in order to expire gradually and beautifully. "When we asked her if she felt ill, she always answered 'Oh, no! only so very tired.' Nothing more" (chapter 28). When she tries to get out of bed she finds she cannot walk and has to hold onto furniture and says, "I can't walk, I am so tired." We are not told where the horse's kick lands, but it was presumably on the abdomen, and the most likely cause of death would have been injury to the spleen or kidneys; in both cases, the pain would have been severe. "Only tired, Nothing more" is fine for the atmosphere of resignation but highly implausible medically.

But of course most fictional children, like most real children, died not of injury but of disease. The disease is seldom named, and contemporary readers probably did not pause to name it; but if asked, they would surely have described it as consumption—that is, pulmonary tuberculosis. Little Eva wastes away, spiritualized and more or less without symptoms: her most definite signs of weakness come when she is told of Prue's death, as if her disease manifests itself primarily as a way of responding to the sufferings of others. The first person to give it a name is her mother, and she does so only indirectly:

> "I don't see as anything ails the child," she would say: "she runs about, and plays."
> "But she has a cough."
> "Cough! you don't need to tell me about a cough. I've always been subject to a cough, all my days. When I was of Eva's age they thought I was in a consumption. Night after night, Mammy used to sit up with me. O! Eva's cough is not anything." (Chapter 24).

Marie's self-pity is of course the novelist's way of directing our sympathy towards Eva. Consumption is what she was thought to have had, and the implicit—indeed, almost explicit—authorial comment here is of course that Eva *has* got it. Marie's crude explicitness saves the novelist from being so indelicate as to name the disease herself.

Paul Dombey's disease is not named either, and the nearest we come to a medical account is the remark made by the apothecary to Mrs. Pipchin:

> Lying down again with his eyes shut, he heard the Apothecary say, out of the room and quite a long way off—or he dreamed it—that there was a want of vital power (what was that, Paul wondered!) and great constitutional weakness. . . . That there was no immediate cause for—What? Paul lost that word. (Chapter 14)

This is an odd passage. The intended effect is clearly that the overheard remark should convey more to us than to Paul, so that the pathos will be heightened by his inability to grasp what is happening to him. We have no difficulty in concluding that the lost word was "alarm," but that tells us little. Indeed, all the apothecary's expressions are so vague that to attribute much meaning to them would argue a medical ignorance and complacency comparable to his. The opportunity to tell the reader tactfully that Paul had consumption has not been taken.

And did he? There are other possibilities: he could have had asthma, or an iron deficiency that would have made him especially susceptible to infection. These are technically possible, but who can doubt that Paul died of consumption, the poetic disease, the disease that killed Keats and Emily Brontë, the disease that spiritualizes its victims, as Susan Sonntag convincingly argues:

> While TB takes on qualities assigned to the lungs, which are part of the upper, spiritualised body, cancer is notorious for attacking parts of the body (colon, bladder, rectum, breast, cervix, prostate, testicles) that are embarrassing to acknowledge.[18]

Cancer, for Sonntag, is the disease that in the twentieth century we do not name, but whose presence we assume when death is generalized, incurable, and vaguely metaphorical. In the nineteenth century it was TB, whose symptoms are much easier to treat euphemistically, and which, because it seems to spiritualize the body, slips easily into the conventions of bodily reticence.

In fictional deaths, then, we find the same tendency to generalize and evade that we saw in the case of real deaths; but there is a qualification to be made. When the novelist's point is not medical but moral or political, he is sometimes prepared to be very specific and very confident. In the opening chapters of Elizabeth Gaskell's *Mary Barton* (1848), John Barton's wife dies in childbirth. Her sister had run away to live as a prostitute, on the edge of society and on the edge of the novel, and this had caused her great distress. When the doctor breaks the news of her death to the husband, he says, "Nothing could have saved her—there has been some shock to the system" (chapter 3). No doctor, examining the body of a woman dying in labor (the doctor does not arrive until she is already dead) could possibly conclude anything about a mental shock: this is not a medical opinion but a nudge from the novelist.

Interestingly enough it is Dinah Mulock, so vague on Muriel's actual death, who is more precise than her contemporaries in the case of smallpox. When John Halifax realizes that little Tommy has brought smallpox into the house, he recalls that he (rather against his wife's wishes) had vaccinated his children (clearly his trust in God had its limits): the virus had taken effect with all but Muriel. We are then told, quite correctly, that "though inoculation and vaccination had made it less fatal among the upper classes, this frightful scourge still decimated the poor, especially children" (chapter 25)—a statement still true, perhaps truer, in the 1850s, when it was written, than at the beginning of the century, when the novel takes place. Though the symptoms are not described in any detail, there is no evasiveness about what the illness is: author and hero share a matter-of-fact interest in smallpox—or perhaps the author assumed it because it was in character for her hero.

But if we want matter-of-factness, no English novelist can touch Flaubert. I have already pointed out the vivid and rather unpleasant detail in which the dead or dying children are described in *l'Education sentimentale*; now I add that Flaubert took the trouble to go and study the symptoms of croup at the hospital Sainte-Eugénie (did that suggest the name of Mme. Arnoux's child, Eugène?). He found the experience tiring and disgusting, and he wrote to his niece, "It's abominable and I'm heartbroken at it; but Art for ever!"[19] This meticulous collecting of authentic detail is associated with the realist school and can cast a certain skepticism over Flaubert's refusal to be thought of as a realist. In the end, despite his staunch assertion "l'Art avant tout!" he found the experience too much to endure and did not have the nerve to watch Dr. Marjolin perform a tracheotomy; conscientiously, he then decided not to have one performed on Eugène, as he had originally intended. Instead, finding in the *Clinique Médicale* of Trousseau, which he studied with great care, a description of the expulsion of false membranes by coughing, with immediate relief for the patient, he put that in the novel as a way of saving the child's life—conveniently ignoring Trousseau's observation that very often another false membrane forms, and the illness begins again.

If realism is, at least in part, the opposite to vagueness, then Flaubert certainly wrote the most realistic account of a child's illness in the nineteenth century novel; and the obvious way to avoid being vague is to observe with clinical accuracy. I have already quoted the description of Eugène's cough, and I now give it again along with the passage from Trousseau's textbook from which it was drawn:

La toux n'est pas sonore, éclatante, mais rauque et sourde comme l'aboiement lointain d'un jeune chien. . . . Après chaque quinte de toux, le sifflement est encore plus marqué; il est produit par une inspiration courte, sèche, comme métallique, se percevant parfaitement à distance.

(The cough is not sonorous or loud, but hoarse and muffled, like the distant barking of a young dog. . . . After each fit of coughing, the whistling sound is yet more marked: it is produced by a short dry intake of breath, a metallic sound perfectly audible at a distance. (Trousseau)

*

La toux ressemblait au bruit de ces mécaniques barbares qui font japper les chiens de carton. . . . Il s'echappait de son larynx un sifflement produit par chaque inspiration de plus en plus courte, sèche et comme métallique.

(The cough was like the noise of those barbarous mechanisms that cause cardboard dogs to yap. . . . A whistling sound escaped from his larynx, produced by the ever shorter intakes of breath, dry and metallic in sound. (Flaubert)[20]

Flaubert has followed his authority carefully and seems to have taken great trouble to get the facts right; he even uses, indirectly, the detail about the distant barking of the dog: Mme. Arnoux is woken by Eugène's coughing, after dreaming that a fierce little dog was biting at her dress and barking louder and louder, so that the distance is now that between sleep and waking. The change from barking to yapping may just be to avoid verbal repetition, but the striking new detail, the barbarous mechanism and the cardboard dogs, have surely nothing to do with accuracy of observation. If realism directs our attention to the signified rather than to the nature of the writing, Flaubert here shows himself not a realist after all: he has indulged in a little stylistic elegance, showing us that precision can manifest itself not only in observation but in the choice of signifiers.

Why?

I now intend to ask, in as cautious a spirit as possible, why child death becomes so prominent in nineteenth century literature, when it was so rare before?

Two kinds of answer are possible, depending on whether we look within the evolving institution of literature or outside it. For many centuries love and adventure were the dominant material of stories, and not until well after the rise of realistic prose fiction are they joined by class relations and the material conditions of the poor (in the Condition-of-England novels of the 1840s), by the hero's work as well as his sexual involvements or picaresque adventures (Balzac, George Eliot), and by family life, in which children figure first as little more than a nuisance (Jane Austen) and then as centers of consciousness in their own right (*Jane Eyre, David Copperfield, The Mill on the Floss*). Death is always important in fiction, because it is both necessary for plot and the main surrogate for plot, a way of confronting characters with a sharply changed situation; so once children are prominent, we will expect them to die.

Does such a cavalier survey of the history of the novel tell us anything important? It is hardly surprising that the subject matter of fiction, like the universe, has a built-in tendency to expand, and it perhaps makes the popularity of fictional child deaths unsurprising; but for explanation, rather than description, of the phenomenon, we surely need to look outside literature. We explain one social phenomenon by looking at others, and the obvious place to look, in this case, will be demography. What can we find out about actual child deaths?

What would we expect to find? Not simply that a lot of children died, since what matters is the comparison between the death rate then and what preceded it. An infant death rate of 154 per thousand seems to us appalling, and in late twentieth century industrialized society it would be, but in 1840 it was not new.[21] To explain change, we must look for what changed. Nor, I suggest, will we expect to find that the death rate increased: an increase in an already familiar occurrence is not likely to bring it to our attention in a dramatically new way. More probably, the new factor will be that fewer children died: if child death can no longer be seen as inevitable, or at any rate normal, it will seem a worse blow when it happens. This would certainly be the case today: turning back to *The Bereaved Parent*, by Harriet Sarnoff Schiff,[22] a modern manual for coping with the death of a child, I am struck by the ongoing assumption that it is a situation almost impossible to accept, by the facts on how often it leads to marital break-up, by the intensity of self-reproach or reproach to one's partner that now seems almost inevitable—all far greater than anything one comes across in Victorian writing. The obvious explanation is that child death is now so unusual in our society, and because unusual, that much harder to bear.[23]

The argument whether the tremendous rise in population of the last two centuries was due to a fall in mortality or a rise in fertility remains unsettled: largely because these two trends are not independent of each other (a fall in the mortality of middle-aged men will increase the length of time married couples stay together and so increase the age-specific fertility of women in their late twenties and thirties—which we know rose in the

eighteenth century). Then there is the question how far the fall in mortality is age-specific, that is, how far infant mortality (death in the first year)
and child mortality (from one year to puberty) decline. There seems general agreement that there was such a decline: "there is little doubt," says
McKeown, "that the reduction of mortality in the eighteenth and early
nineteenth centuries occurred predominantly in childhood."[24]

But we need to be concerned not only with brute fact but with awareness: the way a child death would be perceived by those concerned, especially, of course, the parents, and the emotional impact it would have; and
it is not at all certain that general mortality statistics will tell us this. What
we need to know is how far the death of a middle-class child in, say, 1830
or 1860 was perceived as an unusual—and therefore especially distressing—event. (I say "middle-class," because most of the accounts of child
deaths we have, in fiction and in actuality, are by middle-class writers for
predominantly middle-class readers. There is of course no reason to suppose that working class—or aristocratic—parents grieved any less, but if we
are looking for extra-literary explanations for literary change, then the more
accurate we can make the match the better). The figures we need must be
class-specific and must compare one generation with the preceding one; for
the way a set of parents viewed the death of a child would be influenced by
comparison with the experience of their own parents and grandparents.
Unless we can find evidence as specific as this, demographic speculation
may well be useless.

The Abstract of British Historical Statistics will not help much, both
because it does not record infant mortality rates before 1838 and because it
shows very little decline over the rest of the nineteenth century—which
may well conceal a decline among the well-off and an increase among the
poor. What will help is the study of Quaker demographic history by Vann
and Eversley, *Friends in Life and Death*.[25] This work was undertaken not
only out of loyalty to a particular group, the Quakers, but also because the
Quaker habits of record keeping enable the scholar to discover far more
about their vital statistics than about any other group. Of course there is no
way of testing how far Quaker families were representative—but we do
know they were overwhelmingly middle-class (the Society of Friends having by the late eighteenth century ceased to be a widespread popular
movement among the poor).

Both adult and child mortality declined substantially among Quakers
after 1750. Infant mortality rose in the early eighteenth century, peaked in

the 1720s (as did most British mortality), declined sharply thereafter, and after the mid-century it declined fairly steadily. The drop in child mortality (aged one to fourteen) is fairly similar. "There was a remarkable reduction in infant mortality in the cities in the later eighteenth century, accompanied by a fall in child mortality that was almost as impressive."[26] This reduction may well be specific either to the Quakers or to the middle classes: there is thought not to have been a fall in infant mortality among the working class until the later nineteenth century, with the arrival of widespread smallpox vaccination (inoculation before the introduction of vaccination may well have been ineffective or even harmful, and vaccination did not become widespread until after the mid-nineteenth century). Indeed, the historical demographers disagree about whether infant mortality in the whole population rose or fell in the early nineteenth century, when the sharp increase in urban slum populations must have greatly increased the chances of infection. It is agreed that the decline in mortality was mainly due to the decline in death from infectious diseases (smallpox and TB, the airborne diseases, being easily the most important); but urbanisation may have increased this among the poor while it was decreasing, possibly due to improved nutrition, among the middle classes.

Can we draw any definite conclusion from all this? There is probably enough evidence to enable us to say, if we wish to, that declining infant and child mortality increased sensitivity to child death and thus made it more available as literary material; but there is certainly enough uncertainty about the evidence to make us skeptical of such materialist explanations, on the grounds that they are not specific enough .

But if this drives us back once more to literary explanations for literary change, on the ground that we do not know enough to find a single material cause, we ought at least to realize that isolating the question, as I have done, has a certain artificiality. For it is not just child deaths that are new in literature; it is childhood itself. We have all been children, but one would hardly realize this, reading poetry before Wordsworth, or any literature before Rousseau. And not only literature: why did society concern itself so little with children, establishing only a rudimentary educational system, showing little interest in their exploitation and suffering? Why was there no Lord Shaftesbury before the nineteenth century? My attempt to throw some light on literary change by limiting the inquiry to one topic may teach us something, but the questions expand like a Japanese paper flower in water.

The Twentieth Century

Children die in twentieth century fiction too—less often, and in a very different way. In the first place, they die of meningitis: a peculiarly horrible death. Three such cases, regularly spaced through the first half of the century, show us that we are in a new, frightening age.

In Hermann Hesse's *Rosshalde* (1913), Pierre is the younger son of the painter Johann Veraguth and his estranged wife. Living on the country estate of Rosshalde, which Veraguth had bought and refurbished when they were first married, the couple lead separate lives, unwilling to separate finally because neither is willing to give up Pierre to the other. The first half of the novel depicts the careful efforts of the couple to control their hostility to each other; Pierre falls ill about half-way through and is diagnosed as having meningitis—Hirnhauptentzündung: the word means nothing to Veraguth when the doctor uses it to him, and he even makes bitter fun of the technical term, demanding that it be translated into an answer to the question, Will Pierre die?; and in the next to last chapter, he does. Phil Quarles in Aldous Huxley's *Point Counter Point* (1928) is the only child of the talented intellectual novelist Philip Quarles (who has some resemblance to Huxley himself) and his wife Elinor, who, frustrated at her inability to get any warm and genuine response to her love, has been considering an affair with the fascist politician Everard Webley, who is pursuing her with insistent (and, to her, rather attractive) machismo. The novel is an interweaving of several stories and a host of characters, and the illness and death of Phil (combined as it is with the grotesque murder of Webley) not only leaves Elinor "broken down" but also affects old John Bidlake, her father. Bidlake is a painter of genius, selfish and intensely sensuous, who, suffering from cancer and lost in self pity, has persuaded himself that his own fate is bound up with his grandson's, and he interprets Phil's death as his own death sentence. This is so similar to the obsession of Mr. Rarx in *The Wreck of the Golden Mary* that I find it hard not to believe that the well-read Huxley knew the story. Such borrowing is every author's right, of course, but it does throw an ironic light on Huxley's caustic remarks on Dickens's pathos, which will be discussed in the next chapter.

Thomas Mann's *Doktor Faustus* (1947) is the story of Adrian Leverkühn, the brilliant modern composer, whose pact with the devil is realized on several levels: the contracting of syphilis, a weird and terrifying conversation with his friend Schildknapp, half-identified as a devil figure, and an intermittent suggestion that the story of Adrian is that of Germany itself. Adrian's last work, *Fausti Weheklag*, Faustus's lament, is already taking shape in his head when he is distracted by a Lebenszwischenfall, an event that crops up in his life. His nephew Nepomuk Schneidewein, known as Echo, recovering from measles, comes to spend his convalescence in the house in the country where Adrian is looked after by the motherly Frau Schweigestill and her daughter. The five-year-old child (all three of these children are five or six years old) appears in chapter 44 of the novel and dies in chapter 45.

In each book, there is a larger framework into which the child's death fits. Pierre is the only one of these three children who is a major figure throughout the novel, but in his case too he has a wider function: Veraguth's decision to travel to Asia with his one close friend could lead either to a crisis in the relationship with his wife or to more indecisiveness and resentment; the matter is settled by Pierre's illness, which brings them together only in the sense that they accept the separation and the child's death with a new clarity and decisiveness. Phil's death brings no such resolution, for Huxley's slice-of-life novel is a book that avoids resolutions, and quite as important as the effect of the death on his mother (itself inconclusive) is its lack of effect on the larger world: to most of the characters it means far less than it does to the reader. Indifference is one of the recurring themes of this fitfully cynical novel. The most interesting and also the strangest in its significance for the book as a whole is certainly the death of Echo, because of the way it is made part of the Faustus story. When the narrator tries to speak a few words of comfort to Adrian, he is interrupted: spare yourself the humanist nonsense, he is told, he is taking him ("Spar dir," unterbrach er mich rauh, "die Humanistenflausen! er nimmt ihn"). Adrian regards Echo's death as part of the Devil's bargain: he had sold his soul, and this entitles the Devil to take the object of his love, so that he, Adrian, is responsible for Echo's suffering:

Welche Schuld, welche Sünde, welch ein Verbrechen . . . daß wir ihn kommen ließen, daß ich ihn in meine Nähe ließ. . . Du mußt wissen, Kinder sind aus zartem Stoff, sie sind gar leicht für giftige Einflüsse empfänglich. [27]

What guilt, what a sin, what a crime . . . that we caused him to come here, that I allowed him to be near me. . . . Children are made of tender stuff, they're very susceptible to poisonous influences.

This is crazy but with the craziness of Leverkühn's genius. His later remark, "it is not to be" (es soll nicht sein), that is, that a hopeful theodicy (the ninth symphony, as he elliptically puts it) is now invalidated, has something of the labored theoretic note that lurks in Mann's most powerful writing, but this bitterness at his own purely imaginary responsibility for the child's suffering makes a perfect seam between the self-contained pathetic episode, and the larger Faust-story. Seam: for a seam joins whole panels of cloth, leaving each intact but incomplete, and each child death can—indeed must—be read both as complete in itself and as part of a larger, disquieting whole.

Rosshalde is the only one of these three books that tries to render the child's illness through his own consciousness. The first sign of trouble comes when Pierre wanders through the garden in a kind of intensified childish boredom, "restless between expectation and mistrust . . . in search of something new, some discovery or adventure, no matter what" (unruhig zwischen Erwartung und Mißtrauen, . . . auf der Suche nach irgend etwas Neuem, nach irgendeinem Fund oder Abenteuer).

> Man sollte sich hinlegen und schlafen, dachte er, so lange schlafen, bis alles wieder neu und schön und lustig aussähe. Es hatte ja keinen Sinn, da herumzugehen und sich zu plagen, und auf Dinge zu warten, die doch nicht kommen wollten. (Chapter 10)

> One should be able to lie down and sleep, he thought, and go on sleeping till everything seemed new and beautiful and pleasant again. There was no point in wandering about tormenting oneself and waiting for things that didn't want to happen.

When he does manage to lie down and sleep, he has a dream of alienation, in which he wanders through the garden and finds it "more beautiful than ever, but the flowers seem oddly glassy, large and strange, and the whole shines with a sad, dead beauty" (die Beete waren schöner, als er sie je gesehen hatte, aber die blumen sahen alle sonderbar gläsern, groß and fremdartig aus, und das Ganze glänzte in einer traurig toten Schönheit (chapter 11). When he wakes up, he wants to know why he had vomited when he had not eaten anything bad like half-ripe plums: like any child he is finding, but more painfully than usual, that the world is not fair.

As the illness develops we move outside the child's consciousness to an account of the symptoms as observed. All three novelists describe these in some detail: the vomiting, the violent twisting of the body, and the terrifying scream. Remission, when it comes, brings relief to the sufferer, to the parents, and to the reader; and only Mann offers us no remission. Pierre, after his first bad day, seems to get better, then relapses, then towards the end seems a great deal better, so that his father can read to him, producing a smile, and even remark to the doctor that there seems to have been a miracle; almost immediately after that they hear a shrill scream and rushing to see Pierre find him with hideously distorted mouth, his shrivelled limbs twisting themselves in violent cramps, and his eyes stared in unreasoning terror ("mit gräßlich verzogenem Munde, seine abgemagerten Glieder krümmten sich in wütenden Krämpfen, die Augen stierten in vernunftlosem Entsetzen" [chapter 17]). Soon after that he loses consciousness and dies.

Phil Quarles has only one remission, even more dramatic: "suddenly and without warning" he opens his eyes, and declares he is hungry. He speaks to his parents, makes his father draw for him, eats, drinks and laughs—but has gone completely deaf, and keeps asking, "Why don't you ever say anything?" (chapter 35). As in *Rosshalde*, this prefigures the end, which comes shortly after.

Medically, remission is unlikely in the course of meningitis, but as a plot strategy it is obviously valuable. Plot as a sequence of events demands contrast, and the impact of death is clearly heightened if it is preceded by what could look like recovery, as the death of the tragic hero is often preceded by an apparent resurgence of his earlier, undamaged self. Literary experience could teach the seasoned reader, when Pierre and Phil stage their apparent recovery, that they are about to die; medical knowledge, if the reader considers it reliable in fiction, may already have told him that.

Medical science in the first half of the twentieth century knew more about disease than it had a hundred years earlier, but whether it could do more, until the advent of antibiotics, is doubtful. The doctors attending these three children are more prominent, and more fully treated as characters, than any of their Victorian predecessors, but they are all helpless—and know that they are helpless. To Huxley, this is matter for scorn; to Hesse, for compassion and even a kind of admiration. Huxley's Dr. Crowther, "a small man, brisk and almost too neatly dressed," is treated with contempt from the beginning. He does not share, or even interest himself in, the mother's distress, and for this Huxley punishes him by describing his self-control in terms of physics: "His conversation had been reduced to bedrock efficiency. It was just comprehensible and nothing more. No energy was wasted on the uttering of unnecessary words." Once this figure of speech is introduced, it is grimly repeated. He shakes his head once only, not speaking: "a foot-pound saved is a foot-pound gained." The point is no doubt appropriate: the man who treats the invalid as a predictable machine treats himself the same way. But it is an easy point, and Dr. Crowther is the least interesting of the doctors.

Hesse does not give his doctor a name: he is called the doctor, the physician, the medical officer (der Doktor, der Arzt, der Sanitätsrat), but this is not to score points off him, for he is presented as sympathetic and understanding. He hurries when he is not with a patient, becomes slow and careful when he is; he is interested in Veraguth's renown as a painter, is tactful and understanding when he breaks the news of how serious the illness is—but he is helpless. Both he and Dr. Crowther, when confronted with the child's apparent improvement, say nothing, for both of them know the remission does not mean recovery.

Mann too is aware of the contrast between scientific impersonality and emotional involvement. Echo's scream, heart-rending and piercing, is also referred to as the typical hydrocephalic scream, rendered less unendurable to the doctor because he can diagnose it: the typical leaves us cool, it is only that which we understand as individual which causes us to lose all self-control (das Typische läßt kühl, nur das als individuell Verstandene macht, daß wir ausser uns geraten). The touch of irony here, gentler and subtler than Huxley's, points to the ambivalent attitude toward medical science, which in this book is complicated by the presence of two doctors, the local country physician and the specialist called in from Munich for consultation. Dr. Kürbis is cool in contrast to Adrian and the other heart-broken bystanders, but in contrast to the distinguished Professor von Rotherbuch he appears warm and sympathetic. He had asked for a second opinion, claiming that he was only a simple man and that they were confronted with a case requiring a higher authority (Hier ist ein Aufgebot von höherer Autorität am Platze). This very remark renders him more sympathetic; when the narrator observes that he believes it was uttered with a subdued or sad irony (betrübte Ironie), he is welcoming Dr. Kürbis as a spirit like himself. The Professor, when he arrives, is dignified and slightly condescending, perfectly correct, but helpless: it is made clear that the simple country physician was quite as competent as medical science was capable of being. Science is able to diagnose, to attach learned names to the condition, but even at its most eminent science cannot cure; like theology, it can turn suffering into the typical, which leaves us cool.

And the child? All three children are loved: Phil perhaps only by his mother, Pierre intensely by both parents, Echo by all who know him. The moment he appears at Pfeiffering, Echo wins everyone's heart by his elfin appearance, his charm, and his quaint locutions. He seems a figure from fairy tale, a visitor from the dainty world of the small and the delicate (von Märchen, von Besuch aus niedlicher Klein- und Feinwelt). When the narrator addresses him in a hearty, patronizing tone, he immediately realizes his mistake and realizes that Echo is aware of it too, and aware of his embarrassment. The child, feeling ashamed on his behalf, lets his head sink and pulls down his mouth as one does when biting back a laugh (beschämt für mich, das Köpfchen senkte, indem er den Mund nach unten zog, wie einer, der sich das Lachen verbeißt). For Echo is so sensitive that he feels distress at the distress of others, even attributing regret to those who forbid him something, even stroking them in compassion at their having to deny him, clearly against their will.

Echo's language is quaint and highly individual. He has his own abbreviations, such as "habt" when he has had enough, an abbreviation of "Ich habe es gehabt": Helen Lowe-Porter translates, with her usual ingenuity, as "nuff"—an alternative would perhaps be "had." Echo's careful articulation and archaic vocabulary derive partly from his Swiss father, but mostly seem to be a sign of his unearthliness. He recites children's rhymes with a droll solemnity that makes bystanders laugh, whereupon he looks into their faces, watching the merriment with roguish curiosity (er blickte in die Gesichter dabei, unsere Heiterkeit mit schelmischer Neugier beobachtend). When he goes to bed he recites strange old-fashioned prayers, of which he has a large repertory:

> Swie groß si jemands Missetat,
> Got dennoch mehr Genaden hat,
> Mein Sünd nicht viel besagen will,
> Got lächelt in Seiner Gnadenfüll'. Amen.

> Though my offence be ne'er so great
> The grace of God is greater yet.
> Shall my sins scathe? But surely no,
> See how God's grace doth overflow.

To the archaic language is added Echo's habit of twisting or mispronouncing words ("Swie" for "wie," "swer" for "wer"; "Got" for "Gott"—we might say "Goad" for "God"). Another prayer runs:

> Merkt, swer für den andern bitt'
> sich selber löset er damit.
> Echo bitt' für die ganze Welt
> Daß Got auch ihm in Armen hält.

> Whoso prays for other's weal,
> His own offences he shall heal.
> Echo prays for all mankind.
> So God in his embrace me bind.

This unleashes a discussion between Adrian and Zeitblom, the narrator, in which Adrian observes that disinterestedness is surely suspended once one sees that it is in one's own interest (Uneigennützigkeit ist doch aufgehoben, so bald man sich merkt, daß sie nützlich ist). Zeitblom wonders where Echo learned these strange prayers; Adrian replies that he prefers to let the question rest unasked, assuming that Echo would not be able to tell them anything about it (O nein, ich ziehe es vor, die Frage auf sich beruhen zu lassen, und nehme an, er wüßte mir keinen Bescheid). The suggestion is that Echo, not being altogether of this world, has brought the prayers from the elfin land he inhabited.

Mann's first masterpiece, *Buddenbrooks*, published at the very beginning of the century, which contains the moving death of little Hanno and the consequent extinction of the family (a gentler version of Hardy's "coming universal wish not to live"), is in all essentials a nineteenth century novel. *Rosshalde*, twelve years later, though its theme is that of Yeats ("The intellect of man is forced to choose Perfection of the life or of the work") has not fully crossed the divide that distinguishes nineteenth from twentieth century fiction, the novel of autonomous subject and omniscient narrator from the subversions of modernism. But *Doktor Faustus*, published in 1947, is truly modernist, wrestling with the problem of the artist who rejects tradition only to embrace it in strange and difficult ways, depicting the breakdown of humanist values, and the disturbing connections between aestheticism and barbarism, between artistic experiment and fascism. For some it is *the* modern novel, self-conscious and deeply skeptical;

yet it is Echo, far more than either Hanno or Pierre, who takes us back to the high Victorian sensibility, and recalls Paul Dombey. For it is Echo who is the modern version of the "old-fashioned" child, not only in his ability to disconcert by the mischievous and the unexpected, but also in a very literal sense: he uses old-fashioned language. When it has rained, he delights Adrian by saying "daß der 'Rein' dieser Nacht das Erdrich 'erkickt' habe"; Adrian is fascinated both by the image and by the oddness of the vocabulary. Zeitblom, being a scholar, is able to explain to him that the forms Echo is using are medieval variants, "Rein" or "Reigen" for "Regen," "erkicken" for "erquicken." This makes the passage untranslatable: Lowe Porter, whose efforts to find English equivalents are always heroic and often brilliant, is forced to omit some of it. Perhaps we might say, "last night the ren kickened the earthling." Echo, playing childishly with words, is somehow able to speak medieval German: he is a kind of word-spirit, an embodiment of the language itself—more, indeed, than Paul, who has Toots to do his inventing.

Echo listens to his uncle's musical box as Paul might have, but Dickens would not have added the coolly analytic remark that he listened "always with the same rapt attention, with eyes in which delight, astonishment and a gazing dreaminess mingled in unforgettable fashion" (in immer gleichem Gebanntsein lauschte, mit Augen in dem Amüsiertheit, Erstaunen und tief schauende Träumerei sich auf unvergeßliche Weise mischten). This may not be a Dickensian sentence—Mann the intellectual has far more taste for abstract nouns than Dickens the popular entertainer—but it could be a description of Paul.

And is Echo an angel? He belongs among those who are new to the world, half strange and inexperienced (auf Erden noch Neuen, halb Fremden und Unbewanderten); he is a "holde Erscheinung," a holy apparition; he is childhood itself, conveying a feeling of having come down to be among us (das Gefühl von Herabgestiegensein); he is a little ambassador from the land of the children and elves. There are pagan elements in this, but there are also explicitly Christian elements: he rocks Reason to sleep in dreams that transcend logic, tinged with Christianity (die Vernunft in außerlogische, von unserem Christentum tingierte Träume wiege). Echo lying in his bed to recite his prayers, his shallow hands brought together in front of his breast ("immer vor anbetenden Heiligen seine Händchen zum Kreuzeszeichen [erhoben])" recalls both the Christ child worshipped by saints and little Nell laid to rest. And like the Christ child, he must be taken out of time—as a response to the infinitely sad thought that a child like Echo will grow up and fade into the light of common day. Zeitblom self-deprecatingly admits that as a teacher, given to didacticism, he is especially aware that Echo's charm will, sooner or later, ripen and fall victim to the world, that his Engelsmienchen (his little angel features), with all their individual charming childlike details, will turn into the face of a more or less ordinary boy. No doubt the same would have happened to Paul if death had not rescued him. That was what Mrs. Marcet, with her devilish cuteness, must have realized, and if she had survived to read *Doktor Faustus* she would presumably have predicted Echo's death.

The reason Echo, Phil, and Pierre all die of meningitis is obvious— depressingly obvious: because it is such a horrible death. So it is not surprising to find perhaps the most famous of all child deaths in modern fiction resulting from something equally horrible. The son of M. Othon, judge, at Oran dies of plague in the 4th section of *La Peste*, and we are given a very matter-of-fact account of his sufferings, in the terse dry prose for which Camus was so celebrated.

> Sans mot dire, Rieux lui montra l'enfant qui, les yeux fermés dans une face decomposée, les dents serrées à la limite de ses forces, le corps immobile, tournait et retournait sa tête de droite à gauche, sur le traversin sans drap.[28]

> Without a word, Rieux showed him the child, who, with his eyes closed in his distorted face, his teeth clenched with all his strength, his body immobile, kept turning his head from right to left on the bolster without a sheet.

There is no sensationalism in this clinical writing, except for the deliberately blasphemous climax:

> De grosses larmes, jaillissant sous les paupières enflammées, se mirent à couler sur son visage plombé, et, au bout de la crise, épuisé, crispant ses jambes osseuses et ses bras dont la chair avait fondu en quarante-huit heures, l'enfant prit dans le lit dévasté une pose de crucifié grotesque.

> Large tears, shooting out under the inflamed eyelids, began to run down his face the colour of lead, and at the end of the crisis, exhausted, stiffening his skeletal legs and his arms from which the flesh had melted away in forty-eight hours, the child, lying on the disarranged bed, took on the posture of someone grotesquely crucified.

Plague differs from meningitis in being an epidemic: each death is one of many, not an isolated event. Yet though *La Peste* is a novel about an epidemic, seen as a social and not just a natural occurrence, this death is treated as an individual—and shocking—event. It is described in more detail than any other death in the book, it is watched by all the main characters, and its emotional impact is devastating, not only on Dr. Rieux, the hero, but also on the priest, Father Paneloux, whom it leads to the edge of heresy.

That this death is designed to raise a religious issue is clear from the moment we are told that to Rieux and his friend Tarrou the pain inflicted on innocent children never ceased to seem what it was in truth, that is, a scandal (la douleur infligée à ces innocents n'avait jamais cessé de leur paraître ce qu'elle était en verité, c'est-à-dire un scandale). Nature does not perpetrate scandals: the term implies a world that can be judged morally, a world for which someone is responsible.

In fact it is not God, or Nature, alone that is responsible for the child's suffering. A new vaccine has been devised but not yet tested, and Rieux, deciding that the child is doomed, uses him as the subject for the first trial: it does not save his life, but he does resist longer than one would have expected. When Rieux points this out, Paneloux, who is present, observes that if the child has to die, he will have suffered longer. The remark is a deliberate distraction. Paneloux, who had delivered a fiery sermon when the plague struck, beginning, "My brothers, you are in trouble, and my brothers, you have deserved it" (Mes frères, vous êtes dans le malheur, et mes frères, vous l'avez mérité), suffers as much as anyone watching the child's agony, and his first remark is to single out for condemnation the element in the agony that is due to man. This, however, only postpones his reaction to the real scandal, the suffering inflicted by God. In his second sermon, he deals with this issue: the church this time is less crowded, the delivery less fiery, but for Paneloux it is his supreme confrontation with God. It quite explicitly rejects the stock consolation:

Il lui aurait été aisé de dire que l'éternité des délices qui attendait l'enfant pouvait compenser sa souffrance, mais en vérité, il n'en savait rien. Qui pouvait affirmer en effet que l'éternité d'une joie pouvait compenser un instant de la douleur humaine? (iv, 3)

It would have been easy for him to say that the eternity of delight awaiting the child could make up for his suffering, but in truth he knew nothing about that.

Who in fact could affirm that an eternity of joy could make up for an instant of human pain?

That disposes, in a moment of brusque skepticism, of tomes of Victorian comfort: eternities of delight are the language of conventional piety, which costs nothing; human pain is what we know. But what then is to replace conventional piety? For Rieux the question is set aside, for he goes in for healing, not for theodicy: his is the modest and agnostic task of curing as much suffering as he can. For the Christian, the suffering of the child must not be ignored or minimized; it can only be rejected or accepted. To reject it is to hate God (et qui oserait choisir la haine de Dieu?). But to accept it is to will that suffering. This is the doctrine of Tout ou rien, of all or nothing, and it raises the eyebrows of Paneloux's fellow priests. It derives, surely, from Kierkegaard, whom Camus had read even if Paneloux had not, and it is turned on its head by Leverkühn, for the devil's universe is the universe in which Paneloux hates God.

* * *

How would Victorian readers have responded to these novels? The question may seem so hypothetical as to be pointless, but I have an answer.

In 1850 Elizabeth Gaskell paid a visit to the Bishop of Manchester, and was shown his library:

> Over the door being an exquisitely painted picture of a dead child perhaps Baby's age,—deathly livid, and with the most woeful expression of pain on its little wan face,—it looked too deeply stamped to be lost even in Heaven.[29]

Like so many Victorian parents, she had herself lost a child: "my darling *darling* Willie, who now sleeps sounder still in the dull dreary chapel-yard at Warrington,"[30] and no doubt her grief sharpened the interest with which she looked at the Bishop's picture and listened to the story. The painting was

> so true to the life that an anatomist of that sort of thing on seeing it said "that child has lost its life by an accident which has produced intense pain"—and it was true,—it had been the child of the people with whom the artist lived, and had been *burnt*, had lingered 2 days in the greatest agony, poor darling—and

then died! I would not send my child to be educated by the man who could hang up such a picture as that for an object of contemplation.[31]

She did not know it, but she had taken a step from the nineteenth century into the twentieth: from a culture that represented death as painless, as being received by God, into one that sees it as departing reluctantly and painfully from the only life we actually know. Looking at the Bishop's picture was like reading of little Phil or Nepomuk, and she did not like it.

5

Sentimentality: For and Against

Simple and Honest Hearts

I f England grieved at the death of Princess Charlotte, it gave even more unrestrained signs of grief at the death of Little Nell. *The Old Curiosity Shop* was perhaps the most rapturously received of all Dickens's novels, and its reception meant a great deal to him:

> Some simple and honest hearts in the remote wilds of America, have written me letters on the loss of their children; so numbering my little book, or rather heroine, with their household gods, and so pouring out their trials and sources of comfort in them, before me as a friend, that I have been inexpressibly moved—and am, whenever I think of them—I do assure you[1]

In a speech in Boston a few months later he spoke again of the letters he had received "about that child"

> from the dwellers in log-houses among the morasses, and swamps, and densest forests, and deepest solitudes of the Far West. Many a sturdy hand, hard with the axe and spade, and browned by the summer's sun, has taken up the pen, and written to me a little history of domestic joy or sorrow, always coupled, I

am proud to say, with something of interest in that little tale, or some comfort or happiness derived from it, and my correspondent has always addressed me, not as a writer of books for sale, resident some four or five thousand miles away, but as a friend to whom he might freely impart the joys and sorrows of his own fireside.[2]

These letters from the backwoods of America have unfortunately not survived, and the eager rhetoric with which Dickens builds up the setting that gave birth to them suggests that they have lost nothing, and even gained something, in his retelling. We do have Dickens's reply to one, from a John Tomlin of Jackson, Tennessee, to whom he wrote: "to think that I have awakened a fellow-feeling and sympathy with the creatures of many thoughtful hours among the vast solitudes in which you dwell, is a source of the purest delight and pride to me."[3] Bret Harte's poem "Dickens in Camp"—a description of cowboys round a camp-fire listening to the story of little Nell, read among "the dim Sierras, far beyond, uplifting / Their minarets of snow"—can stand for these lost letters, as it is meant to do, with its hushed awe as "a silence seemed to fall" on the remote scene, and the listeners felt how "their cares dropped from them like the needles shaken / From out the gusty pine."[4] And we do of course have abundant documentation of the book's reception in England, both by the public and by Dickens's friends. Thomas Hood in *The Athenaeum*, writing before Nell died, was much taken by the

> picture of the Child, asleep in her little bed, surrounded, or rather mobbed, by ancient armour and arms, antique furniture, and relics sacred or profane, hideous or grotesque:—it is like an Allegory of the peace and innocence of Childhood.[5]

And Margaret Oliphant, who later grew critical of Dickens's pathos, spoke, in her first retrospective survey of his fiction, with what was surely the common voice of readers:

> Poor little Nell! who has ever been able to read the last chapter of her history with an even voice or a clear eye? Poor little Nell! how we defied augury, and clung to hope for her—how we refused to believe that Kit and the strange gentleman, when they alighted amid the snow at the cottage door, could not do some miracle for her recovery.[6]

The most interesting—and intense—responses, however, came from Dickens's friends. John Forster, Dickens's future biographer, wrote, after hearing Dickens read the concluding chapters:

> I could not say to you last night my dear Dickens how much this last Chapter has moved me. But I cannot resist the impulse of sending this hasty line to say it now. It is little to tell you that I think it is your literary masterpiece. The deeper feeling it has left with me goes beyond considerations of that kind. . . . I felt this death of dear little Nell as a kind of discipline of feeling and emotion which would do me lasting good, and which I would not thank you for as an ordinary enjoyment of literature.[7]

This patronizing attitude to mere literature will turn out to be of great importance as we trace the later fortunes of child pathos. One more voice, perhaps the most interesting of all, is that of Macready, the actor, who had become a close friend of Dickens's, and who wrote:

> I do not know how to write to you about the papers I read last night:—I almost wish to defer any further thought upon them—I have suffered so much in read-ing them I have a recurrence of painful sensations and depressing thought. This beautiful fiction comes too close upon what is miserably real to me to enable me to taste that portion of pleasure, which we can often extract (and you so beautifully do) from reasoning on the effect of pain, when we feel it through the sufferings of others.—You have crowned all that you have ever done in the power, the truth, the beauty and the deep moral of this exquisite picture—but my God—how cruel after all!—it is true that we must be taught in all things through endurance—and the best charity is clear and bright through every les-son you teach.—I have had thoughts and visions of angelic forms and pictures of the last sad truth of our being here, in constant succession through the night.—I cannot banish the images you have placed before us.—Go on, my dear, excellent friend—make our hearts less selfish.[8]

Many years later, after the publication of his *Life of Charles Dickens*, a Mrs. Jane Greene wrote to Forster, describing how her uncle

> was so enchanted with Little Nell that anyone might have supposed she was a *real living* child in whose sad fate he was deeply interested. One evening while silently reading . . . he suddenly sprung from his chair, flung the book violently

on the ground, and exclaimed "The Villain! The Rascal!! The bloodthirsty scoundrel!!!" His astonished brother thought he had *gone mad*, and enquired aghast of whom he was speaking? "Dickens," he roared, "he would *commit murder*! He killed my little Nell—He killed my sweet little child"![9]

Paul's death was as rapturously received as Nell's. The *Westminster Review* spoke for many when it joined the two together:

> The happiest and most perfect of Dickens' sketches is that of 'Little Nell' in the story of *Humphrey's Clock*. Her death is a tragedy of the true sort, that which softens, and yet strengthens and elevates; and we have its counterpart in 'Little Dombey', in the new work of this gifted author.[10]

Both this reviewer and Macready, we can notice, use moral terminology in praising the pathos ("strengthens and elevates," "make our hearts less selfish"), a point that will turn out to be important. And once again the most revealing response to the book comes in private letters, and none more so than that of Francis Jeffrey, the fierce critic of the *Edinburgh Review*, scourge of sentimentality, whom we have already encountered reproaching Wordsworth. Jeffrey's stern outside hid (or hardly hid) a very soft center:

> Oh, my dear Dickens! what a no.5 you have now given us! I have so cried and sobbed over it last night, and again this morning; and felt my heart purified by those tears, and blessed and loved you for making me shed them; and I never can bless and love you enough. Since that divine Nelly was found dead on her humble couch, beneath the snow and the ivy, there has been nothing like the actual dying of that sweet Paul. . . . Every trait so true, and so touching. . . . In reading of these delightful children, how deeply do we feel that "of such is the kingdom of Heaven;" and how ashamed of the contaminations which *our* manhood has received from the contact of earth.[11]

In fairness I ought now to mention that the editors of the Pilgrim edition of Dickens's letters, Madeline House and Graham Storey, are skeptical about assertions of national grief over Nell's death. "For the response of the public in general," they claim, "little evidence has been collected."[12] Since they then go on to cite a good deal of such evidence, their skepticism actually rests on the facts that much else in the novel was praised besides Nell, that some of the evidence does not actually specify the shedding of tears, and that some of the responses are better described as protest than sorrow.

The nature of these protests is worth looking at more closely. Why did Poe think that the death of Nell should have been avoided, even though it was "of the highest order of literary excellence"? And why did Mrs. Greene's uncle get so indignant? Both these readers seem to have responded to the pathos as Dickens wished, then to have added a demurrer on other grounds—ethical in Poe's case, and rather splendidly personal in Mr. Greene's.

It is often maintained nowadays that traditional realist fiction, in which the author decides exactly what happens in the story and tells it to us unambiguously, is authoritarian because it leaves insufficient freedom for the reader. This view, which has become almost a commonplace in some post-structuralist criticism, derives largely from Barthes, for whom what is taken for granted linguistically is the great enemy of freedom. In this view, open-ended narrative is seen as liberating and realism as false to the world which we, the readers, know and in which "profusion, as a result of mass information processes and political generalization, prevents us from finding figures to represent it." The way to free us from what Barthes goes so far as to call the totalitarian power of language is for the author to abdicate, renouncing his power to control a fictive world that only pretends to be a version of the world we inhabit. That is why the death of the author, in Barthes's famous assertion, will be the birth of the reader.[13]

As an example of the application of this view to the novel, we can turn to Thomas Docherty's *Reading (Absent) Character*, which claims that in realist theories of fiction "the reader's activity of creating character and meaning is being elided, and with that elision goes any notion of real interaction in dialogic form, or common production of meaning by the writer and reader working together." So in contrasting the authorial confidence underlying the realist tradition with the epistemological skepticism underlying post-modern fiction ("whereas Dickens has the confidence to begin a novel with a proper name . . . a new novelist such as Nathalie Sarraute . . . refuses to attribute a proper name to her pronominal presences"), Docherty claims that the latter has the advantage of radically involving the reader, not evading his activity, giving him or her "greater existential presence and authoritative or authentic life."[14]

As a theoretical issue, this is too complex to explore fully here: Docherty's position, representative of much post-structuralist thought, perhaps needs to confront more openly than it does the literal sense in which any novelist, realist or modernist, by choosing the words of his text, preempts any actual reader-involvement. Indeed, the reader's struggle to find coherence in a *nouveau roman* could be seen as a more complete enslavement by the writer than anything in the realist tradition, for the power which is exercised by such a writer is more arbitrary and thus more dictatorial. What I do wish to do, however, is to use Mrs. Greene's uncle as an example to test the theory in a crude but telling empirical way, for he both refutes and colorfully confirms it. He refutes it in the sense that Dickens's closure was far from reducing him to a passive role; indeed, it went with intense and vigorous involvement—as has always been the case with the traditional realist-sentimental novel: the readers of Donald Barthelme or Philippe Sollers do not intervene in the narration by writing to the author begging for a particular ending, as did the readers of Richardson's *Clarissa*—or of *The Old Curiosity Shop*—happily ignorant of the theory that their reader-involvement had been "preempted." ("I am inundated," Dickens wrote to his publishers, "with imploring letters recommending poor little Nell to mercy.—Six yesterday and four today!")[15] But at the same time Mrs. Greene's uncle did hold, inarticulately, a version of Barthes's position, in that he resented the outcome imposed by the author. If he happened to have read the facetious "Inquest on the late Master Paul Dombey," published in a comic periodical called *The Man in the Moon* in 1847, he would have come across the same opinion from "Miss Jane Dickybird," who declares that she "thought the author of the dear child's existence very cruel—a nasty, sad, naughty man, for killing such a sweet poppet—of course he killed it. Fie for shame upon him. How could he be so wicked?"[16] In order to say this they postulated, Mr. Greene unthinkingly, and Miss Dickybird's author mischievously, an extreme version of the autonomy of the text: for Dickens can only "murder" Nell if she has an existence independent of him. It would have been as logical for them to have exclaimed, "The hero! the splendid fellow!! He created my Nelly, whom cruel Fate has now snatched away." But so great was Mr. Greene's emotional identification with Nell that it led him to transfer the credit for Nell's existence to the autonomous text, and direct his anger for her death at the author. This anger, it is necessary to point out in reply to House and Storey, is a consequence of, not an alternative to, grief at Nell's death.

As for actual tears, we are brought back to the distinction between inward feelings and outward manifestations. The *Times*'s version of this distinction, when Princess Charlotte died, was quoted in chapter 1:

To assert that we, or that the whole British nation, is at this moment dissolved in tears . . . would be absurd, though many a tear will be shed for her fate by those who have never seen her; but if we say that deep regret, that calm sorrow, produced by pity for her sufferings . . . are universally prevalent, we say no more than every tongue confirms.[17]

There are plenty of tongues to confirm the sorrow for little Nell, entirely, of course, from those who had never seen her; and there is actually more evidence for tears being shed in her case than in Charlotte's and, because her death was not a public occasion, with less restraint. Francis Jeffrey was a sterner and more austere man than Prince Leopold, but he did not find it necessary to make "evident efforts to preserve calmness and fortitude." If he made any efforts, one suspects, it might have been to weep even more.

Sticky Overflowings

In 1895 Oscar Wilde made his famous remark, "One must have a heart of stone to read the death of Little Nell without laughing."[18] It shows, forty-odd years after the novel was published, that we have entered another world—perhaps not completely, since the remark was still intended to shock, but by the twentieth century even the shock has abated. The writing that had so moved the Victorians seemed, a hundred years later, to be (depending on the temperament of the critic) comic or repellent or deplorable. As our first representative of mid-twentieth century opinion I choose Aldous Huxley:

> It is evident that Dickens felt most poignantly for and with his Little Nell; and that he wept over her sufferings, piously revered her goodness, and exulted in her joys. He had an overflowing heart; but the trouble was that it overflowed with such curious and even repellent secretions. . . . The overflowing of his heart drowns his head and even dims his eyes; for, whenever he is in the melting mood, Dickens ceases to be able and probably ceases even to wish to see reality. His one and only desire on these occasions is just to overflow, nothing else. . . . Mentally drowned and blinded by the sticky overflowings of his heart, Dickens was incapable, when moved, of recreating, in terms of art, the reality which had moved him, was even, it would seem, unable to perceive that reality. . . . The history of Little Nell is distressing indeed, but not as Dickens presumably meant it to be distressing; it is distressing in its ineptitude and vulgar sentimentality.[19]

This opinion pervaded both the world of letters and the world of the academy for several generations. F. R. Leavis was no admirer of Huxley, but his comment on little Nell echoes him very closely:

> To suggest taking Little Nell seriously would be absurd: there's nothing there. She doesn't derive from any perception of the real; she's a contrived unreality, the function of which is to facilitate in the reader a gross and virtuous self-indulgence.[20]

And John Carey, no great admirer of Leavis, says of Nell's fidelity to her "disgraceful grandfather" that it "is as sanctimonious as it is improbable," and after quoting Nell's attempts to cheer her grandfather he comments: "this sickly scene carries the usual implications that Dickens is becoming besotted."[21]

An opinion common to three such diverse critics is clearly widespread, and there is no need to document further what can be regarded as the twentieth century orthodoxy on the death of Nell or Paul. It would equally be the orthodox view of the death of Rose Harrington or of Muriel, if kindly oblivion had not (completely in some cases, partly in others) removed these other children from view: the centrality of Dickens has kept him before everyone's eyes and, so, made him the prominent case of child pathos and the victim of the critical reaction. Now by what criterion are these scenes being judged and found so dreadfully wanting? I suggest that each critic has two criteria, one common and one peculiar to himself. All three of them appeal to reality. Huxley uses the term explicitly, Leavis invokes "the real," and Carey finds Nell's devotion "improbable." Reality is always a slippery concept for the philosophically unsophisticated (which is how all these critics present themselves), but some such appeal is inevitable if we are to claim, as part of our criticism of these scenes, that they distort. Reality is both indefensible and unavoidable as a criterion for the literary critic passing judgment.

When it comes to their other criterion, the critics differ sharply. Huxley shows distaste, Leavis shows moral disapproval, and Carey looks at the social implications. So we have Huxley wrinkling his nose at the "curious and repellent secretions," and with the confidence of a novelist whose own fictional child, when dying, "began to scream—cry after shrill cry, repeated with an almost clockwork regularity," he looks down on Dickens as inept and vulgar.[22]

Leavis in contrast shakes an admonitory finger at "gross and virtuous self-indulgence." We need not take seriously his assertion that it would be absurd to take Nell seriously, for he takes her very seriously; hence his stern disapproval. He could be setting out to refute Macready's evident belief that the story of Nell will "make our hearts less selfish," or the strikingly moral terms in which Forster defends it:

> I am not acquainted with any story in the language more adapted to strengthen in the heart what most needs help and encouragement, to sustain kindly and innocent impulses, to awaken everywhere the sleeping germs of good.[23]

This quotation from the *Life* reaffirms the view Forster had already expressed to Dickens in his letter, that the power of the death of Little Nell gives us something more elevated than "an ordinary experience of literature"; and only after dwelling further on the "benevolent" effect of the episode does he turn to "its effect as a mere piece of art."

Leavis's view of literature is, in an important sense, profoundly unhistorical. Relying on his own response, not simply as a twentieth century reader but as a representative reader at any time, he would consider it condescending to make allowance for the fact that Macready and Forster lived in a different age and were familiar with different literary conventions. The exact opposite to this position is represented by Samuel Pickering and Andrew Sanders. The former declares his approach to be "in flagrante delicto historical," and his method is to compare the work of Dickens with that of now unread tracts by forgotten figures (Andrew Reed, John Cunningham, Leigh Richmond, Hannah More) in order to show "that the great tradition of the early nineteenth century English novel is the moral tradition." Both he and Sanders ask us to put aside our own response and replace it, as far as we can, by that of contemporaries. Sanders finds the "easy jests" of modern critics (including Leavis) "grossly unfair" because they demonstrate "a disturbing failure both to sympathize with the nature and intent of Dickens' art and to grasp the tradition in which he is working." Dickens "draws from and adapts a popular literary norm": for Pickering and, less crudely, for Sanders, what matters is that he draws from it; for the Leavisite, what matters is that he adapts it—so much so, that Leavis sees no need to mention the popular norm, since all he is interested in is the way a masterpiece differs from it.[24]

Carey's more sociological analysis relates Nell and her grandfather to Victorian family structure:

In an age without Social Security, when the elderly depended upon the
strength of the family bond for their survival, Nell's unnatural concern about
her grandfather's welfare would particularly endear her to the adult world. For
parents with every intention of becoming a burden to their children, she is the
ideal heroine.[25]

Carey handles ideology with a light touch, but this is an ideological point
all the same. As a contrast with the twentieth century, from within which
we read, it seems to me brilliant, but it will not serve as a contrast with what
preceded. No doubt Victorian parents did have every intention of becoming a burden to their children, but so did those of the eighteenth and the
seventeenth centuries, to go back no further: why are there no little Nells
then? Carey's explanation tells us, perhaps, why Victorians (or at any rate
elderly Victorians) were so besotted with little Nell, but cannot tell us why
such a figure arose then and not earlier.

Sentimentality

I have already introduced the term *sentimentality*, and can no longer
postpone a discussion of it, since that is what is in question here. To begin
with a definition, we cannot do better than quote Jeffrey's reference to the
"gentle sobs and delightful tears" that the last number of *Dombey and Son*
had cost him, to which we can add the "delighted tears" with which
Charles Kingsley's mother read *Uncle Tom's Cabin*.[26] The usual definitions of
sentimentality speak of displaying—or demanding—more emotion than
the situation warrants, but this seems to me misleading. It applies better to
melodrama, which obviously attempts to arouse unwarranted emotion, and
in real life the person who displays excessive emotion is not the sentimentalist but the neurotic. Necessarily, if we are to identify sentimentality
accurately, we must consider the nature of the emotion aroused: a sadness
that has lost all unpleasantness and become a warm glow. If we unpack the
phrasing of Jeffrey and Kingsley, it will yield every important element in
sentimentality: its strong association with the pathetic, the frequent prominence of women and children as subject matter (for they weep more—or
are supposed to), the avoidance of all physically repulsive details (which
would render the sobs and tears less delightful), and even the moral argument: that, on the one hand, sentimentality can be seen as beneficial in its
effects because it sensitizes us to the sufferings of others and arouses feel-

ings of sympathy and compassion but that, on the other hand, it can be seen as morally bad because it allows us to indulge in sorrow as a luxury, enjoying an experience that ought to distress us. This argument has raged since sentimentality began.

A brief historical survey will be useful here. Whether sentimentality has always existed is too large and fascinating a question to engage us now; what we know is that it dates, as a conscious movement, from the later eighteenth century. It was practiced, and defended, by Sterne, Goldsmith, and Cowper (as well as Greuze and Reynolds), found its philosophic basis in Shaftesbury and Adam Smith, was attacked by Johnson, and was ridiculed by Jane Austen. A contributor to the *London Magazine* in 1776 states the case in favor as follows:

> The pleasure which arises from legends of sorrow owes its origin to the certain knowledge, that our hearts are not callous to the finer feelings, but that we have some generous joys, and generous cares beyond ourselves.[27]

We need not pay much attention to the difference between the terms "sensibility," which this writer uses, and "sentimentality," since in the eighteenth century they were, in this context, virtually interchangeable, and either could be used to designate the Man of Feeling, that central figure in the sentimental movement, who is easily moved to tears by the sufferings of others, even, in the novel of that name by Henry Mackenzie, by the sufferings of the old dog Trusty:

> I called to him; he wagged his tail, but did not stir: I called again; he lay down; I whistled, and cried Trusty; he gave a short howl, and died!—I could have lain down and died too; but God gave me strength to live for my children.[28]

—a reminder of continuity, this: Victorian as it sounds, it was written in 1771.

The case in favor of the moral benefit of such a state of feeling can be found in Adam Smith, whose *Theory of Moral Sentiments* defends a morality based not on rationality but on emotion:

> How are the unfortunate relieved when they have found out a person to whom they can communicate the cause of their sorrow? Upon this sympathy they seem to disburthen themselves of a part of their distress: he is not improperly

said to share it with them. He not only feels a sorrow of the same kind with that which they feel, but, as if he had derived a part of it to himself, what he feels seems to alleviate the weight of what they feel. . . . Hence it is that to feel much for others and little for ourselves, that to restrain our selfish, and to indulge our benevolent affections, constitutes the perfection of human nature.[29]

Here is the argument for valuing highly an "indulgence in soothing emotions that turns sorrow into something like pleasure." The case against is made by Johnson, for whom man is led to do good by reason not by sentiment, since human nature is untrustworthy: "If man is by nature prompted to act virtuously and rightly, all the divine precepts of the Gospel . . . had been needless." Johnson's belief in sin led far more strongly to the distrust of feeling than to the distrust of reason. The Man of Feeling is consequently given short shrift:

Sir, it is an affectation to pretend to feel the distress of others, as much as they do themselves. It is equally so, as if one should pretend to feel as much pain while a friend's leg is cutting off, as he does.[30]

It could even be claimed that the inadequacy of sentiment as a basis for morality is adumbrated by Mackenzie himself in the last clause of the quotation above: lying down and dying (or pretending to die, for "could have" means of course "felt inclined to," and does not refer to action) would prevent any attempt to remedy the situation. Indulging in sentiment can therefore be seen as a way of avoiding responsibility, giving oneself the "delight" of tears, instead of acting. And Sterne himself, the greatest of the sentimentalists, offers the same possibility of ambivalence, since his man of feeling, on his sentimental journey through France and Italy, is constantly on the edge of being made a figure of fun. Every sentimental moment in the book is followed or preceded by an ironic undercutting that never completely destroys the reader's sympathy with Yorick but that prevents full identification with him, and certainly prevents any unqualified moral approval.

In sentimentality, grief is so represented that its intensity is mollified and its effect pleasing. If the less comforting elements of an experience are omitted, we can naturally ask if they are in some way implied, even obliquely present, in the writing. Asking this about Florence Dombey, who is clearly sentimentalized, I will look at the scene in chapter 18 in which she tries to comfort her father after Paul's death and is sternly rejected. We are continually assured, in this scene, of the glowing love within her breast; sent back to her room she embraces the dog, Diogenes, and sobs out, "Oh, Di! Oh, dear Di! Love me for his sake!" Presumably she means for Paul's sake, since that is what her father will not do; but it would fit equally well to read it as "love me for Papa's sake, since he will not love me himself." The moral situation here is very plain: Florence loves unconditionally and will not accept, or even see, that her father does not deserve her love—if she accepted that, the love would not be unconditional. But Dickens of course knows that he does not deserve it and tells us so insistently. This means that there is a gap between Florence's view of Mr. Dombey and the author's, and he keeps singing her praises for it. She is praised, in short, for her imperceptiveness.

The figure of the holy fool is not sentimental, because it embodies a paradox: to be foolish in this world can be wisdom by God's standard. But Florence is not a holy fool, because we are not meant to laugh at her or find her ridiculous. Although she fails to see what is in front of her eyes, she receives only credit for that. This is clear if we compare her to the two figures who act as foils to her selfless love, Susan and Toots. Susan Nipper is much more clear-sighted, and knows that Mr. Dombey does not deserve Florence's love—and tells him so. The scene (chapter 44) could easily be made pathetic (for it does cost Susan her place), but it is in fact comic ("I may not be a Peacock; but I have my eyes"), and so there is no danger of Susan displacing Florence as the heroine. Toots, on the other hand, is the holy fool, constantly ridiculous and selflessly devoted. His worship of Florence is expressed in a parody of romantic love: "Miss Dombey, I really am in that state of adoration of you that I don't know what to do with myself. . . . If it wasn't at the corner of the Square at present, I should go down on my knees" (chapter 41). But this devotion is quite compatible with his marrying Susan, as a kind of demonstration that, though it is a sublimation of sexual feeling, the sexual element is not to be taken seriously. Susan and Toots represent two ways of avoiding sentimentality, and Florence is caught between them.

The sentimentalist, we can say, is blinded by his tears, so that he can share Florence's imperceptiveness, even when he knows the truth. If we take the term "blinded" literally, we shall then be using the mimetic criterion invoked by all three of our twentieth century critics, that sentimentality misrepresents reality: a child's death, even when it is not of meningitis, is not so peaceful or so full of uncomplicated uplift as are the deaths of Paul, Eva, Rose, and the rest. But if we take "blinded" more figuratively, we will attack sentimentality by declaring that the experience is distasteful (sticky overflowings) or deplorable (self-indulgence).

Sentimentality can be a quality both of literary and of actual experiences. To show this, I revert to the death of the Tait daughters, discussed in chapter 1, and I will begin with a linguistic point. That sentimental writing will be heavily adjectival is only to be expected, and of all the sentimentalizing adjectives dear to the Victorians—*sweet, soft, delightful, darling,* etc.—the most effective will be those that do not name warm feeling directly but attach it to what passes for description, and the prime candidate here is *little*. It is a word that has cropped up often enough in our quotations. Paul is "little Dombey" at school, he is Dr Blimber's "little friend" (of course that is ironic, but only at Dr Blimber's expense: the Doctor has through his condescension hit on the right word), and when discussed by Mrs. Pipchin and the apothecary, he is (repeatedly) "the little fellow." In the case of little Eva and little Nell, the adjective has been incorporated into the child's name. But I have come across nothing quite as concentrated as Mrs. Tait's account of the aftermath of Chatty's death, which contains "a little sweet talk" with her daughters, the "little funeral" is to be on Monday, the dead child is "the little one," the children gather flowers from "their own little gardens," a friend sends flowers as "her little offering of love," the placing of the wreath on "little Susan's" head is a "little scene," in the nursery "one little bed" was gone, she takes a last look at the "little form," and so on—twelve usages in just under three pages.[31] Diminutive size is associated with harmlessness, with helplessness, and so with pathos, and there is not a single usage whose connotations are of size only.

Sentimentality, then, minimizes the ugliness of death in order to make sadness pleasing. Mrs. Tait does not completely ignore the unpleasantness (Susan's "little body was quite stiff, the arms and legs twitching, the eyes open, but no sight for anything more in this world"), but she devotes far more space to Catty's more peaceful death. May also suffered a great deal, and at one time they could hardly hold her in bed. Yet more prominence is given to the peacefulness that follows and to the ultimate peaceful departure: "then her summons came, and the brightness of those beautiful eyes closed for ever on this world of sin and sorrow, and opened in Heaven."[32]

But there is of course one crucial and obvious difference between sentimentality in literary representation and in the representation of actual grief: in the first case it could be the entire experience, but not in the second. For the reader of a novel, there is no substratum of actual grief that is being rendered more gentle and delightful: his response is equal to his reading of the text. It would be an affront to Mrs. Tait's grief, however, to reduce it to the sentimentalizing undoubtedly present in the writing: it would amount to saying that she had no experience outside the text, not as a philosophical point but as a kind of insult. What we can say is that she is assimilating it to the less painful emotion that might be offered by a novelist. The experience of the novel reader is sentimental; that of Mrs. Tait is sentimentalized.

But, like most distinctions between fact and fiction, this is less clear-cut than it at first appears. What are we to make of Macready, who reacted to Nell much as Jeffrey reacted to Paul but who added, "this beautiful fiction comes too close upon what is miserably real to me to enable me to taste [the] portion of pleasure?"[33] He had recently lost his own daughter: hence the "recurrence of painful sensations." Macready's experience in reading *The Old Curiosity Shop* can therefore be seen not only as the arousing of vicarious grief but also as a modification of real grief: hence his reluctance to read the episode—though it clearly did not enter his head that he could put it down unread. Jeffrey too, though not recently, had lost the only child of his first marriage. And what we know to be the case with them could in some sense be true of any reader: if he (or she) had not lost a child, her friends or relatives might have, and she could very probably in the nineteenth century (though improbably today) have watched a child die. Contrariwise, the Catherine Tait who watched her children die had certainly read sermons, probably read novels, and had thought about the meaning of death, so that her grief was culturally formed. Real and vicarious grief do not exist independently of each other.

Not many Victorians were able to describe the death of their child without some touch of sentimentality; it may, indeed, be a need that parents will feel in any age. But there are different degrees, and different ways, of yielding to or resisting it, and for a contrast I turn (perhaps surprisingly) to Tennyson. The first child of Alfred and Emily Tennyson was still-born on Easter Sunday 1851; "I would not send the notice of my misfortune to the *Times*," Tennyson wrote, "and I have had to write some sixty letters." (We can wonder if the letters were the burdensome consequence of his refusal to publish his grief, or if the refusal to publish was obscurely motivated by the need to write to all his friends about it). The longest account that has survived speaks of his grief with something like surprise:

I have suffered more than ever I thought I could have done for a child still born:
I fancy I should not have cared so much if he had been a seven months spin-
dling, but he was the grandest looking child I had ever seen. Pardon my saying
this. I do not speak only as a father but as an Artist—if you do not despise the
word from German associations. I mean as a man who has eyes and can judge
from seeing. I refused to see the little body at first, fearing to find some pallid
abortion which would have haunted me all my life—but he looked (if it be not
absurd to call a newborn babe so) even majestic in his mysterious silence after
all the turmoil of the night before.[34]

He drops at times into the usual sentimental vocabulary ("dear little nameless one"), but in a passage like this there is a kind of double presence—
the grieving father, and the detached, curious observer, surprised at what
he sees and even at his own feelings, able to slip in a touch of self-congrat-
ulation (he knows what an artist—a real one—needs to notice), able to
analyse his own feelings. Perhaps this is more self-centered than Mrs. Tait's
conventional vocabulary, but it is also more independent, and it enables
Tennyson to be very direct about the cause of death: "the child got suffo-
cated in being born"—he wrote a variant of this sentence several times.
There is even a sprightliness about the prose: "The whole night before he
was born he was vigorously alive, but in being born he died." All this, without undermining the emotion, diverts the language from the commonplace,
and the result is perhaps more, not less, moving. The contrast is very striking with the gushing poem he wrote about the event ("Little bosom not yet
cold"), which uses "little" three times in its thirteen lines and which he had
the sense not to publish. Who would expect Tennyson of all people—the
consummate poetic artist who hated writing letters—to be more skilled,
less conventional, in letters than in poetry?

Woman Power: Rehabilitating Sentimentality

The whirligig of taste has performed many somersaults, but none more
drastic than that concerning the sentimental child death. Sentimentality,
which entered literature so self-consciously in the later eighteenth century,
rode high in mid-Victorian times but by the twentieth century had disappeared from high culture, though it remained very much alive in popular culture—and the savagery with which Huxley and Leavis attack it may be partly
directed at the "romantic" novels and tear-jerking films of their own day.
Only in the last decade has there been a serious attempt to rehabilitate it.

The new case for sentimentality is feminist: it claims that the sentimental tradition is important because it is a way of empowering women.
This view belongs primarily to American academic discourse, the tradition
that it rehabilitates is above all that of the American sentimental novel, and
the novel it concentrates on is, of course, *Uncle Tom's Cabin*. Much of the
basis for this new view is set forth by Ann Douglas in *The Feminization of
American Culture*, which maintains that sentimentality can be seen as "a
strategy by which many women and ministers espoused at least in theory
to (*sic*) so-called passive virtues, admirable in themselves, and sorely
needed in American life."[35] The most vigorous and influential proponent in
literary studies is Jane Tompkins, whose book *Sensational Designs* defends
Harriet Beecher Stowe, along with other popular women novelists of the
time, against "the male-dominated scholarly tradition that controls both the
canon of American literature . . . and the critical perspective that interprets
the canon for society." This tradition has "taught generations of students to
equate popularity with debasement, emotionality with ineffectiveness,
religiosity with fakery, domesticity with triviality, and all of these, implic-
itly, with womanly inferiority." In contrast to this, Tompkins argues that
"the work of the sentimental writers is complex and significant in ways
other than those that characterize the established masterpieces." To do this,
she quite explicitly shifts her literary criteria, seeing literary texts "not as
works of art embodying enduring themes in complex forms, but as
attempts to redefine the social order." Seeing them in this way enables us
to attach these works to "a cultural myth which invests the suffering and
death of an innocent victim with just the kind of power that critics deny to
Stowe's novel: the power to work in, and change, the world." Stowe writes
out of a conviction that "historical change takes place only through religious conversion, which is a theory of power as old as Christianity itself."
The sentimental novel should then be seen as an agent of cultural change
which "represents the interests of middle-class women."[36] This approach
will enable the reader, if he lays aside his "modernist" prejudices, his bias
against "melodrama," "pathos" and "sunday school fiction," to appreciate
the sentimental novel on its own terms:

> The vocabulary of clasping hands and falling tears is one which we associate
> with emotional exhibitionism, with the overacting that kills off true feeling
> through exaggeration. But the tears and gestures of Stowe's characters are not
> in excess of what they feel; if anything they fall short of expressing the experi-
> ences they point to—salvation, communion, reconciliation.[37]

The work of Ann Douglas, which lies behind this, is both more ambitious and more complex. Its argument that American mass culture in the twentieth century is partly a result of an extensive process of feminization in the nineteenth would lead us far from the present topic, and I will look only at her defense of sentimentalism as a valuable agent of cultural change, which is more qualified than Tompkins's. Douglas considers sentimentalism a way of protesting against "a power to which one has already in part capitulated. . . . It always borders on dishonesty, but it is a dishonesty for which there is no known substitute in a capitalist country." And so she points out that "Little Eva's beautiful death, which Stowe presents as part of a protest against slavery, in no way hinders the working of that system"; and she is critical too of the language of sentimentality, which she describes as "rancid," and contrasts with that of Romanticism, which though it may sometimes sound grandiose to our ears, has a relationship to its age that is fundamentally healthy. But she too treats sentimentalism as an aspect of feminization and an agent of cultural change.[38]

There is now quite a body of criticism that derives from and develops this position, treating sentimentalism in general, and *Uncle Tom's Cabin* in particular, as an intervention in American culture that sets out to resist its predominantly masculine and aggressive ethic. Gillian Brown claims that "abolishing slavery means, in Stowe's politics of the kitchen, erasing the sign and reminder of the precariousness of the feminine sphere."[39] Jean Fagan Yellin claims that Stowe's female exemplar, "powerless on earth, powerful in heaven, . . . is less an advocate of mundane emancipation than a model of heavenly salvation. As her conversion of Topsy demonstrates, she is a spiritual, not a political liberator."[40] And Elizabeth Ammons, too, defends the novel as a cultural intervention to which feminine values are central. Emphasizing the Christ-like qualities of both Eva and Tom, she treats this as part of the feminization of Christianity: since Tom's qualities are all feminine, she describes him as "the ultimate heroine of *Uncle Tom's Cabin*." Stowe thus offers "the maternal Christ, the divine motherly love and light" as the means to "lead America out of the night of slavery."[41]

The extension of this agenda from women's fiction to women's poetry is best represented by *The Contours of Masculine Desire*, by Marlon Ross, a learned and trenchant attempt to undermine the male canon of Romanticism and cause us to change drastically our notion of literary history. Corresponding to the rehabilitation of *Uncle Tom's Cabin*, Ross argues for serious consideration of a neglected phenomenon of the early nineteenth century, the rise of the "female affectional poets":

> Reclaiming these first women poets does not simply mean that we should
> attach them to the house of romantic poetry for the sake of liberal inclusive-
> ness. . . . It means more fundamentally that we must re-examine romanticism
> itself, and enriched with the knowledge garnered from these recovered sources,
> that we must rewrite their history and in so doing rewrite our own.

The female poet closest to the concerns of this book is Felicia Hemans,
whose celebration of the affections is explicitly linked by Ross to the feminine, and the modern refusal to take her poetry seriously is seen as "a way
of fighting off the feminization of literature which is so integral and influential an aspect of the literary process since the mid-eighteenth century. By
reclaiming Hemans' affectional poetics, then, we are representatively also
reclaiming the power of the 'feminine' within literature and within ourselves."[42] At this point, Ross explicitly claims alliance with the agenda of
Sensational Designs.

This campaign has not, so far, done much for the reputation of Hemans,
but it has at least had the effect of bringing *Uncle Tom's Cabin* back into print
and onto the syllabus of courses in American Literature. If the literary
canon is now determined not by the judgment of the common reader with
whom the critic rejoices to concur, as Johnson believed, but, as American
professors universally believe, by the academic profession, then Harriet
Beecher Stowe has rejoined the canon. How permanent this rehabilitation
will be depends on whether the whirligig can ever be made to keep still.

I Take My Stand

That then is the story of readers' responses to the sentimental child
death, which I have told as objectively as I can; now in conclusion it is time
to abandon neutrality and take a stand.

When we put next to each other the Victorian and the modern response
to child pathos, each completely confident of its rightness and passing dia-
metrically opposed judgments, what do we see? Is one of these groups simply mistaken? Are there universal criteria by which their judgments can be
compared and one of them preferred? Or are we seeing judgment passed
by one age upon another, to be followed no doubt by the judgment of a
future age on the later one? (If the feminists I have cited are representative
of the future, this process has already begun.) This example raises, more
neatly and in more extreme form than any other example I know, the ques-

tion of value judgments in literature, or, as it is now generally referred to, the question of the canon.

To this question must be added a meta-question: what are we doing when we ask this? Are we ourselves performing a disinterested historical inquiry, or will our answer be in its turn determined by our own position? Not many literary scholars nowadays believe in disinterested, value-free inquiry, but there has been a marked shift in the nature of the disbelief. For Leavis, for the New Critics, and in slightly different form for Carey, there is no escaping the pursuit of judgment; literary criticism that does not commit itself to the primacy of quality—merely descriptive criticism—must remain superficial and even mechanical. But to the new historicists, the feminists, and other schools that practice the hermeneutics of suspicion, the inescapable commitment is not aesthetic but ideological. Deconstructing traditional artistic value judgments in order to discover their underlying political motivation, today's radicals see the claim to artistic autonomy, and the independence of artistic judgment from politics, as itself ideologically determined, as one of the strategies of power. This is very clear in Tompkins, who sets the two conceptions of literary judgment against each other with perfect clarity:

> In modernist thinking, literature is by definition a form of discourse that has no designs on the world. It does not attempt to change things, but merely to represent them, and it does so in a specifically literary language whose claim to value lies in its uniqueness. . . . I will ask the reader to set aside some familiar categories for evaluating fiction—stylistic intricacy, psychological subtlety, epistemological complexity—and to see the sentimental novel not as an artifice of eternity answerable to certain formal criteria and to certain psychological and philosophical concerns, but as a political enterprise.[43]

It is even possible to find in Dickens himself some support for the view of a literary text as the exercise of power: after a private reading of *The Chimes* in 1844 (the first beginnings of what eventually grew into the famous public readings), he wrote to his wife, "If you had seen Macready last night, undisguisedly sobbing and crying on the sofa as I read, you would have felt, as I did, what a thing it is to have power."[44] This statement assumes a conception of the artist as performer, controlling the responses of the audience—the same conception as Thackeray assumed when he said of the death of Paul, in a mixture of envy and admiration, "There's no writing

against such power as this—one has no chance!"[45] This is very different
from the claim, admitted even by Huxley—indeed, used as part of his
indictment—that Dickens himself felt the sufferings of Nell and exulted in
her joys. It is the difference between an expression theory of literature—
which believes that the author identifies with his own creations, and that
the emotions he strives to express are his own—and a rhetorical theory,
which concentrates on the emotions of the reader, and can even lead to the
idea of the artist as showman, proud of his total control over audience
response. There is abundant evidence for both in Dickens, and it is striking that he expresses the latter in terms of power—though of course he sees
it as the empowering of himself as an individual, not (as would a Fou-
cauldian analysis) as the representative of a group.

Ross, who shares Tompkins's diagnosis that the dismissal of sentimentality is a strategy of masculine power, argues for a less confrontational conclusion:

> My argument is not so much for a new canon of literature as for a more radical,
> non-canonical approach to how we think about literature and its history. . . .
> Recognizing that writing history is always a process of partly arbitrary selection,
> I do not desire simply to set up yet another canon, consisting of these specific
> women writers on whom I have chosen to focus in this study.[46]

To rewrite history is always exhilarating; and there is a certain grudging
tameness about the traditionalist argument that insists that a fair-sized baby
is being thrown out with the patriarchal bath water. But I now have to play
that grudging role, since I believe that the radicalism represented by
Tompkins and Ross, though it may justify some interrogation, and possible
modification, of the previously established canon, does not require its abandonment: ideological factors do influence aesthetic judgments, and it is
important to see how this happens, but that does not mean that art should
be seen as nothing more than a disguise for ideology.

It is necessary first of all to remind ourselves of a point glossed over by
many of the new radical critics, the long existence of writing with the
explicit purpose of changing the world, that is, of didactic writing. Many of
the recent critical theories that see literature as the agent of cultural intervention seem to me to be asking for a return to didacticism and to be subject to the many criticisms that modern criticism has brought against it.

The abandonment of didacticism is, I believe, the most important single change in the long history of criticism. It is, on the one hand, virtually

impossible to find before the nineteenth century a statement of the nature and purpose of literature that does not include the claim that it promotes virtue or improves the world. In what Tompkins calls "modernist" thinking about literature (which clearly includes a good deal of Romantic and realist thinking as well) it is, on the other hand, difficult to find statements that do. Of course the presence of didactic claims does not mean that the value of the work lies in its didactic function, any more than the fact that so much art, music, and literature was for centuries in the service of the church means that it can only be judged by Christian standards. This is a familiar critical problem, perhaps the most familiar problem of literary criticism, and it does not disappear when we turn to women's writing.

There are two central objections to didactic views of literature, both familiar and both, in my view, irrefutable. The pragmatic objection derives from the fact that the purpose of didactic writing lies outside itself: it aims to influence our moral attitudes and even our behavior, to win converts for Christ, to cause us to treat our friends with more consideration, to vote socialist (or conservative), and so on. The site of its success or failure is not confined to the textual experience and may even be independent of it. However enthusiastic our praise of a work's intentions, it will not have succeeded in carrying them out unless it has, in some degree, changed the world. *Uncle Tom's Cabin* is interesting here, because the case that it succeeded in doing this is probably stronger than with any other novel ever written. Tompkins's claim that critics have denied to the novel "the power to work in and change the world" is quite misleading: criticism has disputed the artistic value of the novel, but conservative and liberal critics alike have agreed about its practical effect. Lincoln's famous compliment to Stowe, as the little lady who started this big war, sounds like evidence that her book succeeded, if not in its direct purpose (for it was not the intention of this pacific writer to start a war), at least in a cognate one. But even this example is not exactly hard evidence, and it is difficult, if not impossible, to demonstrate that the novel did speed up abolition, or that Dickens did speed up any actual social reforms (the evidence, in that instance, points rather against the claim). These may seem—indeed are— crude criteria, but unless we locate the site of didactic impact *outside* the textual experience, we cannot claim that a work is promoting virtue, converting to Christ, or helping to emancipate the slaves.

Ideological readings of literature are not of course to be equated with didactic readings, since they do not look at the stated moral purpose of the work but at how the work illustrates the intermeshing of art and power, how by carrying out an apparently aesthetic purpose, art actually serves the interests of a dominant group. But this is still to locate the ultimate function outside the work; and I am often struck by how often, in both Marxist and feminist critics, the oblique ideological function attributed to a work merges into, or is even replaced by, a direct didactic one—as is the case in *Sensational Designs*.

The second objection is that didactic, along with ideological, theories are not specific to literature. If *Uncle Tom's Cabin* is to be seen "as a political enterprise," then we need to ask how it differs from those forms of writing that aim directly at moral or political improvement: insofar as literature promotes virtue, it does not differ from sermons; insofar as it is an agent of reform, it does not differ from political speeches or pamphlets. If aesthetic effect were completely reducible to didactic or ideological function, we would be left with no criteria for distinguishing poems from pamphlets. The expansion of interest that now causes us to look at Spenser's *Short View of Ireland* as well as *The Faerie Queene*, at Poor Law Reports and Queen Victoria's letters as well as Dickens's novels, is wholly to be welcomed (and this book is a modest contribution to it); but that should lead us to look not only at functional parallels but also at differences. When we grant that a poem or a novel may serve an ideological function, we must still go on to ask how it differs from those forms of writing with nothing but that function, and these differences will not be merely formal or superficial (composed of lines that rhyme or of events that are fictitious). One of the great achievements of literary criticism (both modernist and Romantic) has been to explore how carefully the masterpieces conceal and complicate their ideology, how richly they dissolve it into a more complex experience. There is no need to make a simple choice, between denying all ideological function to literature and admitting no other function.

The usual reply to this is that ideological criticism (the hermeneutics of suspicion) must operate not, or not only, on the level of individual judgment but in the construction of criteria for judging. If there are aesthetic criteria for preferring James and Dickens to Stowe and Sewell (and a fortiori to the pamphleteers), these very criteria, when examined, will be seen to serve an ideological purpose. The trouble with this reply is that it has to grow evasive on what aesthetic principles serve what function. If realism is a way of asserting bourgeois culture, so is fantasy. If complexity and subtlety, even indirection, can be seen as the ideals of conservative criticism, so too can immediacy and raw power. The aesthetic standards of bourgeois,

patriarchal, or white literary criticism are so varied, and so full of contradic-
tions, that it is almost impossible to set up an alternative set of criteria for
proletarian, feminist, or black literature. Tompkins's rejection of stylistic
intricacy, psychological subtlety, and epistemological complexity could easily be seen as a conservative strategy, offering to readers a directness of
experience that will reinforce their stereotypes and discourage any questioning of the established world view. Indeed, the death of Little Eva is a
very questionable example of enacting a philosophy of reform and a radical
cultural intervention: to radical movements, dying is a form of defeat; only
to an otherworldly ideology can it be seen as victory.[47]

Next, it is necessary to question the version of cultural history put forward by the critics we are discussing. Does sentimentality belong to the
female sphere? Behind Hemans lies Wordsworth, behind Stowe lies Dickens. Hemans was a passionate disciple of Wordsworth ("During the last
four years of her life she never, except when prevented by illness, passed a
single day without reading something of Wordsworth's"[48] and Wordsworth's
claim to be considered a poet of the affections was universally admitted.
Ross's attempt to place Hemans in a specifically female tradition therefore
involves an ingenious attempt to "contradict" the view of her as a female
Wordsworth, but most of what she sees as a contrast looks, to the unpreju-
diced eye, like similarity.[49] Tompkins's book, dealing only with the American experience, ignores the history of sentimentality and the enormous
importance of Dickens in Victorian culture and does not, therefore, confront the question of the male sentimentalist at all. Virtually all the testi-
monies to the emotional impact of Nell and Paul quoted earlier in this
chapter came from men, and in the case of Mrs. Greene's uncle the sentimental response seems to belong more to the man than to the woman.
Within the novels there is very little to identify the pathos as predominantly feminine. "Anyone familiar with Victorian life," writes Philip
Collins, "can remember many anecdotes of the manly tear being shed";[50]
and indeed the changing meanings of "manly" show the changing fortunes
of sentimentality. Nowadays its usual opposite is *womanly* or *effeminate*, and
one of its main characteristics is emotional control; but early Victorian man-
liness was contrasted quite as much with childishness or beastliness, and
even when contrasted with effeminacy did not necessarily exclude weeping, so that "manly tear" was not then the oxymoron it has since become.
It is not even clear that *Uncle Tom's Cabin* itself should be placed all that
firmly in a feminine tradition. Not only is Tom a man, but the main exam-

ple of resistance to sentimentality is Eva's mother Marie. Furthermore, she uses explicitly feminine attitudes and clichés to justify her indifference, telling St. Clare that he speaks like a man and does not understand a mother's feelings—in every way exploiting her identity as part of a misunderstood woman's world.

Of course there is a reply, but as usual it raises a problem as serious as the one it resolves. That is to distinguish the female from the feminine and to claim that feminization is not gender specific. Thus Elizabeth Ammons claims that "Eva's father is admirable in direct proportion to the extent of his womanishness (his inclination to follow the dictates of his heart rather than his head)" and that Marie, on the contrary, exhibits a kind of masculine selfishness.[51] I have already quoted, as an extreme example of this position, Ammons's claim that Tom is the ultimate heroine of the novel.

The issue raised here is central to feminist criticism and has tended to divide the movement. Is feminism to identify itself in contradistinction to men or to patriarchy? Is it to tell the story of women—all women—or the story of radical challenges to masculine values? In the first case, it will concentrate on what women actually said and did, collecting its material by using the purely mechanical criterion of the sex of the writer; in the second, it will look for subversions of the dominant ideology, whomever they come from, and will be comparatively uninterested in the writings of conservative women. Charlotte M. Yonge and Queen Victoria are important figures for the first, John Stuart Mill and Henrik Ibsen for the second.

Both these tendencies are of great value, and neither can simply be rejected. But we can say that the dichotomy should not be used for the purposes of slippery argument, gliding from one to the other when the going gets awkward; also that the first can never be completely eliminated, for if "femininity" is as common among men as among women then the term itself has become misleading, and we can fall back on perfectly adequate vocabulary such as the contrast between reason and feeling, toughness and sensitivity. To call Tom the heroine of *Uncle Tom's Cabin* is a striking paradox, but we need to preserve our awareness that it is a paradox. Sentimentality cannot be equated with femininity unless there really is some correlation with gender.

An Experiment in Criticism

So is evaluation possible, desirable, inevitable—or even impossible but desirable? The question is about evaluation of literary quality, distinct from the value of the doctrinal or political position of a work. Though literary judgments may be governed more than we used to admit by ideological considerations, I refuse, for the reasons given, to translate them into a mere screen or rationalization for ideology.

I begin by observing that evaluation is inescapable for practical purposes. The British Library and the Library of Congress contain hundreds of times as many novels as any person can read in a lifetime; publishers receive more manuscripts than they can possibly publish, and they publish more than one reader can possibly keep up with. Anthologists, teachers and common readers have to select the poems they will look at (or require others to look at). An evening at the theater can only be spent seeing one play. Choices must always be made, and so a filter is necessary. The game we play of which books to take to our desert island, or the grim reality of the political prisoner grateful to lay his hands on even a single volume, are ways of releasing ourselves from this need, but at the price of no longer belonging to society. For the most part, choosing the most worthwhile is an essential task. But to show that it is pragmatically necessary proves only that it is pragmatically possible, not that the choice can be principled and objective.

It is of course possible to study the past without passing value judgments: that is what historians do. The historian of Victorian religion or cabinet government may or may not feel emotionally involved with his subject, and historians differ on whether this is inevitable, optional, or undesirable. But insofar as he is detached from his subject, the historian's experience is quite different from that of the Victorian evangelical trembling in fear of hell or the politician scheming for office. Should the historian of literature be equally detached, making no choice between those who loved Wordsworth and those who preferred Hemans? Sould he rigorously exclude his own concern for and love of poetry? If we set out to explore (either as detached historians or as ideological unmaskers) what lay behind the preferences of past readers, we are removing ourselves from their concern with poetry: we are no longer studying literature, but what people have thought about literature. Literature matters to its readers, or they would not read it; but to the detached observer it no longer matters. There is no doubt a place for both kinds of critic, but the deconstruction of why poetry matters to its readers requires the existence of readers; if poetry ceases to matter to anyone, there will no longer be an object of study.[52]

To discover whether evaluation is necessary not just for practical purposes but in order to perceive fully what a text is like, I propose to conduct a small experiment. For this, I must ask the reader to turn back to the discussion of Lydia Sigourney's poem in chapter 2: for convenience, I here give the text again:

The Mother's Sacrifice

"What shall I render Thee, Father Supreme,
For thy rich gifts, and this the best of all?"
Said the young mother, as she fondly watched
Her sleeping babe. There was an answering voice
That night in dreams:—
                    "Thou hast a tender flower
Upon thy breast—fed with the dews of love:
Send me that flower. Such flowers there are in heaven."
But there was silence. Yea, a hush so deep,
Breathless and terror-stricken, that the lip
Blanched in its trance.
                    "Thou hast a little harp,—
How sweetly would it swell the angels hymn!
Yield me that harp."
                    There rose a shuddering sob,
As if the bosom by some hidden sword
Was cleft in twain.
                    Morn came—a blight had found
The crimson velvet of the unfolding bud,
The harp-strings rang a thrilling strain, and broke—
And that young mother lay upon the earth
In childless agony. Again the voice
That stirred her vision:
                    "He who asked of thee,
Loveth a cheerful giver." So she raised
Her gushing eyes, and, ere the tear-drop dried
Upon its fringes, smiled—and that meek smile
Like Abraham's faith, was counted righteousness.

The language of this poem is totally commonplace: virtually every adjective is predictable: God's gifts are "rich," the mother watches "fondly," the babe is a "tender" flower. It is written in the stock poetic diction of the nineteenth century, which is based mainly on archaism. The use of "thee" and "thou" in the opening sentence is defensible as the usual language of prayer; God's use of "thou hast" is perhaps defensible as the language God spoke in Victorian times. But for the baby to become a "babe" takes us into the unacknowledged poetic diction of the age, as, in a slightly different way, does the image of the heart "cleft" by a sword, which owes nothing to experience and derives unmodified from older poems. The babe as flower we met with in Theodora's poem and before that in Hemans's: there cannot be many nineteenth century poems of child pathos in which the child is not a flower. All these poems are totally uninteresting poetically—as we can see if we put them next to Wordsworth:

> She dwelt among th' untrodden ways
>> Besides the springs of Dove,
> A maid whom there were none to praise
>> And very few to love.
> A violet by a mossy stone
>> Half hidden from the eye . . .

—where the simple language conceals very precise discriminations (none to praise/few to love: there is no flattery, no writing of complimentary verses, in that rural culture, but there is family affection, though circumscribed) and precise observation (that violet has been seen, as Sigourney never saw her flower). This contrast shows us how totally uninteresting "The Mother's Sacrifice" is as a poem.

The preceding can be regarded as an optional first paragraph of our discussion of the poem. It is openly evaluative, and I believe it is a typical piece of New Criticism or of the *Scrutiny* school—as stock an example of that as the poem is of Victorian pathos. An attempt to rehabilitate the poems of Sigourney (or Hemans) would have to take one of two forms: either disputing the accuracy of this analysis or claiming that though the poem is correctly described, these attributes can be seen as virtues because they place the poem so firmly in the feminine tradition. The preferred strategy of Ross, and the only strategy of Tompkins, is the second: this then shifts the debate from the particular qualities of that poem to the ideological function of such poems. Evaluation is no longer a filter.

If the evaluative paragraph I have added is, as I have proposed, optional, it is not essential for the argument that followed. In that argument I examined the moral and theological function of the poem, describing it as containing a reversal of the duck-rabbit kind, claiming that consolatory writing (not only poems) about the death of a loved one constantly tends towards such reversals. That argument belongs to cultural history; whereas my optional paragraph belongs to literary criticism strictly conceived, and is concerned with the poetic quality of the lines. The two issues are theoretically distinct: it is quite conceivable that a poem of great subtlety and originality could be a duck-rabbit. I have therefore written two accounts of the poem, one concerned with artistic quality, the other with ideological function. They are independent of each other, but I believe them both.

Synchronic Discrimination

And so to the question that I have kept postponing, conscious that the attempt to answer it, though important, may be impossible: Is the rejection of sentimentality an example of historical relativism (one age rejects the values of a previous age) or can it be granted some sort of timeless validity? Even if we give the first answer we may still share the rejection, for we do not need to grant absolute or timeless status to our beliefs in order to hold them. But when one age reads a past age, the difference between these two positions is clearly important.

If the question can be answered, it will be in one way only: we need to discriminate within the same age. If we can find Victorian critics who share the modern condemnation, or if we can find some nineteenth century child pathos that, as modern readers, we admire, then the global confrontation between two solid blocks of history has, at least, been broken down.

There was of course one group of critics in the nineteenth century who condemned the sentimental deathbeds, for what at a first glance seem very different reasons from the twentieth century: these were the Evangelicals. An article on "Modern Novels" in the Christian Remembrancer in 1842 has a good deal to say about *The Old Curiosity Shop*, objecting "most strongly to the way in which [Nell's] dying and her death are worked up." It praises the writing ("nearly the best composition we ever encountered in our author's pages"), but then objects:

If we except her haunting the old church, not a single christian feature is introduced. The whole matter is one tissue of fantastic sentiment, as though the growth of flowers by one's grave, and the fresh country air passing over it, and the games of children near it, could abate by one particle the venom of death's sting. . . . To work up an elaborate picture of dying and death, without the only ingredient that can make the undisguised reality other than "an uncouth hideous thing"; to omit all reference to that by means of which alone the one enemy has "grown fair and full of grace, much in request, much sought for as a good"; this is not dealing fairly by us.[53]

This critic is trying hard to be fair. He assures us anxiously that he is "far indeed from demanding the direct introduction of religion in a novel," but insists that once the author has raised our expectations, once he has forced us to think about death and what it means, there can be only one way of dealing with it. Dickens might have protested that his intentions *were* Christian; but the softened, emotive religiosity that he offers does not, for this critic, count as Christianity. For him, an example of a Christian writer is not Dickens but George Herbert, someone whose poems are built firmly on doctrine.

That is obviously not the objection of Huxley, or of Leavis, or of Carey—or is it? It may not be as wholly unrelated to theirs as at first appears, for what this critic dislikes is a kind of self-indulgence, a pleasure which the author takes in contemplating his own sweetening of death. We do not need to accept Christian doctrine to accept that death *is* a hideous uncouth thing, any more than we need accept it to value Herbert's poem. And looking at the rest of this critic's discussion of *The Old Curiosity Shop*, I find myself developing a respect for him. His remarks on Quilp are astonishingly shrewd: he obviously enjoyed the "jollifications with rum punch and such like" and declares that he is a man of genius and that Mrs. Quilp was in love with him. This is true, and almost Freudian; and at other moments he is Dostoyevskian too: "If a man be neither saintly nor sensual, we believe there is nothing left for him but to be satanic"—this might be about Stavrogin! I am therefore willing to grant him the honor (if honor it is) of being a proto-modern; and I claim him confidently as evidence that not all Victorians were besotted by sentimentality.

Then there is Fitzjames Stephen, whose cool detachment on child deaths has already been quoted and who wrote of Nell's death,

> He gloats over the girl's death as if it delighted him; he looks at it . . . touches, tastes, smells and handles as if it was some savoury dainty which could not be too fully appreciated.[54]

This is indistinguishable from the twentieth century objections quoted earlier: there is the same accusation of self-indulgence, the same distaste as in Huxley, the same moral disapproval as in Leavis.

Or there is the *Saturday Review*, not often friendly to Dickens, which wrote in 1858:

> No man can offer to the public so large a stock of death-beds adapted for either sex and for any age, from five and twenty downwards. There are idiot death-beds where the patient cries ha!ha! and points wildly at vacancy—pauper death-beds, with unfeeling nurses to match—male and female children's death-beds, where the young ladies or gentlemen sit up in bed, pray to the angels, and see golden water on the walls. In short, there never was a man to whom the King of Terrors was so useful as a key figure.[55]

There is nothing here about Dickens's sticky secretions: he is seen purely as the showman "offering to the public" a set of tricks that are "useful" to him: Dickens's vast sales are surely being hinted at here. The *Saturday Review*er clearly considers himself removed from this gullible public.

"Children are not diminutive angels," declared Francis Jacox firmly in 1868, expressing a decided preference for "troublesome, ill-behaved children over the good little boys and girls . . . who never dirty their pinafores, and decline eating their dinner till grace has been said." He chooses the child death as the prime example of what he dislikes:

> It has been said that if anybody can get a pretty little girl to die prattling to her brothers and sisters, and quoting texts of Scripture with appropriate gasps, dashes, and broken sentences, he may send half the women in London, with tears in their eyes, to Mr Mudie's or Mr Booth's.[56]

I have already quoted Henry James on *Our Mutual Friend*, who also treats the author as showman and performer, not as giving us the overflowings of his own heart (he "has been accustomed to draw alternate smiles and tears, according as he pressed one spring or another"); and I suggested that the James we see in that hostile notice belongs very much to the Victorian Age.

This is important for the present argument, since what we need is not alien spirits who by some freakish time-warp are found to have stumbled into the sensibility of a later age. They would be of much less interest to us than these men of their time who disliked the child-pathos. I ought to add here that Philip Collins, from his unrivalled knowledge of the period, suggests that sentimentality may have been on the decline from about 1860.[57] No doubt there are epicycles on the somersaults performed by the whirligig of taste, but there is also no doubt that Dickens remained popular throughout his life, that readers continued to prefer his earlier novels, and that the audiences at his readings in the 1860s, though they may have sobbed less than Macready, were still spellbound by the death of Paul.

But though this evidence is important, in showing us that negative modern judgments are not necessarily completely locked up in their own time, it is in a sense only negative evidence. Positive evidence would be a case of nineteenth century child pathos that is artistically acceptable to the modern reader.

Huxley himself gives us a clue here, when he picks out Dostoyevsky's account of the death of Ilyusha as "agonizingly moving." The date of *The Brothers Karamazov* (1880) places it, perhaps, just within the cultural world of Dickens, and the way in which the death of Ilyusha is represented is without doubt pathetic and redemptive: it moves to tears, and it brings out the best in the survivors. It is known that Dostoyevsky had read *Dombey and Son*, and there are a large number of parallels between the two deaths. We are given a description of the dead child with many of the icons of pathos: the heart-broken grief of the father, the dying wish of the child, and a very moral sermon delivered by Alyosha after the funeral. I even notice (through, I must admit, the mists of translation) the presence of our touch-stone adjective, "little." This is surely enough to locate the episode firmly within the topos of child-pathos—firmly but not simply, for it is surrounded by a far more complex set of circumstances than the death of Paul or Eva or Helen Burns. There is, in the first place, the use of the dog Zhutchka. When Paul Dombey was alive he took to a "blundering, ill-favoured, clumsy, bullet-headed dog, . . . far from good-tempered and certainly not clever, [with] hair all over his eyes, and a comic nose" called Diogenes, and after his death this dog is presented to Florence, to whom he is dearer, because of the link with Paul, "than the most valuable and beautiful of his kind." It is a typical Dickensian blend of comedy and pathos. Diogenes may well have given the idea for Zhutchka, the dog who is brought to cheer the dying Ilyusha—but with a difference. Ilyusha had taken a fancy to Zhutchka, who is lost; and when he is ill, Kolya Krassotkin turns up with a dog called Perezvon, which he insists on bringing to the child's bedside, despite protests, and appears to taunt Ilyusha about the loss until he produces the dog who turns out to be none other than Zutchka, to Ilyusha's delight.

This episode is a conventional example of child sentimentality, except for two elements. First, the trick of Kolya's that produces such delight in the sick child is very nearly disastrous:

> Ilyusha could not speak. White as a sheet, he gazed open-mouthed at Kolya, with his great eyes almost staring out of his head. And if Krassotkin, who had no suspicion of it, had known what a disastrous and fatal effect such a moment might have on the sick child's health, nothing would have induced him to play such a trick on him.[58]

The trick has also been a trick on the reader. Keeping us in suspense, in order to arouse in us the same surprised delight that Alyusha felt, is a normal and effective writing strategy: but what is effective rhetorically might be dangerous in actuality, and Dostoyevsky, in telling us this, is being critical not only of Kolya but also of the fictional technique that he has made use of.

Second, there is the reason Zhutchka was lost. He had been tormented by being offered a piece of bread with a pin inside it, which he had snapped up, and then run off howling; it had been assumed that he was dead, but, as it happened, he had spat the pin out. Such cruelty is quite conceivable in Dickens and would be presented with indignation, the death of the child being offered as a redemptive contrast to it—as is done by Dostoyevsky, except that the bread with a pin was thrown to the dog by Ilyusha himself! He had repented and cried bitterly, then, when reproached, shouted defiantly that he would throw bread with pins to all the dogs—"all—all of them." There is no neat division here between saintly child and surrounding evil, and we are all the more justified in speaking of redemption.

Then there is Kolya, a character with no real equivalent in any of the comparable deathbeds. He is a precocious, self-justifying lad of about fourteen ("I am not thirteen, but fourteen, fourteen in a fortnight"!), who acts out his own moodiness in his dealings with Ilyusha: he stays away and refuses to visit him when urged by Alyosha, insisting when he does go that it is of his own volition only, showing off his knowledge, trying to make a fool of anyone who answers him, yet at the same time taking enormous pains to be kind to Ilyusha. Kolya's own development is as important a theme as Ilyusha's death and keeps intermeshing with it, then spinning off into impulsive, self-regarding conversations with Alyosha.

If we ask how all this differs from a Dickensian child death, the obvious answer will be its complexity. Pathos depends on simplification. Dostoyevsky achieves this at particular moments, but just as he surrounds his dying child with disturbed, immature, and involved bystanders, he surrounds the pathos with sordidness, hostility, and selfishness, not just as foils but as parts of a complex effect.

This would appear to imply—what in a sense is obviously true—that a full appreciation of the death of Ilyusha must rest on a complete response to the whole novel; and indeed it may not sound like much of a defense of the episode in itself to insist that its sentimentality is redeemed by the complexity of the context. Literary criticism obviously needs to respect the wholeness of a novel or poem; but I have written this book in the belief that to single out parts, and compare the same theme in book after book, also has its value. When we compare whole novels by Dickens and Dostoyevsky, the immeasurable superiority of Dostoyevsky's account of the spiritual growth of his heroes is matched only by the immeasurable superiority of Dickens's comic inventiveness and linguistic exuberance. In Dickens's case, we have seen how this invades and transforms the sentimentality of Jenny Wren radically, of Paul Dombey in part, of little Nell hardly at all.

In order to ask whether there is a comparable redemption of local sentimentality in Dostoyevsky's case, I shall look at a particular moment in some detail; and in order to draw together the whole discussion I shall do this by way of a comparison with comparable passages from the two deathbeds by which we have already lingered so long, those of Eva and Paul. I begin with Eva.

Topsy gave the short, blunt laugh that was her common mode of expressing incredulity . . .

"No; she can't bar me, 'cause I'm a nigger!—she'd's soon have a toad touch her! There can't nobody love niggers, and niggers can't do nothin'! *I* don't care," said Topsy, beginning to whistle.

"O Topsy, poor child, I love you!" said Eva, with a sudden burst of feeling, and laying her little, thin, white hand on Topsy's shoulder. "I love you, because you haven't had any father, or mother, or friends;—because you've been a poor, abused child! . . . I wish you would try to be good, for my sake;—it's only a little while I shall be with you." The round keen eyes of the black child were overcast with tears;—large, bright drops rolled heavily down, one by one, and fell on the little white hand. Yes, in that moment, a ray of real belief, a ray of heavenly love, had penetrated the darkness of her heathen soul! She laid her head down between her knees, and wept and sobbed,—while the beautiful child, bending over her, looked like the picture of some bright angel stooping to reclaim a sinner. (Chapter 25)

It hardly needs saying, by now, that this is a conventional scene. Eva is an angel; both children have "little" hands; the adjectives are predictable, and the paired monosyllables ("round keen eyes," "large bright drops") are like a ritual of pathos, as is the tautology of paired monosyllabic verbs, "wept and sobbed." Contemporaries loved it; we mock or are embarrassed. Contemporaries saw Eva's references to her impending death as redemptive, we, if feeling unkind, can see them as emotional blackmail.

For one last time I shall use Jane Tompkins as a foil. Here is her commentary on this passage:

> The rhetoric and imagery of this passage—its little white hand, its ray from heaven, bending angel and plentiful tears—suggest a literary version of the kind of polychrome religious picture that hangs on Sunday-school walls. Words like "kitsch," "camp," and "corny" come to mind. But what is being dramatized here bears no relation to these designations. By giving Topsy her love, Eva initiates a process of redemption whose power, transmitted from heart to heart, can change the entire world.[59]

The distinction this commentary fails to make is crucial. It could be argued either that Stowe's passage is not kitsch or camp or corny or that kitsch, camp, and corny are categories that modern criticism uses to keep the political power of *Uncle Tom's Cabin* at bay. In the first case, it would be necessary to make the distinction by pointing to elements in the writing that are not kitsch (which I take to mean, here, achieving sentimental effects through cliché) but that produce a more complex, ironic, or exploratory effect. There is one such detail, but Tompkins does not mention it. By the second argument, literary criteria have been openly replaced by political criteria, and the artistic case against the passage has been conceded but dismissed as unimportant; and in that case, the defense would apply not only to *Uncle Tom's Cabin* but to all sentimental writing, whether in sensational novels, pamphlets, or sermons. A great deal is then being rehabilitated, and we have certainly lost our filter.

Next to this episode I place, first, *Dombey and Son*:

> "And who is this? Is this my old nurse?" said the child, regarding with a radiant smile, a figure coming in. Yes, yes. No other stranger would have shed those tears at sight of him, and called him her dear boy, her pretty boy, her own poor blighted child. No other woman would have stooped down by his bed, and taken up his wasted hand, and put it to her lips and breast, as one who had some right to fondle it. No other woman would have so forgotten everybody there but him and Floy, and been so full of tenderness and pity. "Floy! this is a kind, good face!" said Paul. "I am glad to see it again. Don't go away, old nurse! Stay here." (Chapter 16)

The moral positives are exuded by the dying child in Stowe, and are conveyed to him in Dickens: whereas Eva is the source of uplift, Paul is the occasion for it. We can therefore say that *Dombey and Son* is, here, more pathetic than *Uncle Tom's Cabin*: Paul's helplessness makes him the object of love and the cause of grief, whereas Eva is already an angel. That is a difference in conception, but in execution Dickens is even more predictable than Stowe, for he lacks the degree of life injected into the passage by Topsy, who is of course more interesting before she is subjected to Eva's virtue than after; her discontent does at least provide the one touch of liveliness in the passage, the (true) claim that the virtuous Ophelia would "sooner have a toad touch her." Is this the best touch because it is verbally interesting (a toad, even just as a simile, is a welcome visitor among the so predictable adjectives), or for political reasons, because it is a trace of our knowledge that for all Eva's goodness there are still white folks, even well-meaning ones, who find a black child repulsive. Paul has not even a toad to liven him up: the wise child who answered back to Mrs. Pipchin, or who wanted to know "What's money?" has by now disappeared completely. What made Jeffrey and Macready weep, we now see, was the utter predictability of it all.

As a confirmation of this, I will quote the enthusiastic tribute of one John Hollingshead, written in 1857, listing some of the much loved "creations of Dickens's fancy"—all of whom turn out to be dying children:

Even now I love to picture him far from the din of the critical Babel, surrounded by those delicate and beautiful creations of his fancy, that ideal family, the children of his pen. There, in the twilight of his study, do I see him sitting with his arm round Nell, the favourite child. Her face seems worn and sad, but when she looks up in his eyes, it then becomes suffused with heavenly light. At his feet rest poor little Dombey and his sister, hand in hand, and nestling to the father who has called them into birth. Poor Joe is there, the fungus of the streets, crouching like a dog beside the fire, grateful for food and warmth and shelter. I hear the clumping of a little crutch upon the stairs, and in hops Tiny Tim, the crippled child.[60]

This totally conventional tribute may seem, at first, without any interest for us; yet it is remarkable for one thing, so obvious that it might easily escape our notice. Nell's face "seems worn and sad, but when it looks up in his eyes, it then becomes suffused with heavenly light." Offered this sentence without explanation, we would surely assume it came from the novel; it could be slipped into one of Dickens's own chapters without difficulty. Hollingshead, a man of, we presume, no particular literary talent, can go on writing *The Old Curiosity Shop*—or rather, it would be truer to say, Dickens won his success by writing in a style that his admirers can go on writing. The only difference between Hollingshead's paragraph and the novels is that the privations and sufferings of the children are here turned to cosy happiness: Paul and Florence have not got hard-hearted Mr. Dombey for a father, but soft-hearted Mr. Dickens. The coziness was of course implicit in the original hardness: Paul and Florence and Nell suffer so that the reader can comfort them, and the language for doing so is offered him by the book.

Dostoyevsky has far more than a verbal toad to offer us.

Kolya hurriedly pulled out of his satchel the little bronze cannon. He hurried, because he was happy himself. . . . Kolya held the cannon in his hand so that all could see and admire it. Ilyusha raised himself, and, with his right arm still round the dog, he gazed enchanted at the toy. The sensation was even greater when Kolya announced that he had gunpowder too, and that it could be fired off at once "if it won't alarm the ladies." Mamma immediately asked to look at the toy closer, and her request was granted. . . . A magnificent explosion followed. Mamma was startled, but at once laughed with delight. . . .

"Oh, give it to me! No, give me the cannon!" mamma began, begging like a little child. Her face showed a piteous fear that she would not get it. Kolya was disconcerted. The captain fidgeted uneasily.

"Mamma, mamma," he ran to her, "the cannon's yours, of course, but let Ilyusha have it, because it's a present to him, but it's just as good as yours. Ilyusha will always let you play with it, it shall belong to both of you, both of you."

"No, I don't want it to belong to both of us, I want it to be mine altogether, not Ilysuha's," persisted mamma, on the point of tears.

"Take it mother, here, keep it!" Ilyusha cried. . . . "Ilyusha darling, he's the one who loves his mamma!" she said tenderly, and at once began wheeling the cannon to and fro on her lap again. (Part iv, book 10, chapter 5).

The central figure of any child death must surely be the mother, and most of the real deaths described in chapter 1 were narrated by the mother. It is astonishing, then, how few of the fictional deaths involve mothers. Neither Little Nell nor Paul; Eva's mother is carefully placed in opposition to the sympathy and pathos; Helen Burns is an orphan; even in *The Daisy Chain*, though Flora is involved, the real grief for the child seems to be that of Dr May, the grandfather. Only in the case of Dickens is there any obvious explanation—if we can call it that. Happy families in Dickens are hardly ever biologically normal—father or mother (usually mother) is often missing and replaced by a substitute. This can be seen either as a rhetorical device to assert that family values are more enduring than the family itself (as is done here through the very motherly figure of Polly Toodle, the "old nurse"), or as the expression of a profound uncertainty (real families are never real families).

Dostoyevsky does give us a mother; but in a manner that subverts the family coherence as much as anything in Dickens. Ilyusha's mother is a half-wit, with the mental age and emotional development of a child, and in this scene she not only takes the child's cannon, she usurps his role as the object of pity. The childishness that makes her into a pathetic figure also makes her a disturbing element, so that she both arrogates the pathos to herself and destroys it altogether by her egoism. The result is a deep ambivalence, a twisted and disturbing pathos.

Dostoyevsky, then, is using much the same material as Dickens and some of the same material as Stowe: it is easy to find details in his narrative that locate it among the sticky secretions—or the beautiful fictions that transcend mere literature (depending whose judgment we use). But whereas Dickens redeems his novels for sophisticated modern readers by elements of grotesque comedy and linguistic vitality that coexist but hardly interact with the sentimentality, Dostoyevsky creates an effect that never drops into the mere simplicity of the sentimental. Sentimentality cannot tolerate the mixing of pathos with the sardonic and the disturbing which he offers us. There are no angels in his scene.

CONCLUSION

On My First Son

Farewell, thou child of my right hand, and joy;
My sin was too much hope of thee, lov'd boy,
Seven years tho'wert lent to me, and I thee pay,
Exacted by thy fate, on the just day.
O, I could lose all father, now. For why
Will man lament the state he should envy?
To have so soon scap'd world's, and flesh's rage,
And, if no other misery, yet age?
Rest in soft peace, and, ask'd, say here doth lie
Ben Jonson his best piece of poetry.
For whose sake, henceforth, all his vows be such,
As what he loves may never like too much.[1]

Ben Jonson wrote this epitaph on his son in 1603. We know nothing about the son except what the poem tells us: that he was seven years old and that his name was Benjamin (which in Hebrew means "son of the right hand"). The epitaph has become one of Jonson's best known and best loved poems, and takes us back, with a shock of recognition, to parental grief four hundred years ago.

It is a simple and formal poem: the heroic couplets announce formality, and the poet, for all his grief, will not break up his lines to weep. A skilled craftsman, he pays his child the compliment of not abandoning his skill when he writes the epitaph, so the lines move smoothly and deploy the caesura with care and thoughtfulness: most of the lines (3 and 4, for instance) pause after the sixth syllable, for regularity, whereas line 1 pauses after the second, to single out the opening word, "Farewell," and lines 2, 5 and 8 after the eighth, to highlight the two concluding monosyllables. The only slight technical imperfections are the two elisions in line 3, and the omission of definite articles in line 7, in both cases to keep the number of syllables down to ten. (The apparent awkwardness of the last line disappears when we realise that "like" is used in the sense of "please": may no earthly love-object mean too much to me.)

Twenty-two years later, Milton wrote an elegy "On the Death of a Fair Infant Dying of a Cough." Its stanzas are even more impeccable:

> O fairest flower no sooner blown but blasted,
> Soft silken primrose fading timelessly,
> Summer's chief honour if thou hadst outlasted
> Bleak winter's force that made thy blossom dry;
> For he being amorous on that lovely dye
>   That did thy cheek envermeil, thought to kiss
> But killed alas, and then bewailed his fatal bliss.[2]

I omit the rest of the poem, whose complicated playing with classical mythology is of great interest to the student of Milton but seems frigidly ingenious in a poem on his dead niece. But the technical mastery is unquestionable and impressive: the difficult ABABBCC rhyme-scheme is adhered to faultlessly over eleven stanzas. This decorum is a kind of respect for the dead, like turning up carefully dressed for the funeral. The alliteration so carefully deployed in the first stanza is like a touch of extra elegance in the dress; once it is noticed, there is no need to insist on it, and it is much less prominent in the later stanzas.

We now have quite a number of poems on dead children from the seventeenth and eighteenth centuries, written by mothers, for the most part women of no great literary skill or aspirations, now unearthed and published by feminist scholars. Here for instance are two of the halting couplets of Mary Carey, who lost all but three of her many children:

> In that then; this now; both good God most mild,
> His will's more dear to me, than any child:
>
> I also joy, that God hath gained one more;
> To praise him in the heavens, than was before.[3]

Ann Bradstreet's poems are better known, and more competent. They include several on the death of grandchildren, such as these lines "In memory of my dear grand-child Elizabeth Bradstreet, who deceased August, 1665, being a year and a half old":

> Farewell dear babe, my heart's too much content,
> Farewell sweet babe, the pleasure of mine eye,
> Farewell fair flower that for a space was lent,
> Then ta'en away unto eternity.
> Blest babe why should I once bewail thy fate,
> Or sigh thy days so soon were terminate;
> Sith thou art settled in an Everlasting state.[4]

As a postscript to this book, I offer this short glimpse of earlier poetry on the death of children for several reasons. First, to qualify the assertion made in chapter 4 that the theme of child death does not appear in literature before the nineteenth century. This is true of fiction, but not altogether true of poetry, a fact that should not surprise us. Lyric poetry has always dealt with a subject matter both wider and narrower than narrative fiction: narrower in that it tends to deal in crises, wider in that it deals with every kind of crisis. We would therefore expect children to appear in poetry when they form a crisis in the lives of adults—that is, when they are born and when they die. There may not be many poems on child death before the nineteenth century, but those that there are do not seem anomalous.

Second, this enables us to look again at cultural change. Why is it so clear that these poems belong to an earlier age? They do, after all, contain many of the ingredients of Victorian consolatory poems:

> Think what a present thou to God hast sent,
> And render him with patience what he lent.

Here is Milton telling the mother that she has suffered no real loss. Bradstreet expresses the same sentiment—and so, as we saw in chapter 2, do Sigourney and "Theodora." Jonson's poem makes the claim, now familiar to us from Hemans, that it is better to die young and escape the snares of the world and the flesh. Yet we could not mistake the poems of Jonson or Milton or Bradstreet for post–Romantic poems.

Partly the reason lies in the technical accomplishment I have already commented on. The nineteenth century was not yet an age of free verse, but although metrical craftsmanship was still practised, we can detect a reluctance to show off one's skill too openly, lest it seem unfeeling. Jonson and Milton feel no such inhibition, and Milton's elegy is full of ingenious mythological conceits. A much more restrained conceit opens Jonson's epitaph on the boy actor Salomon Pavy:

> Weep with me all ye that read
> > This little story,
> And know, for whom a tear you shed,
> > Death's self is sorry.[5]

—just enough wit to give the poem distinction, without appearing to drown grief in cleverness.

Even more subtle is the delicate hint of paganism in the poem on his son:

> To have so soon scaped world's and flesh's rage,
> And, if no other misery, yet age?

The Christian reason it is better to die young concerns sin: that to live in this fallen world, with our fallen nature, is to be surrounded by snares, and we have seen much of this in Hemans's poetry as well as in a good deal of fiction. Jonson's poem sets out to say this, using biblical phrasing, and then, unobtrusively, shifts; after the world and the flesh should, of course, come the devil, but in his place we have a half-acknowledged diversion into a purely pagan reason for dying young: that one avoids the pain of growing old. It is not easy to imagine that effect in a Romantic or Victorian poem.

Third, this excursus gives us the opportunity to compare men's writing with women's and so return to the issue raised in earlier chapters, on the relation between texts and emotion. For it is striking, in this comparison, that the men are so much more accomplished than the women—striking, but hardly surprising in male-dominated society. Mary Carey's groping poem does not contain any grief—it insists effusively that God's will must be accepted; Anne Bradstreet's lines are completely conventional; and the truly moving statements of grief are found in Jonson, with his subtle rhythms, capturing the broken but controlled voice of the sorrowing parent. Indeed, the very technical skill of the poem becomes a sign of the emotion in its most striking and subtle line: the description of the child as "Ben Jonson his best piece of poetry." This line, telling us that he is more proud of having made the child than of making any poem, unfolds in the mind as we reflect on the different kinds of making involved. The poet deserves credit for writing well but hardly for so natural and impulsive an act as making a child, so that the line expresses a kind of humility: the deed that I deserve no credit for is my finest achievement. And the more skilfully written the poem, the more is being renounced.

Again I return to the point made in my first two chapters, that there are two ways in which we can read off emotion from texts. I have no difficulty in believing (the point was well made by Sara Coleridge) that mothers love their children more intensely than fathers (though in the case of Anne Bradstreet there is a complication: do women love their grandchildren more than men love their sons?) The fact that Jonson is a more talented poet than either of these women does not mean that he loved his son (let alone Salomon Pavy) more than Mary Carey and Anne Bradstreet loved their offspring. A way of making this point would be to distinguish between the meaning of the poem when written, and the meaning of the act of writing it. If we hold an expression theory of poetry (if, that is, we think that skill is not enough), then we shall believe that Jonson wrote out of his own grief because he wrote so well (and, perhaps, that Milton was carrying out a literary exercise unmoved); but we have then to remind ourselves that emotion is not enough either, and that the inferiority of Mary Carey or Anne Bradstreet as poets gives us no reason to doubt the intensity of their grief.

When Robert Graves was a student, he was informed, "a little stiffly," that the essays he wrote for his English tutor "are, shall I say, a trifle temperamental. It appears, indeed, that you prefer some authors to others."[6] The opinionatedness of Graves the student, shocking to the academic mind in 1920, became academic orthodoxy in the mid-twentieth century, under the influence of the New Criticism in America and the Scrutiny school in Britain. I argued in chapter 5 that some authors are indeed better than others but that this position cannot be defended with the ready confidence of, say, F. R. Leavis or Yvor Winters. In the first place, poetic technique at its crucial moments becomes almost untraceably subtle, and rare is the critic who can put his finger (as De Quincey did) on just what gives a poem its brilliance; and second, the hermeneutics of suspicion has alerted us to the ways in which literary judgments may contain disguised politics.

What was described a generation ago as the making of value judgments is now referred to as the establishing of a canon. The task is the same, but the shift in terminology indicates a shift in how it is conceived. Making a value judgment is done by the individual for him- or herself; it implies open-minded reading, followed by unconstrained judgment. A canon, however, is established for others, by means of authority: it assumes a group with cultural power, who legislate. It shifts attention away from the individual act of judgment to the social, even political, situation served by (and governing) that act. So whereas the skeptic thought, a generation ago, that value judgments in literature were unreliable because they were simply rationalizations of individual prejudice, today's skeptic mistrusts them as rationalizations of ideology. A modern Graves would be told by his tutor not that he was temperamental but that he was naive.

And now I add a further complication, the difficulty of disentangling literary judgments not only from ideology but also from history, of distinguishing between (to use E. D. Hirsch's terminology) interpretation and criticism. For I do not know how far the discussion I have just been conducting has been an attempt to recover ways of thinking and feeling that belong to the seventeenth century and how far it has been about what these poems can say to us today. The distinction is clear in theory, almost impossible to sustain in practice.

There is another distinction I must briefly return to. The discussion of religion in the first two chapters was about its function in providing consolation. That it serves this function cannot, I think, be denied, and I regard Freud's little essay, "The Future of an Illusion," as containing a masterly insight. Though I doubt if many Christians accept Freud's position, it would be perfectly logical for them to do so: if religious ideas are "illusions, fulfilments of the oldest, strongest and most insistent wishes of mankind," it is always possible to maintain that God endowed humanity with these wishes so that we would discover his existence. Freud is scathing about those who reduce God to an "insubstantial shadow" and "persist in calling 'deeply religious' a person who confesses to a sense of man's insignificance and impotence in the face of the universe," and claims that "he who humbly acquiesces in the insignificant part man plays . . . is irreligious in the truest sense of the word." Freud's contrast between the religious and the truly irreligious may, however, be little more than a verbal distinction, for the God of many mystics (as I briefly suggested in chapter 2) *is* an insubstantial shadow, and the religion of many modern Christians could be described as a sense of man's insignificance. Are these so very different? Both may be felt as a spiritual experience. I have therefore written this discussion from a strictly agnostic standpoint, declining to discuss the existence of God or the truth or falsehood of Christianity, and I have discussed only the social and emotional function of religion for the bereaved. Furthermore, the disrespectful terminology I have occasionally used—the duck-rabbit, the smile on the Cheshire cat—testify to my belief that discussions of this kind are better if they shake free of too much respect; but respect is not the same as reverence, and such stylistic disrespect is quite compatible with a reverence for religious experience—or a belief in God.

* * *

I would like to give the last word to a grieving parent—to John Todd, at the bedside of his daughter Martha, aged sixteen months:

> I go to her bedside and gaze, and hear her short groans, as long as I can stay, and then go away to weep. . . . I know we ought not to refuse to give this dear one, this sweet child, back to her Maker and Father: she must be better off than with us; but oh! the agony of breaking the heart-strings.

—or to Anne Grant, who lost a son of four years, and wrote:

> It was my first affliction; and consolation was distressing to me, because I knew how little any one but a suffering parent can enter into that distress where a child, too young to interest any but those about him, is taken away from the evil to come.[7]

Both these parents are on the edge of refusing consolation, the edge which (as we saw in chapter 1) Margaret Oliphant stepped over. If our story is to end not with attempts at consolation but with the grief that consolation cannot always reach, then the last word should go to those who cannot make use of it, the stricken mothers who retreated into silence and even despair: Mary Wordsworth and Mary Shelley.

A book about the words that deal with grief should respect silence; and in telling the story of child deaths, real and fictitious, I have sometimes felt that in the face of material so powerful and moving it was unnecessary to say anything, that I should simply pass on the texts to my readers without comment. A brief example of what this would have produced can be seen in the bibliographical note, and it is now clear to me that these quotations gain in interest from the discussion surrounding them. That is, at any rate, one justification for my having gone ahead and written a book instead of just compiling an anthology. I hope the book will be perceived as a sounding box in which the voices of the bereaved and the memory of the dead still resonate.

Notes
Bibliography
Index

NOTES

Quotations from novels are identified by chapter rather than page, since different readers are likely to have different editions of these; date of original publication is given in the bibliography.

Chapter 1

1. *Times*, 7 Nov. 1817 (all future newspaper references are to 1817 unless otherwise stated).

2. "An Address to the People on the Death of the Princess Charlotte" (1817) in *Shelley's Prose; or, The Trumpet of a Prophecy*, ed. David Lee Clark. Albuquerque: University of New Mexico Press, 1954), 165.

3. Lord Shaftesbury to the House of Commons, 7 June 1842: Parliamentary Debates 3rd Series LXIII, 1321–1352. (Text taken from Robert A. Rosenbaum, *Earnest Victorians* (New York: Hawthorn Books, 1961).

4. Friedrich Engels, *The Condition of the Working Class in England in 1844* (German edition 1845; English translation 1886; reprint, London: George Allen & Unwin, 1952), 289–291.

5. John Skinner's Journal of a Somerset Rector covers the years 1803–1834; text taken from Robert Cecil, *The Masks of Death* (Lewes: Book Guild, 1991), 113.

6. Thomas Carlyle, *Chartism* (1839), chapter 1. In *Critical and Miscellaneous Essays*, Edinburgh Edition (London: Chapman & Hall, 1902), 112.

7. All quotations in this section are from the *Memoir of Catherine and Craufurd Tait*, ed. William Benham (London: Macmillan, 1879). Mrs Tait's narrative is on pages 159–243.

8. Rev. G. L. Prentiss, D.D., *The Life and Letters of Elizabeth Prentiss* (London: Hodder & Stoughton, 1883), 133, 137.

9. William Canton, *The Invisible Playmate: A Story of the Unseen* (1894), *WV Her Book* (1896), *In Memory of WV* (1901). Quotations from one-volume Everyman edition (London: J. M. Dent & Sons, 1911).

10. Paul Ricoeur, *Hermeneutics and the Human Sciences*, ed. John B. Thompson (Cambridge: Cambridge University Press, 1981), esp. part ii.

11. Both quotations from *Josephine Butler, An Autobiographical Memoir* (Bristol: J. W. Arrowsmith, 1909), 49, 51.

12. Josephine Butler, *Recollections of George Butler* (Bristol: J. W. Arrowsmith, 1892), 157.

13. Josephine Butler to her son Stanley; quoted in Margaret Forster, *Significant Sisters* (London: Secker & Warburg, 1984), 176.

14. Margaret Oliphant, *Autobiography* (1899), ed. by Elisabeth Jay (Oxford: Oxford University Press, 1990).

15. This has of course become one of the most controversial issues in recent literary theory, under the influence of Derrida in philosophy and Foucault and Hayden White in the writing of history, as well as innumerable literary theorists. A fierce but intelligent and well-documented attack on the decontructionist insistence that there is no escape from textuality can be found in J. G. Merquior, *From Prague to Paris* (London: Verso, 1986). Entering into this theoretical issue would clearly be beyond the scope of this book, but it is natural, even necessary, nowadays to ask oneself where one stands. The naive realist belief, that access to the thoughts and feelings of the past is unproblematic, is everywhere in retreat, but it is important not to replace it by an equally naive post-structuralism, claiming that such access is impossible and that all we can understand is our own way of constructing it. "The remedy for bad history," asserts Melchior, "is more and better history—a far cry from wholesale distrust." If there is no absolute signified, this does not mean that there is no signified at all or that language is ultimately about itself.

16. The Kipling papers are in the University of Sussex Library. The passages quoted are in boxes 19/2, 19/3, and 19/4.

17. Leonard Huxley, *Life and Letters of Thomas Henry Huxley* 2 vols. (London: Macmillan, 1900), 1:213–220.

18. Harriet Sarnoff Schiff, *The Bereaved Parent* (New York: Viking, 1977), 114–115.

19. *The Journal of Emily Shore* (London: Kegan Paul, 1891). The quotations occur on 280, 319, and 352.

20. See the introduction to the bibliography for references to other child deaths.

21. *Times*, 6 Nov. 1817.

22. Florence Nightingale, *Notes on Nursing* (London: D. Appleton & Co., 1860). Quotations occur on 26 and 10.

23. Charles E. Rosenberg, "Florence Nightingale on Contagion: The Hospital as Moral Universe," in *Healing and History: Essays for George Rosen*, ed. Charles E. Rosenberg (Kent, England: Dawson, 1979; New York: Science History Publications, 1979).

24. Nightingale, *Notes on Nursing*, 32.

25. Susan Sontag, *Illness as Metaphor* (New York: Farrar, Strauss & Giroux, 1978), ch. 7. See also Sontag's *AIDS and Its Metaphors* (New York: Farrar, Strauss & Giroux, 1989).

Chapter 2

1. Text from *The Poetical Works of Mrs. Hemans* (London: Chandos Classics, n.d.), 407.

2. *Memoir of Mrs. Hemans*, by her sister (Philadelphia: Lea & Blanchard, 1839), 153.

3. The first two quotations are from an anonymous poem, "Weep not for her," in *The Recognition of Friends in Heaven*, by the Bishop of Ripon and others (London: 1866), the third from "A Dirge" by Felicia Hemans, 435.

4. "On an Infant which died before Baptism", *Poems* (Oxford: Oxford University Press, 1935), 312. Other Coleridge poems are taken from the same edition.

5. Sara Coleridge to her husband, 1 Nov. 1798. Text of Sara's letters, and that of Poole, taken from Molly Lefebure, *The Bondage of Love: A Life of Mrs. Samuel Taylor Coleridge* (London: Victor Gollancz, 1986).

6. Samuel Taylor Coleridge, *Select Letters*, ed. H. J Jackson (Oxford: Oxford University Press, 1988), 72.

7. Philippe Ariès, *The Hour of our Death* (Baltimore: Penguin, 1983), 471.

8. Rev. Norman MacLeod, "Social Life in Heaven," in *The Recognition of Friends in Heaven*.

9. Elizabeth Stuart Phelps, *The Gates Ajar* (Boston: Fields, Osgood & Co., 1870).

10. In Britain, for example, it was contemptuously dismissed "by a Dean" in *The Gates Ajar Critically Examined* (London: Hatchards, 1871).

11. Colleen McDannell and Bernhard Lang, *Heaven: a History* (New Haven, Conn.: Yale University Press, 1988).

12. Ariès, 471, 536ff.

13. Rev. W. S. Thomson, in *Recognition of Friends in Heaven*, 77.

14. Sigmund Freud, *The Future of an Illusion* (1928), ch. 6 (New York: Doubleday, 1957), 51.

15. It is always interesting to find the Victorians anticipating modern views; so I here observe that Freud's argument can be found in W. R. Greg's contribution to the "Modern Symposium," in the journal *The Nineteenth Century* in 1877. He informs us that he has read most of the pleadings in favor of the doctrine of the Future State, "but these pleadings, for the most part, sound to anxious ears little else than the passionate outcries of souls that cannot endure to part with hopes on which they have been nurtured and which are intertwined with their tenderest affections." (*The Nineteenth Century* 2: 508).

16. C. S. Lewis, *A Grief Observed* (1961): Bantam edition (New York: 1976), 28.

17. Louis de Blois (1506–1565), *The Spiritual Mirror*. Quoted in Patrick Grant, *A Dazzling Darkness: An Anthology of Western Mysticism* (London: Collins, 1985), 340.

18. T. S. Eliot, East Coker, section 3, *Collected Poems* (London: Faber & Faber, 1963), 201.

19. Angela of Foligno (ca. 1248–1309), *The Divine Consolation* III, 7, in Grant, *A Dazzling Darkness*, 229.

20. Henry Vaughan, "The Night," *Silex Scintillans* (1655), part ii.

21. *Memoir of the Life of Elizabeth Fry, with extracts from her journal and letters* (1847) (London: Library of the Society of Friends), 237.

22. *The Young People's Treasury and Little Gleaner* 18, n.s. (1896): 107.

23. "Theodora," in *The Recognition of Friends in Heaven*, 71.

24. *The George Eliot Letters*, ed. Gordon S. Haight, 7 vols. (New Haven: Yale University Press, 1955), 4:183.

25. *Our Little Ones in Heaven, with an Introduction by the Late Rev. Henry Robbins, MA* (London: Sampson Low, Son & Co., 1858), 212–216.

26. "The Mother's Sacrifice," by Lydia Sigourney. (Much reprinted, e.g., in *Our Little Ones in Heaven*, 45). This is by no means Sigourney's only poem on a dead child. In fact there are so many that her biographer Gordon Haight claims that having devised a formula for such poems she used it "over and over again with a monotonous similarity of metaphor." The "formula" involves a conclusion in which the spirit of the dead child flies heavenward to "seek [its] place Amid yon cherub train." Since she lost her first three children at birth, we can assume that the monotony of the formula is due to lack of talent not lack of feeling. See Gordon S. Haight, *Mrs Sigourney* (New Haven: Yale University Press, 1930).

27. Josephine Butler, *Autobiographical Memoir*, 53–54.

28. Shelley, "To William Shelley" (1819). *Poetical Works* (Oxford: Oxford University Press, 1905), 581. Other Shelley poems taken from the same edition.

29. Walt Whitman, *Song of Myself* (1855), #6, *Complete Poetry and Collected Prose* (New York: Library of America, 1982), 194.

30. Richard Holmes, *Coleridge: Early Visions* (Baltimore: Penguin, 1989), 224.

31. Wordsworth, "The Childless Father" (1800): *Poetical Works*. ed. Ernest De Selincourt and Helen Darbishire, 6 vols. (Oxford: Oxford University Press, 1940–1959), vol. 2. All other Wordsworth poems taken from this edition.

32. Wordsworth, *Poetical Works*, 1:360 .

33. Edited text of the poem is in W. J. McTaggart, *England in 1819: Church, State and Poverty* (London:, 1970).

34. Richard Holmes, *Shelley: The Pursuit* (1974; London: Penguin, 1987), 563.

35. Dorothy Wordsworth to Catherine Clarkson, 5 Jan. 1813, *Letters of William and Dorothy Wordsworth: The Middle Years*, ed. Ernest de Selincourt (Oxford: Oxford University Press, 1973), 531. All the following quotations from the Wordsworths' letters are from this volume.

36. DW to Catherine Clarkson, Sept. (1st week) 1813, 571.

37. DW to Jane Marshall, 24 Jan. 1813, 545.

38. DW to Catherine Clarkson, 8 April 1813, 554.

39. Wordsworth to Samuel Rogers, 12 Jan. 1813, 540.

40. Wordsworth to Basil Montagu, 1 Dec. 1812, 524.

41. Miscellaneous Sonnets, no. 25 (1830) *Poetical Works*, 3:51.

42. Ibid, 423.

43. "There was a Boy" (1798), published in *Lyrical Ballads* (2d edition, 1800), then placed first among the "Poems of the Imagination" in 1815; also incorporated into *The Prelude* (see *Poetical Works*, 2:206).

44. Francis Jeffrey, review of Poems by the Reverend George Crabbe, *Edinburgh Review*, April 1808, 135.

45. George Crabbe, *The Parish Register* (1807) part iii, 199ff.

46. "Remains of Henry Kirke White—with an Account of his Life by Robert Southey (London: Vernor Hood & Sharpe, 1807).

47. Coleridge, Letter to Wordsworth, 10 Dec. 1798. See *The Prelude* in *Poetical Works*, 2:546.

48 De Quincey, "William Wordsworth," in *Taits Magazine*, 1839. See *De Quincey as Critic*, ed. John E. Jordan (London: Routledge, 1973), 443.

49. The suggestion that Wordsworth can be seen as a poet of the primary imagination derives from A. D. Nuttall, *A Common Sky* (London: Chatto & Windus, 1974), chap. 3: V (119ff.).

50. Among the ingenious critics I will single out Geoffrey Hartman, who offers several explanations for why the boy dies: first and simplest, readers would wonder why the boy is worth writing about: "There was a boy—and what happened to him?" (This could be seen as a kind of anticipatory reply to Jeffrey); seond, the poet is mourning the loss of a prior mode of being (this would connect the poem to the Immortality Ode); third—and most interesting and puzzling—"growing further into consciousness means a simultaneous development into death." A similar point seems to be made by Kenneth Johnston when he suggests "that this death somehow represents a triumph for the imagination." These suggestions have a convincing ring to them; yet because Book 5 of *The Prelude* is about education, we would expect it to demonstrate preparation for life, not anticipations of death. The mysterious power of the episode seems to elude the poem's argument. See Geoffrey H. Hartman, *Wordsworth's Poetry 1787–1814* (Cambridge, Mass.: Harvard University Press, 1964), 1:2; and Kenneth R. Johnston, *Wordsworth and The Recluse* (New Haven: Yale University Press, 1984), 142.

Chapter 3.

1. *Dealings with the Firm of Dombey and Son* . . . (1848), chapter 1. All Dickens quotations are taken from *The Oxford India Paper Dickens*, 17 vols. (Oxford: Oxford University Press, n.d.).

2. Tennyson to Robert Monteith, 24 April 1851, *The Letters of Alfred Lord Tennyson*, ed. Cecil Y. Lang and Edgar F. Shannon, Jr. (Cambridge, Mass.: Harvard University Press, 1981–1990), 15.

3. E. Conder, in *Joseph Conder: a Memoir* (1857); quoted in Leonore Davidoff and Catherine Hall, *Family Fortunes: Men and Women of the English Middle Class 1780–1850* (Chicago: University of Chicago Press, 1987), 331.

4. Josiah Gibbins in *Records of the Gibbins Family* (1911); quoted in Davidoff and Hall, 331.

5. Many of the apocryphal New Testament writings consist of sayings attributed to Jesus. The first of these is from the pseudo-Matthew, ch. 18, the second from the Gospel of Thomas, ch. 9.

6. *The English Dialect Dictionary* (Oxford: Oxford University Press, 1905), s.v. "old.".

7. Frances Hodgson Burnett, *Sara Crewe, or What Happened at Miss Minchin's* (London: F. Warne & Co., 1888).

8. *The Journal of Emily Shore* (London: Kegan Paul, 1891), 5.

9. Walt Whitman, "Out of the Cradle Endlessly Rocking" (1855), *Complete Poetry and collected Prose* (New York: Library of America), 393.

10. Garrett Stewart, *Death Sentences: Styles of Dying in British Fiction* (Cambridge, Mass.: Harvard University Press, 1984), chapter 2. Stewart's discussion of the death of Mrs. Gradgrind shows the interest but also, very clearly, the limitation of his approach. Here is the sentence from *Hard Times*: "The light that had always been feeble and dim behind the weak transparency went out; and even Mrs Gradgrind, emerged from the shadow in which man walketh and disquietetch himself in vain, took upon her the dread solemnity of the sages and patriarchs." Once again Stewart fastens on a grammatical oddity—also, as it happens, inserted at proof stage. He writes:

> Since even in the revised version we cannot at first understand "emerged" as anything but an intransitive form, we think we are engaged upon the main action of the clause, the shadowy Mrs. Gradgrind's emergence from the Valley of the Shadow in a still finite verb phrase, only to realize that the sentence must in fact parse as turning about a faintly false passive with unstated agent—"having (been) emerged"—dependent upon the subsequent main verb phrase, "took upon." This strained passive aura is evocatively in phase with Mrs. Gradgrind's diminished force of character yet again (and quintessentially) in death. Somewhere, unsaid, betweeen "went out" and the grammatical disembodiment of "emerged" lies the evasive interval of death.

The "strained passive aura" could indeed be regarded as "evocatively in phase" with the diminution and death, but then so could any syntactical break or subversion of our grammatical expectationsa—the breaks and subversions that are so common in the style of the inimitable Dickens. Once Stewart has established (or at any rate claimed) a parallel between syntactical breaks and death, it can easily become a formula to be applied mechanically, and the sophisticated critical vocabulary cannot altogether conceal this.

11. The importance of religion in the commonplaces of the Victorian death-bed

scene is well shown in Margarete Holubetz, "Death-bed Scenes in Victorian Fiction," *English Studies* 1 (1986): 14–34.

12. Steven Marcus, *Dickens: From Pickwick to Dombey* (London: Chatto & Windus, 1965).

Of the many discussions of little Nell and her death in recent Dickens criticism, the one that is most necessary for me to notice is that of Andrew Sanders, in *Charles Dickens: Resurrectionist* (London: Macmillan, 1982), a book overlapping considerably with the concerns of this chapter and using some similar extra-literary material to set Dickens" death-scenes in context. (Sanders does not confine himself to child deaths). For all its learning and persuasiveness, this book advances a thesis quite incompatible with mine, since Sanders insists on Dickens's Christian orthodoxy, finding in the novels unambiguous confirmation of the claim he made in his last letter (and often before) that he had always striven in his writings "to express veneration for the life and lessons of our Saviour." Pious (even Pecksniffian) remarks like this are not difficult to find in Dickens, and to use them as a criterion for interpreting his fiction is to subordinate art to uplift, ignoring the nuances with which belief is advanced, retracted, hinted at, turned into metaphor, or kept just beneath the surface, which I have tried to explore. The very suggestion that Dickens's novels are vehicles for "veneration" has a ring of the absurd. It is shrewd of Sanders to observe that the pseudo-medievalism of Nell's death is an attempt to exploit a set of properties to which Dickens normally felt considerable aversion; but then to claim that this is the *only* reason for the distaste felt by so many critics—even denying the presence of any sentimentality—is to use an incidental point as a distraction from the main effect. Sanders stresses the importance of angels but sees their function and existence as much less problematic than I do. A much fuller development of these criticisms can be found in the excellent review of Sanders's book by Garrett Stewart in the *Dickens Quarterly* 1 (1984): 97–105. I return to this question when discussing the reception of Nell and Paul in chapter 5.

13. Mrs. Tait's narrrative, 213 (see chapter 1, note 7).

14. Michel Serres's book is *Angels: A Modern Myth* (Paris: Flammarion, 1995). See the article by Justine Picardie, "A Host of Angels" in the *Independent on Sunday*, 24 Dec. 1995.

15. Nina Auerbach, *Woman and the Demon* (Cambridge, Mass.: Harvard University Press, 1982), 82.

16. Mrs. Stone, *God's Acre: Historical Notices Relating to Churchyards* (London: 1858), 394.

17. *Recognition of Friends in Heaven* (see chapter 2, note 8).

18. Philippe Aries, *The Hour of Our Death* (Baltimore: Penguin, 1983), 471, 543 (see also chapter 2, note 7).

19. Dickens to Thomas Latimer, 13 March 1841, *Letters*, Pilgrim edition (Oxford: Clarendon Press, 1965–), 1:257.

20. John Forster, *The Life of Charles Dickens* (London: Chapman & Hall, 1872), book 2, ch. 7.

21. Ibid., book 5, ch. 5.

22. Edmund Wilson, "Dickens: The Two Scrooges," in *The Wound and the Bow: Seven Studies in Literature* (Boston: Houghton Mifflin, 1941).

23. Dickens to George Thomson, 8 May 1837, *Letters*, 1:257.

24. Dickens to Richard Johns, 31 May 1837, *Letters* 1:263; and to W. Harrison Ainsworth, 17 May 1837, *Letters*, 1:260.

25. Dickens to John Forster, 8 Jan. 1841, *Letters*, 2:181.

26. Garrett Stewart, *Dickens and the Trials of Imagination* (Cambridge, Mass.: Harvard University Press, 1974), chapter 4 (esp. p. 214).

27. Alexander Welsh, *From Copyright to Copperfield* (Cambridge, Mass.: Harvard University Press, 1987), 14.

28. Henry James, Review of *Our Mutual Friend*, *Nation*, 21 Dec. 1865. Text from *Charles Dickens: A Critical Anthology*, ed. Stephen Wall (Harmondsworth, England: Penguin, 1970), 166.

29. James R. Kincaid, *Child Loving: the Erotic Child and Victorian Culture* (New York: Routledge, 1992). Since Kinkaid's position is radically deconstructive, interested not directly in the nature of child-loving or in the meaning of Victorian texts but only in our way of reading them and in our reasons for denying the sexual element, it is very difficult to discover what his view of pedophilia or his reading of the novels actually is. Certainly there is nothing in his book that would enable one to maintain, as I do, that the representation of Jenny contains sexual elements absent from that of Nell.

30. Robert M. Polhemus, "Comic and Erotic Faith Meet Faith in the Child: Charles Dickens' *The Old Curiosity Shop*," in *Critical Reconstructions: The Relationship of Fiction and Life*, ed. Robert M. Polhemus and Roger B. Henkle (Stanford, Calif.: Stanford University Press, 1994).

31. Charles Dickens, *The Public Readings*, ed. Philip Collins (Oxford: Clarendon, 1975), 33.

32. "Dr Marigold's Prescriptions", first published in *All the Year Round*, Christmas number, 1865.

33. *The Public Readings*, 280.

34. Philip Collins, personal communication.

35. "The Wreck of the Golden Mary" (1856): collected in *Christmas Stories*.

36. Fitzjames Stephen in *Cambridge Essays*, contributed by members of the University (London: 1855), 154.

37. Alan Horsman, Introduction to *Dombey and Son* (Oxford: Clarendon, 1974), 20.

38. Karl Marx, *Capital* (1867), 3 vols. (Moscow: Foreign Languages Publishing House, 1961), 1:259.

39. Henry Mayhew, *London Labour and the London Poor* (1851). Text from *London's Underworld . . .* , ed. Peter Quennell (London: Spring, 1958), 222.

40. A survey of the vast body of Dickens criticism obviously lies beyond the scope of a book on child deaths; but because I have touched on so many points that recent criticism has dealt with, I will briefly mention a few more critics whose concerns overlap strikingly with mine. Alexander Welsh, in *The City of Dickens* (Oxford: Oxford University Press, 1971), which I am inclined to think the finest critical book on Dickens, explores the ambiguous parallel between death and the domestic hearth: "the power of an angel to save implies, even while it denies, the eventuality of death." Frances Armstrong, in *Dickens and the Concept of Home* (Ann Arbor: University of Michigan Press, 1990) quotes a number of Victorian poems and essays to illustrate the religious and psychological function of home. Her discussion of Dickens's novels is uncritical—she treats all examples as uniformly successful—but for this very reason it gives an excellent account of Dickens's intentions. Anny Sadrin, in *Parentage and Inheritance in the Novels of Charles Dickens* (Cambridge: Cambridge University Press, 1994) explores the theme of the wrong kind of love shown in Dombey's relationship not only with Paul but with other, vicarious sons and throws a great deal of light on Dickens's treatment of the moral complexities involved in the rituals of succession. My chapter, however, is less concerned with moral concepts, since I believe that these (along with Mr. Dombey) get pushed aside when Paul takes center stage in order to die.

Chapter 4.

1. Into the description of the dead Nell in *The Old Curiosity Shop*, chapter 71, I have interpolated the third sentence, which is from the description of Muriel in chapter 28 of *John Halifax, Gentleman*, by D. M. Mulock (Mrs. Craik) (London, 1856).

2. Florence Montgomery, *Misunderstood* (1869), 10.

3. Mary Sherwood, *The Fairchild Family* (part i, 1818; part ii, 1842; part iii, 1847). I have used the Pilgrim edition (London, n.d.) which has 542 pages (no chapter divisions). Augusta Noble dies on pp. 82–84.

4. *Memoir of the Life of Elizabeth Fry, with Extracts from Her Journals and Letters*, 233 (see chap. 2, note 21).

5. Charlotte Brontë, *Jane Eyre* (1848) chapter 7.

6. Elisabeth Jay, *The Religion of the Heart: Anglican Evangelicalism and the Nineteenth-Century Novel* (Oxford: Clarendon, 1979). Jay's excellent discussion of evangelical deathbeds and how they relate to child deaths in fiction overlaps both with the present discussion and with my next chapter. See her chapter on "Practical Piety," especially pp. 162–67.

7. Thomas Traherne, *Centuries of Meditations* (posthumously published in 1908), iii, 2 (Oxford: Oxford University Press, 1958), 110.

8. Thackeray to Mrs Carmichael-Smith, March 1839, *The Letters of William Makepeace Thackeray*, ed. Gordon Ray, 4 vols. (London: Oxford University Press, 1945), 1:380 .

9. David Grylls, *Guardians and Angels: Parents and Children in Nineteenth-Century Literature* (London: Faber & Faber, 1978), esp. ch. 1.

10. E. M. Sewell, *Amy Herbert* (1844), ch. 29.

11. Harriet Beecher Stowe, *Uncle Tom's Cabin* (1852), ch. 27.

12. Thomas Hardy, *Tess of the D'Urbervilles* (1891), chapter 14, and *Jude the Obscure* (1896) V iii–VI ii.

13. Gustave Flaubert, *l'Education sentimentale* (1869), part ii, ch. 6 (my translation).

14. Johann Wolfgang von Goethe, *Die Wahlverwandschaften* (1809), part ii, chap. 13.

15. Alfred Lord Tennyson, "As through the land", from *The Princess* (1847).

16. *Human Documents of the Victorian Golden Age,* ed. E. Royston Pike (London: Allen & Unwin, 1967), 229–230.

17. See chap. 5, esp. 187, 189–208, for discussion of "little."

18. Susan Sonntag, *Illness as Metaphor* (New York: Farrar, Strauss & Giroux, 1978), 18n.113.

19. Gustave Flaubert, Letter to his niece Caroline, March 1868. *Correspondance,* 9 Vols. (Paris: Louis Conard, 1926–1933), 5:359.

20. The relevant passages from the *Clinique Médicale* of Trousseau are quoted, along with the corresponding passages from the novel, in the edition of René Dumesnil (Paris: Société les Belles Lettres, 1958), 2:349.

21. B. R. Mitchell, *Abstract of British Historical Statistics* 36. Infant death rates begin in 1839: they were 151 per 1000 in that year, 154 in 1840, and they hardly changed until the end of the century.

22. Harriet Sarnoff Schiff, *The Bereaved Parent* (New York: Viking, 1977), 114-115.

23. If we turn to the leading authorities on historical demography in order to establish whether child deaths became less common in the nineteenth century, we find that the obstacles to arriving at an answer are almost insurmountable. The publications of the Cambridge Group for the History of Population and Social Structure, and especially the monumental work by E. A. Wrigley and R S. Schofield, *The Population History of England, 1551–1871: A Reconstruction* (Cambridge, Mass.: Harvard University Press, 1981), offer state-of-the-art discussions of the reliability of parish registers and bills of mortality, of the possibilities of back projections and generalized inverse projections, and of the difficulties of family reconstruction, which, like most discussions of methodology, are intended for other demographers and result largely from the fact that there is not enough information to give full and reliable answers to the direct questions with which we began: what happened to infant

mortality between 1750 and 1850 and how is that related to family size and social class? Less up-to-date works such as Thomas McKeown's *The Modern Rise of Population* (London: Edward Arnold, 1976) are more likely to provide answers— whose reliability, of course, the layman is not competent to judge.

24. McKeown, *Modern Rise of Population*, 52.

25. Richard Vann and David Eversley, *Friends in Life and Death: The British and Irish Quakers in the Demographic Transition 1650–1900* (Cambridge: Cambridge University Press, 1992).

26. Ibid., 242.

27. Chapter 45. All the quotations from *Doktor Faustus; das Leben des deutschen Tonsetzers Adrian Leverkuhn, erzahlt von einem Freunde* (Stockholm: Bermann-Fischer, 1947) occur in chapters 44 and 45. My translations.

28. Albert Camus, *La Peste* (1947) part iv, section 3. My translations.

29. Letter to Eliza Fox, 26 April 1850: *The Letters of Mrs Gaskell* (Manchester: Manchester University Press, 1966), 112.

30. Letter to Anne Shaen, 24 April 1848, Ibid., 57.

31. To Eliza Fox, Ibid., 112–113.

Chapter 5.

1. Dickens to Lewis Gaylord Clark, 28 Sept. 1841: *Letters*, Pilgrim edition (Oxford: Clarendon Press, 1965–), 2:394.

2. Speech in Boston, 1 Feb. 1842: quoted in *Letters*, 2:394.

3. Dickens to John Tomlin, 23 February 1841. Ibid 2:217.

4. Bret Harte, "Dickens in Camp" (1870), *Complete Poetical Works* (New York: P. F. Collier & Son, n.d.), 209.

5. Thomas Hood on *The Old Curiosity Shop*, *The Athenaeum* 680, 7 Nov. 1840: 887.

6. Margaret Oliphant, "Charles Dickens," *Blackwoods Magazine*, April 1855, in *Dickens: The Critical Heritage*, ed. Philip Collins (London: Routledge, 1971), 331.

7. Forster to Dickens, 16 Jan. 1841, *Letters*, 2:187.

8. Macready to Dickens, 25 Jan. 1841, *Letters*, 2:193.

9. Mrs Jane Greene to Forster, c. 1872, *Letters*, Preface to vol. 2, x.

10. "H" in *Westminster Review*, April 1847, 5–11, in *Dickens: The Critical Heritage*, 225.

11. Jeffrey to Dickens, 31 Jan. 1847, from Francis Jeffrey, Francis Jeffrey, *Life of Lord Jeffrey, with a Selection from His Correspondence. By Lord Cockburn*, Edinburgh, 1852, in *Dickens: The Critical Heritage*, 217.

12. *Letters*, Preface to vol. 2, ix.

13. See, inter alia, *Roland Barthes par Roland Barthes* (Paris: Seuil, 1980), 51, 88, 142, 146; "The Death of the Author," in *Image, Music, Text*, trans. Stephen Heath (London: Fontana/Collins, 1977); "Literature and Signification," in *Critical Essays*,

trans. Richard Howard (Evanston, Ill.: Northwestern University Press, 1972). I have discussed the issue further in "Literature: Coroner's Report," *Southern Humanities Review* 23 (Summer 1989): 201–216.

14. Thomas Docherty, *Reading (Absent) Character* (Oxford: 1982), xiii, 31.

15. Dickens to Messrs. Chapman and Hall, 24 Nov. 1840, *Letters*, 2:153.

16. Anon., *The Man in the Moon*, March 1847, 155–160, in *Dickens: The Critical Heritage*, 221.

17. *Times*, 7 Nov. 1817.

18. The remark was made to Ava Leverson. See Richard Ellman, *Oscar Wilde* (London: Penguin, 1988), 441.

19. Aldous Huxley, "Vulgarity in Literature," *Collected Essays* (New York: Bantam, 1960), 113.

20. F. R. Leavis, *Dickens the Novelist* (Chatto & Windus, 1970).

21. John Carey: *The Violent Effigy* (London: Faber, 1973), 140.

22. See the discussion of *Point Counter Point* in chap. 4.

23. John Forster, *The Life of Charles Dickens* (London: Chapman & Hall, 1872), book 2, chap. 7.

24. Samuel Pickering, Jr., *The Moral Tradition in English Fiction 1785–1850* (Hanover, New Hampshire: University Press of New England, 1976); Andrew Sanders, *Charles Dickens: Resurrectionist* (London: Macmillan, 1982), chapter 3, note 12.

25. Carey, *The Violent Effigy*, 140.

26. Harriet Beecher Stowe, *The Writings*, Riverside edition, 16 vols. (New York: Houghton Mifflin, 1896), 1:lxxii.

27. Anon., "The Birth of Sensibility," *London Magazine* 45 (1776): 95.

28. Henry Mackenzie, *The Man of Feeling* (1771), ch. 34.

29. Adam Smith, *The Theory of Moral Sentiments* (1757), part i, section 1, chapters 2, 5.

30. James Boswell, *Life of Samuel Johnson* (1791), 2 vols., ed. G. Birkbeck Hill (Oxford: Oxford University Press, 1934–1950), 2:469.

31. *Memoir of Catherine and Craufurd Tait*, ed. William Benham (London: Macmillan, 1879), 183–186.

32. Ibid., 242.

33. See note 7.

34. Tennyson to Robert Monteith, c. 24 April 1851: *Letters of Alfred Lord Tennyson*, 6 vols. (Oxford: Oxford University Press, 1987), 2:15.

35. Ann Douglas, *The Feminization of American Culture* (1977): (New York: Avon, 1978), 11.

36. Jane Tompkins, *Sensational Designs: The Cultural Work of American Fiction* (Oxford: Oxford University Press, 1985), chapter 5, passim. [not in bibligraphy]

37. Ibid., 132.

38. Douglas, *Feminization of American Culture*, 12.

39. Gillian Brown, "Domestic Politics in *Uncle Tom's Cabin*," *American Quarterly* 36 (1984): esp. 506.

40. Jean Fagan Yellin, "Doing it Herself: *Uncle Tom's Cabin* and Women's Role in the Slavery Crisis," in *New Essays on Uncle Tom's Cabin*, ed. Eric J. Sundquist (Cambridge: Cambridge University Press, 1986), 94–95.

41. Elizabeth Ammons, "Stowe's Dream of the Mother-Saviour: *Uncle Tom's Cabin* and American Women Writers before the 1920s," in *New Essays on Uncle Tom's Cabin*; see also Mary Kelley, "The Sentimentalists: Promise and Betrayal in the Home," *Signs* 4 (Spring 1979): 434ff.

42. Marlon Ross, *The Contours of Masculine Desire: Romanticism and the Rise of Women's Poetry* (New York: 1989). I have thought it best to discuss a small number of critics carefully rather than attempt a survey of the feminist rehabilitation of senti-mentality; but I will add Glennis Stephenson, "Poet Construction: Mrs Hemans, L. E. L., and the Image of the Nineteenth Century Woman Poet," in *ReImagining Women*, ed. Shirley Neuman and Glennis Stephenson (Toronto: 1993).

43. Tompkins, *Sensational Designs*, 125.

44. Quoted in George Ford, *Dickens and His Readers* (Princeton: 1955), 20. This is the best discussion of the reception of little Nell that I have come across.

45. quoted in *The Letters and Private Papers of W. M. Thackeray*, ed, Gordon Ray 4 vols. (London: Oxford University Press, 1945), 2:266.

46. Ross, *Contours of Masculine Desire*, 13–14.

47. There is a further objection to the didactic/ideological position of Tompkins that may sound like an intrusion into her personal beliefs, though I do not know how else to put it. Artistic criteria do not require us to admire only authors we agree with: much of the project of Romantic and modern aesthetics can be seen as an attempt to describe those qualities of a literary work that do not depend for their value on its moral or political purpose. But the critic who judges didactically or ideologically can-not do this. If we value a work primarily for its political function, we need to value that function. When therefore Tompkins praises Uncle Tom's Cabin for vindicating "the notion that historical change takes place only through religious conversion," that the true goal of its rhetorical undertaking "is nothing less than the establish-ment of the kingdom of God on earth," it seems to me crucial that she indicate whether she accepts this goal. I have no doubt that she accepts the goal of abolishing slavery, but she is quite right to point out, as she does here, that for Stowe this had to be done by religious conversion. If Tompkins does not share this view, then her political defense of the book seems made in bad faith.

48. This sentence from Chorley's *Memorials of Mrs Hemans* (1836) is quoted by Ross on 305.

49. To document fully what seem to me the weaknesses of Ross's argument would take us too far from the concerns of this book: I will just offer one general

observation and one detailed criticism. In general: all the qualities that Ross attribut-es to Hemans in order to distinguish her from Wordsworth seem to me either trivial or to be found in Wordsworth. As an example of how her program can lead her to sweeping assertions, I cite her praise of Hemans for using *we* instead of the egoistic *I*: "In place of the romantic's self-possessing control of the reader's vision, she offers consciously and repeatedly the shared experience of an italicised 'we.' She offers the potential of shared desire for a humanity that can never escape the power and vul-nerability of their shared affection" (309). When does a poet write "I" and when "we"—and why? The question is fascinating—and more complicated than is here admitted. Why should Wordsworth, that great user of the first person singular, begin a sonnet, "The world is too much with us," continue, "We have given our hearts away," and move to the singular only when he indignantly exclaims, "Great God! I'd rather be / A pagan, suckled in a creed outworn"? Not only is it doubtful whether Hemans uses *we* more often than Wordsworth (it occurs in none of the poems Ross has just mentioned as creating "her own distinct vision of the relation between nature and humanity"); it is even more doubtful whether the use of *we* is less egois-tical and more truly concerned with shared experience: it could equally be seen as an insensitive assumption that others are like me. And as for the italicising of *we*, does that not suggest the uncertainty of a writer who protests too much? A political agenda damages our reading if it leads the critic to drag in thoughtlessly such tricky points of technique to support an ideological case.

50. Philip Collins, "The Decline of Pathos," *English Studies Today*, Fifth Series (Dublin 1970).

51. Elizabeth Ammons, "Stowe's Dream," 167n.39.

52. This is why Ross's plea for a "noncanonical" approach to literary study, though attractive, is in an important sense anti-literary. To open up the canon in accordance with new ideological and political positions can certainly be liberating— but not only for those who hold the new positions. It is important, in the end, to ask what the established writers, canonized by a conservative tradition, can offer to the radical and what the forgotten writers, unearthed by the radical, can offer to the reader previously satisfied with the established canon. This is one of the most fruit-ful questions confronting criticism today; and I do not want to see it ruled out of court by either conservatives or radicals.

53. "Modern Novels," *The Christian Remembrancer* (Dec. 1842), 591–592.

54. Fitzjames Stephen, *Cambridge Essays* contributed by members of the University (London: 1855), 174. And see George Ford, *Dickens and his Readers*, chap-ter 3 (passim). *Cambridge Essays*, contributed by members of the University (London, 1855), 154

55. *Saturday Review*, 8 May 1858, 474, in *Dickens: The Critical Heritage*, 383. This article may also be by Fitzjames Stephen.

56. Francis Jacox, "About Goody Children," *Temple Bar* (Aug. 1868), 138.

57. Philip Collins (see note 50).

58. Fyodor Dostoyevsky, *The Brothers Karamazov* (1880), trans. Constance Garnett (London: Heinemann, 1912), part iv, book 10, ch. 5.

59. Tompkins, *Sensational Designs*, 131.

60. John Hollingshead, "Mr Dickens and his Critics," *The Train* (Aug. 1857), in *Dickens: The Critical Heritage*, 377.

Conclusion.

1. Ben Jonson, "On My First Son" (*Epigrams* 45, 1616). Text of this and the other Jonson poem from *Poems of Ben Jonson*, ed. George Burke Johnston (London: Routledge and Kegan Paul, 1954).

2. John Milton, "On the Death of a Fair Infant Dying of a Cough" (1625). Text from *The Poems of John Milton*, ed. John Carey and Alastair Fowler (London: Longmans, 1968).

3. Text of Mary Carey from *Kissing the Rod*, an Anthology of 17th Century Women's Poetry, ed. by Germaine Greer et al. (London: Virago, 1988).

4. Anne Bradstreet, "In Memory of My Dear Grand-Child Elizabeth Bradstreet" (1665). Text from *Poems of Anne Bradstreet*, ed. Robert Hutchinson (New York: Dover, 1969).

5. Jonson, "Epitaph on S. P. A child of Q El Chapel" (*Epigrams* 122).

6. Robert Graves, *Goodbye to All That* (London: Jonathan Cape, 1929). The remark is quoted by F. R. Leavis as epigraph to *The Common Pursuit* (London: Chatto & Windus, 1952).

7. Linda Pollock, *A Lasting Relationship: Parents and Children over Three Centuries* (Hanover: University Press of New England, 1987), 118, 129.

BIBLIOGRAPHY

Here, finally, are some of the striking child deaths I have come across in memoirs and letters, excluding those I have used in the text, which are, of course, documented in the notes. (A similar list, with which I have avoided overlap, can be found in Linda Pollock's *A Lasting Relationship: Parents and Children over Three Centuries* [Hanover and London: University Press of New England, 1987], pages 123–135.) Such a list obviously makes no claim to completeness, but each has at least a mite of interest, and they all contribute to a sense of what the subject meant to people in the nineteenth century. I give where possible the date, age, and cause of death, a quotation from the comments, and at least one source.

HENRY GURNEY AGGS (1846: 19: typhus). "This dear youth early evinced a retiring and thoughtful demeanour, with a marked ingenuousness of character. . . . His complaint was considered a feverish cold, that, with attention, would soon pass off . . . until fourth-day evening, the 25th of 11th month, when there was an increase of fever. . . . He spoke to his mother with deep and affectionate feeling, especially mentioning a book which he wished to be destroyed, if he would not recover.—'I have never read it through, it is an improper book; I have laid it aside; it was given to me by—, but I wish no-one to read it. Do thou burn it, dear mamma.' . . . On First-day morning, the 13th, seeing the light breaking through the curtains, he turned to his Father who was watching by his side, and said sweetly, 'the dawning of the sabbath.' . . . About a quarter before seven in the evening, his redeemed spirit gently passed from the body" (*The Annual Monitor for 1848*, or *Obituary of the Members of the Society of Friends for 1847*). Among the obituaries regularly appearing in *The Annual Monitor* (York, 1842–) are several of young people (of which this is a representative sample) and occasionally of children.

MARTIN BENSON (1878: 17: tubercular meningitis). "He closed his eyes as for sleep, and then turned his head a little towards the room, awoke afresh, and gazed with a beautiful expression at a part of the room where nothing visible stood: plainly saw something and exclaimed, 'How lovely.' These words were the last he uttered."—E. W. Benson (father). "My dear Arthur, Martin is dead. . . . Martin is

239

gone to hefen. . . . I am so happy that Martin is gone to Jesus Christ. I hope we shall all go to HIM very soon. He is Saint Martin now."—Hugh Benson (brother, aged 6). David Newsome, *Godliness and Good Learning* (1961).

DAUGHTER OF WILLIAM BRADBURY (1839: ?: ?). Dickens's letter of condolence speaks of "the certainty of a bright and happy world beyond the Grave, which such young and untried creatures (half Angels here) must be called away to . . .—the happiness of being always able to think of her as a young and promising girl, and not as one whom years and long sorrow and suffering had changed—above all the thought of one day joining her again where sorrow and separation are unknown." *Letters of Charles Dickens*, Pilgrim edition, 1:515.

LIONEL BURNETT (1890: 15: consumption). "He has a mournful little way of calling 'Mamma' that would bring me to him if I were dying on my bed. If I move away from his side he says, 'Oh! *where* are you going? Don't go, Mamma darling.'" Ann Thwaite, *Waiting for the Party: The Life of Frances Hodgson Burnett* (1974).

ELDEST SON AND THREE YOUNG DAUGHTERS OF SIR THOMAS FOWEL BUXTON (1820: 10 and younger: "inflammatory disorder," whoooping cough and measles). "'Though he slay me, yet will I trust in him.' I have much desired her life, but willingly do I resign her into the hands of the Lord, praying Him that He would mercifully make her death the means of turning me more nearly to the Lord." *Memoirs of Sir Thomas Fowell Buxton* (1860).

SON OF J. W. CROKER (1820: "of tender years": "water on the brain"). "He takes nothing; he has an odd kind of nervous sighing or groaning, very frequent." *Correspondence and Diaries of John Wilson Croker* (1885).

ELIZABETH, ELDEST SISTER OF THOMAS DE QUINCEY (1791: 9: a "spark of fatal fire fell upon that train of predispositions to a brain complaint which had hitherto slumbered within her"). "I wearied the heavens with my inquest of beseeching looks. Obstinately I tormented the blue depths with my scrutiny, sweeping them for ever with my eyes, and searching them for one angelic face that might, perhaps, have permission to reveal itself for a moment. . . . I saw white fleecy clouds [that] . . . grew and shaped [them]selves into visions of beds with white lawny curtains; and in the beds lay sick children, dying children, that were tossing in anguish, and weeping clamorously for death." *Autobiography* of Thomas De Quincey (1834–51).

DORA DICKENS (1851: 8 months: ?). Dickens wrote to his wife: "Little Dora, without being in the least pain, is suddenly stricken ill. . . . I do not—why should I say I do, to you my dear!—I do not think her recovery at all likely. . . . I cannot close without putting the strongest entreaty and injunction upon you to come home with perfect composure—to remember what I have so often told you, that we never can expect to be exempt, as to our many children, from the afflictions of other parents— and that if—if—when you come, I should even have to say to you 'our little baby is dead,' you are to do your duty to the rest, and to shew yourself worthy of the great trust you hold in them." (Dora was already dead when he wrote this letter.) *Letters*, Pilgrim edition (6:353).

LAMBTON DURHAM (1831: 13). "Why did it fall on this heavenly boy, whilst I and so many others, who would be no loss to the world, are spared? I can think of nothing else, and am quite unnerved for the battle I have to fight."—Lord Grey (grandfather). *Life and Letters of Lord Durham*, ed. Stuart J. Reid (1906).

WILLIE GASKELL (1845: 10 months: ?). Three years later his mother wrote: "I have just been up to our room. There was a fire in it, and a smell of baking, and oddly enough the feelings and recollections of three years ago came over me so strongly—when I used to sit up in the room so often in the evenings reading by the fire, and watching my darling darling Willie, who now sleeps sounder still in the dull dreary chapel-yard at Warrington." *The Letters of Mrs Gaskell* (1966).

JESSY GLADSTONE (1850: 4: meningitis). "In April of [1850] a little daughter, between four and five years old, had died, and was buried at Fasque. The illness was long and painful, and Mr Gladstone bore his part in the nursing and watching. He was tenderly fond of his little children, and the sorrow had a peculiar bitterness. It was the first time that death entered his married home" (John Morley, *The Life of William Ewart Gladstone*, 1908). "Gladstone was reported as being 'for some hours in a state of such violent grief as to cause positive alarm to those around him. Then, suddenly, his sense of duty got the upper hand; thence forward he was perfectly calm, and returned in all respects to the demeanour and habits of his everyday life.'. . . He reported to Catherine: 'I have kissed the coffin where it lies: but the stones will not be laid down until tomorrow is over; and therefore my last visit is not paid'" (Richard Shannon, Gladstone, 1984). I should add that Morley follows the account of Jessy's death with an account of the death of Gladstone's father, which he regards as having had a far deeper effect on him.

SON OF WILLIAM HARCOURT (1862: ?: "fever and brain disorder"). The father wrote to Thomas Hughes, in reply to a letter of condolence: "I really feel as if all my heart strings were snapped. My happiness was so wrapped up in the little boy that I feel it must be very long before either mind or body can rally from the shock. My wife bears up with an angelic courage. Women behave better in their trials because they are better. Watts did for me yesterday a sketch from the cold clay which Perugino might have envied. It really is my little darling as he lived. I shall write on his grave, 'For this angel doth always behold the face of my father which is in heaven.'" (A. G. Gardiner, *The Life of Sir William Harcourt*, 1923).

FANNY HAYDON, second daughter of Benjamin Robert Haydon, the painter (1831: 2 years 9 months & 12 days: "suffusion of the brain"). "The life of this child has been one continued torture: she was weaned at three months from her mother's weakness and attempted to be brought up by hand. This failed, and she was reduced to a perfect skeleton." Haydon engaged a wet nurse, but had pangs of conscience when he realized that the nurse's own child was being sacrificed. "When the nurse's time was up, Fanny withered . . . and today, after two convulsive fits, expired without a gasp." She was buried in Paddington new churchyard. "Two trees weep over her grave. No place could have been more romantic and secluded."

Haydon lost three more children, Alfred (1833: 7: ?), Harry, "my favourite child" (1834: 4: ?) and Georgiana (1835: 1-2: ?). He passed four days "sketching Harry's dear head in the coffin—his beautiful head! What a creature! With a brow like an ancient god!" As he watched Georgy "in her convulsions, her beautiful head had a look of power and grief no-one could forget. It's dreadful work. I tried to sketch her dear head but could not. The look was of another world, as if she saw sights we could not see and heard sounds unfit for our mortality. Sweet innocent!" *Autobiography and Journals of B. R. H.* (1853; ed. Malcolm Elwin, 1950).

EFFIE HUGHES (1856: ?; scarletina). Effie had a "lurking mischief" in the head, which might well cause serious illness before the age of 14-15; "she could never have been so fit for God's kingdom again or he would have left her to go gleaming about the house with her little golden head rejoicing our hearts."—Thomas Hughes (father) to Lord Goderich. British Library Add MS. 435547. (I owe this reference to Norman Vance).

FANNY PEABODY (1844: ?: scarlet fever). Shortly after the death of her mother, Amelia Peabody, which seems to have been a far greater blow to William Peabody; Fanny "improved in character" after her mother's death. *Sermons by the late Wm. B. O. Peabody, with a memoir by his brother* (Boston, 1849).

MARY SHAFFNER (1866: 10 months: pneumonia). Her mother, finding it difficult to accept the death, remarks on her "plump and natural" appearance in her coffin. Diary of Carry Frances Shaffner, quoted in *Victorian Women*, ed. Hellerstein, Hume, and Offen (1981).

HERBERT SOUTHEY (1816: 10: illness "of a strange and complicated nature—subsequent examination showing a great accumulation of matter at the heart"). "Death has so often entered my doors, that he and I have long been familiar. The loss of five brothers and sisters (four of whom I remember well), of my father and mother, of a female cousin who grew up with me and lived with me; of two daughters, and of several friends . . . have very much weaned my heart from this world." *Life & Correspondence of Robert Southey* (1850).

HARRIET STREATFIELD (1842: 7: ?). Her grandnmother, Elizabeth Fry, spoke at the funeral, expressing thankfulness "that the lamb taken was a believing child, one rather peculiarly impressed with the fact of redemption. and forgiveness of sins through Christ; and in practice, an obedient gentle-spirited creature, and according to the measure of so young a child, unusually full of good works and alms deeds, for she gave much to the poor, whose tales of woe, (whether true or false, she did not stop to inquire,) always touched her." *Memoir of the Life of Elizabeth Fry* (1847).

The following bibliography is selective and includes only works actually cited or used.

I. Primary.

Brontë, Charlotte. *Jane Eyre*. 1848.

Burnett, Frances Hodgson. *Sara Crewe, or What Happened at Miss Minchin's*. 1888.

———. *Giovanni and the Other*. New York, 1892.

Butler, Josephine E. *An Autobiographical Memoir*. Bristol: J. W. Arrowsmith, 1909.

———. *Recollections of George Butler*. Bristol: J. W. Arrowsmith, 1892.

Buxton, Sir Thomas Fowell: Memoirs. London, 1860.

Camus, Albert. *La Peste*. 1947. Text from Camus, *Théatre, Récits, Nouvelles*. Bibliotheque de la Pléiade. Paris: NRF, 1962.

Canton, William. *The Invisible Playmate*. 1894; *W. V. Her Book*. 1896; *In Memory of W. V.* 1901. Reprinted together in Everyman's Library. London: J. M. Dent & Sons, 1911.

Cecil, Rev. Richard. *Remains*. Arranged by Josiah Pratt (with memoir by Mrs. Cecil). N.d.

Clissold, Rev. Henry. *The Happy Land, or Examples of Early Piety*. London, 1854.

Coleridge, Samuel Taylor. *Poems*. Oxford: Oxford University Press, 1935.

———. *Selected Letters*. Ed. H. J. Jackson. Oxford: Clarendon, 1988.

Croker, John Wilson. *Correspondence and Diaries*. London: John Murray, 1885.

Davidson, R. T., and William Benham. *Life of Archbishop Tait*. London: Macmillan, 1891.

De Quincey, Thomas. *Autobiographic Sketches*. In *Works*, vol 1, ed. David Masson. London, 1896.

Dickens, Charles. (Note: All quotations from Dickens's novels are taken from the Oxford India Paper Dickens, 17 vols., n.d.)

———. *Nicholas Nickleby*. 1839.

———. *The Old Curiosity Shop*. 1841.

———. *A Christmas Carol*. 1843.

———. *Martin Chuzzlewit*. 1845.

———. *Dombey and Son*. 1848.

———. "A Child's Dream of a Star," 1850. In *Reprinted Pieces*, 1858.

———. *Christmas Stories*. 1850–1867.

———. *Bleak House*. 1853.

———. *Hard Times*. 1854.

———. *Little Dorritt*. 1857.

———. *A Tale of Two Cities*. 1859.

———. *Great Expectations*. 1861.

———. *The Uncommercial Traveller*. 1861.

———. *Our Mutual Friend*. 1864.

————. *Letters*. Pilgrim edition, ed. Madeline House, Graham Storey et al. Oxford: Oxford University Press, 1969ff.

Dostoyevsky, Fyodor. *The Brothers Karamazov*. 1880. Trans. Constance Garnett. London: Heinemann, 1912.

Flaubert, Gustav. *L'Education sentimentale*. 1869.

[Fry, Elizabeth]. *Memoir of the Life of Elizabeth Fry, with Extracts from her Journal and Letters*. Ed. her daughters. London: W. & F. G. Cash, 1853.

Forster, John. *The Life of Charles Dickens*. London: Chapman & Hall, 1872.

Gaskell, Elizabeth. *Mary Barton*. 1848.

————. *Letters*. Ed. J. A. V. Chapple and Arthur Pollard. Manchester: Manchester University Press, 1966.

Goethe, Johann Wolfgang von. *Wilhelm Meisters Lehrjahre*. 1796.

————. *Die Wahlverwandschaften*. 1809.

Grant, Patrick, ed. *A Dazzling Darkness: An Anthology of Western Mysticism*. London: Collins, 1985.

Greg, W. R. "A Modern Symposium," *The Nineteenth Century* 2 (1877): 508.

Hardy, Forence Emily. *The Life of Thomas Hardy* (1928, 1930). Single volume edition. London, 1962.

Hardy, Thomas. *Tess of the D'Urbervilles*. 1891.

————. *Jude the Obscure*. 1895.

Haydon, Benjamin Robert. *Autobiography and Journals*, ed. Malcolm Ewin. London: MacDonald, 1950.

Hemans, Mrs. Felicia. *Poetical Works*. Chandos Classics, n.d.

Hesse, Hermann. *Rosshalde*. 1914.

Huxley, Aldous. *Point Counter Point*. 1928.

[Huxley, Thomas Henry]. *Life and Letters of Thomas Henry Huxley*, by his son Leonard Huxley. London: Macmillan, 1900.

[Jeffrey, Francis]. *Life of Lord Jeffrey, with a Selection from His Correspondence. By Lord Cockburn*. Edinburgh, 1852.

Lewis, C. S. *A Grief Observed*. London: Faber & Faber, 1961.

Mackenzie, Henry. *The Man of Feeling*. 1771.

Mayhew, Henry. *London Labour and the London Poor*. 4 vols. 1851–1861.

Mann, Thomas. *Buddenbrooks*. 1901.

————. *Doktor Faustus*. 1947.

Montgomery, Florence. *Misunderstood*. 1869.

Mozley, J. B. *Sermons Preached before the University of Oxford*. London, 1876.

Mulock, D. M. (Mrs. Craik). *John Halifax, Gentleman*. 1856.

Oliphant, Margaret. *The Autobiography of Margaret Oliphant*. Ed. Elisabeth Jay. Oxford: Oxford University Press, 1990.

Phelps, Elizabeth Stuart. *The Gates Ajar*. 1870.

Robbins, Rev. Henry, ed. *Our Little Ones in Heaven*. London, 1858.

Sewell, E. M. *Amy Herbert*. 1844.

Shelley, Percy Bysshe. *Poetical Works*. Oxford: Oxford University Press, 1905.

———. *Letters*. Oxford, 1964.

———. *Shelley's Prose; or, The Trumpet of a Prophecy*. Ed. David Lee Clark. Albuquerque: University of New Mexico Press, 1954.

Sherwood, Mary. *The Fairchild Family*. Part 1, 1818; part 2, 1842; part 3, 1847.

Shiff, Harriet Sarnoff. *The Bereaved Parent*. New York, 1977.

Shore, Emily. *Journal*. London, 1891.

Sontag, Susan. *Illness as Metaphor*. New York: Farrar, Strauss & Giroux, 1978.

———. *AIDS and Its Metaphors*. New York: Farrar, Strauss & Giroux, 1989.

Southey, Robert. *Life and Correspondence*. 6 vols. London, 1849–1850.

Stowe, Harriet Beecher. *Uncle Tom's Cabin*. 1851.

———. *The Pearl of Orr's Island*. 1862.

———. *The Writings*. Riverside edition, 1896. Reprinted, Hildersheim and New York, 1975.

Stone, Mrs. *God's Acre, or Historical Notices Relating to Churchyards*. London, 1858.

Smith, Adam. *The Theory of Moral Sentiments*. 1757.

Tennyson, Alfred. *The Letters of Alfred Lord Tennyson*. Ed. Cecil Y. Lang and Edgar F. Shannon, Jr. Oxford: Clarendon, 1987.

———. *The Poems of Tennyson*. Ed. Christopher Ricks. Harlow, Longmans, 1969.

White, Henry Kirke. *Poems* (with Memoir). London, 1803.

———. *Remains—with an Account of His Life by Robert Southey*. London: Vernon, Hood & Sharpe, 1807.

Wood, Mrs. Henry. *East Lynne*. 1861.

Wordsworth, William. *Poetical Works*. Ed. Ernest de Selincourt and Helen Darbishire. Oxford: Oxford University Press, 1926–1959.

———. *The Letters of William & Dorothy Wordsworth: The Middle Years*. Ed. Ernest de Selincourt. Oxford: Oxford University Press, 1973.

Yonge, Charlotte M. *The Daisy Chain, or Aspirations: A Family Chronicle*. 1856.

The Young People's Treasury: a Monthly Magazine for the Young. [N.a.] London, 1896.

II. Secondary.

Ammons, Elizabeth. "Stowe's Dream of the Mother-Saviour: Uncle Tom's Cabin and American Woman Writers before the 1920s." In Eric J. Sunquist, *New Essays on Uncle Tom's Cabin*. Cambridge: Cambridge University Press, 1986.

Ariès, Philippe. *Centuries of Childhood*. 1960; Baltimore: Penguin 1973.

———. *The Hour of our Death*. 1977; Baltimore: Penguin, 1983.

Armstrong, Frances. *Dickens and the Concept of Home*. Ann Arbor, Mich.: UMI Research Press, 1990.

Bradley, Ian. *The Call to Seriousness: The Evangelical Impact on the Victorians*. London: Jonathan Cape, 1976.

Brockington, C. Fraser. *Public Health in the Nineteenth Century*. London: E. & S. Livingstone, 1965.

Brown, Herbert Ross. *The Sentimental Novel in America, 1789–1860*. Durham, N.C.: Duke University Press, 1940.

Carey, John. *The Violent Effigy: A Study of Dickens' Imagination*. London: Faber & Faber, 1973.

Cecil, Robert. *The Masks of Death: Changing Attitudes in the Nineteenth Century*. Lewes: Book Guild, 1991.

Chadwick, Owen. *The Victorian Church*. Oxford: Oxford University Press, 1970.

———. *Victorian Miniature*. London: Hodder & Stoughton, 1960.

Chesterton, G. K. *Charles Dickens: a Critical Study*. London, 1906.

Collins, Philip. "Dombey & Son: Then and Now," *The Dickensian* 63: 83 ff.

———. *The Decline of Pathos*. English Studies Today. 5th series. Dublin, 1960.

———, ed. *Charles Dickens: The Critical Heritage*. London: Routledge, 1971.

———, ed. *Charles Dickens: The Public Readings*. Oxford: Oxford University Press, 1975.

Coveney, Peter. *The Image of Childhood*. Baltimore: Penguin, 1967.

Cutt, M. Nancy. *Mrs Sherwood and Her Books for Children*. Oxford: Oxford University Press, 1974.

———. *Ministering Angels: a Study of Nineteenth Century Evangelical Writing for Children*. London: Five Owls, 1979.

Davidoff, Leonore and Catherine Hall. *Family Fortunes: Men and Women of the English Middle Class 1780–1850*. Chicago: University of Chicago Press, 1987.

Docherty, Thomas. *Reading (Absent) Character*. Oxford: Oxford University Press, 1983.

Douglas, Ann. *The Feminization of American Culture*. New York: Avon, 1977.

Fisher, Philip. *Hard Facts: Setting and Form in the American Novel*. New York: Oxford University Press, 1985.

Ford, George H. *Dickens and His Readers: Aspects of Novel-Criticism since 1836*. Princeton, N.J.: Princeton University Press, 1955.

Forster, Margaret. *Significant Sisters*. London: Secker & Warburg, 1984.

Gardiner, Alfred George. *The Life of Sir William Harcourt*. London: Constable, 1923.

Gay, Peter. *The Bourgeois Experience: Victoria to Freud*. New York: Oxford University Press, 1984–1986.

Grylls, David. *Guardians and Angels*. London: Faber & Faber, 1978.

Haight, Gordon S. *Mrs. Sigourney*. New Haven, Conn.: Yale University Press, 1930.

Hartman, Geoffrey H. *Wordsworth's Poetry, 1781–1814*. Cambridge, Mass.: Harvard University Press, 1964.

Hellerstein, Erna Olafson, et al., eds. *Victorian Women: A Documentary Account of Women's Lives* in Nineteenth-Century England, France, and the United States. Brighton: Harvester, 1981.

Holmes, Richard. *Coleridge's Early Visions*. London: Hodder & Stoughton, 1989.

———. *Shelley: The Pursuit*. London: Weidenfeld & Nicholson, 1974.

Holubetz, Margarete. "Death-bed Scenes in Victorian Fiction," *English Studies*. Vol. 1. Lisse, Netherlands, 1986.

Horsman, Alan. Introduction to *Dombey & Son*. Oxford: Clarendon, 1974.

Huxley, Aldous. "Vulgarity in Literature" (1931). In *Music at Night, and Other Essays*. New York: Bantam, 1960.

Jay, Elisabeth. *The Religion of the Heart: Anglican Evangelicalism and the Nineteenth Century Novel*. Oxford: Clarendon, 1979.

———. *Mrs. Oliphant: A Fiction to Herself. A Literary Life*. Oxford: Oxford University Press, 1995.

Johnson, Edgar. *Charles Dickens: His Tragedy and Triumph*. Boston: Little, Brown and Co., 1952.

Johnston, Kenneth R. *Wordsworth and the Recluse*. New Haven, Conn.: Yale University Press, 1984.

Kaplan, Fred. *Sacred Tears: Sentimentality in Victorian Literature*. Princeton, N.J.: Princeton University Press, 1987.

Kelley, Mary. "The Sentimentalists: Promise and Betrayal in the Home," *Signs* 4 (Spring 1979): 434–446.

Kincaid, James R. *Child-Loving: The Erotic Child and Victorian Culture*. London: Routledge, 1992.

Leavis, F. R. and Q. D. Leavis. *Dickens the Novelist*. London: Chatto & Windus, 1970.

Lefebure, Molly. *The Bondage of Love: a Life of Mrs. Samuel Taylor Coleridge*. London: Victor Gollancz, 1986.

MacDannell, Colleen. and Bernhard Lang. *Heaven: A History*. New Haven, Conn.: Yale University Press, 1988.

McKeown, Thomas. *The Modern Rise of Population*. London: Edward Arnold, 1971.

Marcus, Steven. *Dickens: From Pickwick to Dombey*. London: Chatto & Windus, 1965.

Miller, J. Hillis. *Charles Dickens: The World of His Novels*. Cambridge, Mass.: Harvard University Press, 1958.

Morley, John. *Death, Heaven and the Victorians*. Pittsburgh: University of Pittsburgh Press, 1971.

———. *Life of Gladstone*. London: Edward Lloyd, 1908.

Newsome, David. *Godliness and Good Learning: Four Studies on a Victorian Ideal*. London: John Murray, 1961.

Plowden, Alison. *Caroline and Charlotte: The Regent's Wife and Daughter*. London: Sidgwick & Jackson, 1989.

Polhemus, Robert M. "Comic and Erotic Faith Meet Faith in the Child: Charles Dickens' 'The Old Curiosity Shop.'" In *Critical Reconstructions: The Relationship of Fiction and Life*, ed. Robert M. Polhemus and Roger B. Henkle. Stanford, Calif.: Stanford University Press, 1994.

Pollock, Linda. *A Lasting Relationship: Parents and Children over Three Centuries.* Hanover, N.H.: University Press of New England, 1987.

Qualls, Barry V. *The Secular Pilgrims of Victorian Fiction.* Cambridge: Cambridge University Press, 1982.

Reid, Stuart J. *Life and Letters of Lord Durham.* London, 1906.

Rosenberg, Charles E. *Healing and History.* New York: Dawson, 1979.

Rowell, Geoffrey. *Hell and the Victorians.* Oxford: Clarendon, 1974.

Sadrin, Anny. *Parentage and Inheritance in the Novels of Charles Dickens.* Cambridge: Cambridge University Press, 1994.

Sanders, Andrew. *Charles Dickens, Resurrectionist.* London: Macmillan, 1982.

Shannon, R. T. *Gladstone.* London: Hamish Hamilton, 1982.

Slater, Michael. *Dickens and Women.* London: J. M. Dent & Sons, 1983.

Stewart, Garrett. *Dickens and the Trials of Imagination.* Cambridge, Mass.: Harvard University Press, 1974.

———. *Death Sentences. Styles of Dying in British Fiction.* Cambridge, Mass.: Harvard University Press, 1984.

Sundquist, Eric J., ed. *New Essays on Uncle Tom's Cabin.* Cambridge: Cambridge University Press, 1986.

Thwaite, Ann. *Waiting for the Party: The Life of Frances Hodgson Burnett.* London: Secker & Warburg, 1974.

Tompkins, Jane. *Sensational Designs: The Cultural Work of American Fiction.* New York: Oxford University Press, 1985.

Todd, Janet. *Sensibility: An Introduction.* London: Methuen, 1986.

Vann, Richard T. and David Eversley: *Friends in Life and Death: The British and Irish Quakers in the Demographic Transition 1650–1900.* Cambridge: Cambridge University Press, 1992.

Walvin, James. *A Child's World: A Social History of English Childhood 1800–1914.* Baltimore: Penguin, 1981.

Welsh, Alexander. *The City of Dickens.* Oxford: Oxford University Press, 1971.

———. *From Copyright to Copperfield: The Identity of Dickens.* Cambridge, Mass.: Harvard University Press, 1987.

Wheeler, Michael. *Death and the Future Life in Victorian Literature and Theology.* Cambridge: Cambridge University Press, 1990.

Wilson, Edmund. "Dickens: The Two Scrooges." In *The Wound and the Bow: Seven Studies in Literature.* Boston: Houghton Mifflin, 1941.

Wrigley, E. A., and R. S. Schonfield. *The Population History of England 1541–1841.* Cambridge, Mass.: Harvard University Press, 1981.

Yellin, Jean Fagan. "Doing it Herself: *Uncle Tom's Cabin* and Woman's Role in the Slavery Crisis." In *New Essays on Uncle Tom's Cabin,* ed. Eric J. Sundquist. Cambridge: Cambridge University Press, 1986..

INDEX

Entries refer only to substantive discussion, not passing mention. The deaths of real children are usually indexed under the name of the parent.

ANGELS AND ABSENCES

was composed
electronically in Caslon 540 types,
with display types in Caslon Open Face and Type Embellishments Three.
The book was printed on 60-pound Natural Smooth acid-free, recycled
paper, with Multicolor Presidential Blue antique finish endpapers,
Smyth sewn, and bound over 88-point binder's boards in
Holliston 53556 Purple cloth, by Braun-Brumfield.
The dust jackets were printed in three colors
by Vanderbilt University Printing Services.
Book and jacket designs are the work of Gary Gore.
Published by Vanderbilt University Press
Nashville, Tennessee 37235

DATE DUE
